International and Development Education

The *International and Development Education Series* focuses on the complementary areas of comparative, international, and development education. Books emphasize a number of topics ranging from key international education issues, trends, and reforms to examinations of national education systems, social theories, and development education initiatives. Local, national, regional, and global volumes (single-authored and edited collections) constitute the breadth of the series and offer potential contributors a great deal of latitude based on interests and cutting-edge research. The series is supported by a strong network of international scholars and development professionals who serve on the International and Development Education Advisory Board and participate in the selection and review process for manuscript development.

SERIES EDITORS
John N. Hawkins
Professor Emeritus, University of California, Los Angeles
Co-Director, Asian Pacific Higher Education Research Partnership (APHERP), East-West Center

W. James Jacob
Associate Professor, University of Pittsburgh
Director, Institute for International Studies in Education

PRODUCTION EDITOR
Weiyan Xiong
Program Coordinator, Institute for International Studies in Education

INTERNATIONAL EDITORIAL ADVISORY BOARD
Clementina Acedo, *Webster University, Switzerland*
Philip G. Altbach, *Boston University, USA*
Carlos E. Blanco, *Universidad Central de Venezuela*
Oswell C. Chakulimba, *University of Zambia*
Sheng Yao Cheng, *National Chung Cheng University, Taiwan*
Ruth Hayhoe, *University of Toronto, Canada*
Wanhua Ma, *Peking University, China*
Ka Ho Mok, *Lingnan University, Hong Kong*
Christine Musselin, *Sciences Po, France*
Yusuf K. Nsubuga, *Ministry of Education and Sports, Uganda*
Namgi Park, *Gwangju National University of Education, Republic of Korea*
Val D. Rust, *University of California, Los Angeles, USA*
Suparno, *State University of Malang, Indonesia*
John C. Weidman, *University of Pittsburgh, USA*
Husam Zaman, *Taibah University, Saudi Arabia*
Yuto Kitamura, *Tokyo University, Japan*

Institute for International Studies in Education
School of Education, University of Pittsburgh
5714 Wesley W. Posvar Hall, Pittsburgh, PA 15260 USA

Center for International and Development Education
Graduate School of Education & Information Studies, University of California, Los Angeles
Box 951521, Moore Hall, Los Angeles, CA 90095 USA

Titles:

Higher Education in Asia/Pacific: Quality and the Public Good
Edited by Terance W. Bigalke and Deane E. Neubauer

Affirmative Action in China and the U.S.: A Dialogue on Inequality and Minority Education
Edited by Minglang Zhou and Ann Maxwell Hill

Critical Approaches to Comparative Education: Vertical Case Studies from Africa, Europe, the Middle East, and the Americas
Edited by Frances Vavrus and Lesley Bartlett

Curriculum Studies in South Africa: Intellectual Histories & Present Circumstances
Edited by William F. Pinar

Higher Education, Policy, and the Global Competition Phenomenon
Edited by Laura M. Portnoi, Val D. Rust, and Sylvia S. Bagley

The Search for New Governance of Higher Education in Asia
Edited by Ka-Ho Mok

International Students and Global Mobility in Higher Education: National Trends and New Directions
Edited by Rajika Bhandari and Peggy Blumenthal

Curriculum Studies in Brazil: Intellectual Histories, Present Circumstances
Edited by William F. Pinar

Access, Equity, and Capacity in Asia Pacific Higher Education
Edited by Deane Neubauer and Yoshiro Tanaka

Policy Debates in Comparative, International, and Development Education
Edited by John N. Hawkins and W. James Jacob

Curriculum Studies in Mexico: Intellectual Histories, Present Circumstances
Edited by William F. Pinar

Increasing Effectiveness of the Community College Financial Model: A Global Perspective for the Global Economy
Edited by Stewart E. Sutin, Daniel Derrico, Rosalind Latiner Raby, and Edward J. Valeau

The Internationalization of East Asian Higher Education: Globalizations Impact
Edited by John D. Palmer, Amy Roberts, Young Ha Cho, and Gregory Ching

University Governance and Reform: Policy, Fads, and Experience in International Perspective
Edited by Hans G. Schuetze, William Bruneau, and Garnet Grosjean

Mobility and Migration in Asian Pacific Higher Education
Edited by Deane E. Neubauer and Kazuo Kuroda

Taiwan Education at the Crossroad: When Globalization Meets Localization
Edited by Chuing Prudence Chou and Gregory Ching

Higher Education Regionalization in Asia Pacific: Implications for Governance, Citizenship and University Transformation
Edited by John N. Hawkins, Ka Ho Mok, and Deane E. Neubauer

Post-Secondary Education and Technology: A Global Perspective on Opportunities and Obstacles to Development
Edited by Rebecca Clothey, Stacy Austin-Li, and John C. Weidman

Education and Global Cultural Dialogue: A Tribute to Ruth Hayhoe
Edited by Karen Mundy and Qiang Zha

The Quest for Entrepreneurial Universities in East Asia
By Ka Ho Mok

The Dynamics of Higher Education Development in East Asia: Asian Cultural Heritage, Western Dominance, Economic Development, and Globalization
Edited by Deane Neubauer, Jung Cheol Shin, and John N. Hawkins

Leadership for Social Justice in Higher Education: The Legacy of the Ford Foundation International Fellowships Program
Edited by Terance W. Bigalke and Mary S. Zurbuchen

Curriculum Studies in China: Intellectual Histories, Present Circumstances
Edited by William F. Pinar

The Transnationally Partnered University: Insights from Research and Sustainable Development Collaborations in Africa
By Peter H. Koehn and Milton O. Obamba

Curriculum Studies in India: Intellectual Histories, Present Circumstances
Edited By William F. Pinar

Private Universities in Latin America: Research and Innovation in the Knowledge Economy
Edited by Gustavo Gregorutti and Jorge Enrique Delgado

Research, Development, and Innovation in Asia Pacific Higher Education
Edited by John N. Hawkins and Ka Ho Mok

Research, Development, and Innovation in Asia Pacific Higher Education

Edited by
John N. Hawkins and Ka Ho Mok

RESEARCH, DEVELOPMENT, AND INNOVATION IN ASIA PACIFIC HIGHER EDUCATION
Copyright © John N. Hawkins and Ka Ho Mok, 2015.

All rights reserved.

First published in 2015 by
PALGRAVE MACMILLAN®
in the United States—a division of St. Martin's Press LLC,
175 Fifth Avenue, New York, NY 10010.

Where this book is distributed in the UK, Europe and the rest of the world, this is by Palgrave Macmillan, a division of Macmillan Publishers Limited, registered in England, company number 785998, of Houndmills, Basingstoke, Hampshire RG21 6XS.

Palgrave Macmillan is the global academic imprint of the above companies and has companies and representatives throughout the world.

Palgrave® and Macmillan® are registered trademarks in the United States, the United Kingdom, Europe and other countries.

ISBN: 978–1–137–45708–0

Library of Congress Cataloging-in-Publication Data

    Research, development, and innovation in Asia Pacific higher education / edited by John N. Hawkins and Ka Ho Mok.
      pages cm. — (International and development education)
    Includes index.
    Summary: "Hawkins and Mok explore the relationship between higher education, research, innovation, and governance as a complex yet critical aspect of higher education development"— Provided by publisher.
      ISBN 978–1–137–45708–0 (hardback)
      1. Education, Higher—East Asia. 2. Education, Higher—Research—East Asia. 3. Education, Higher—Aims and objectives—East Asia.
    I. Hawkins, John N., editor of compilation. II. Mok, Ka Ho, 1964– editor of compilation.

LA1143.R47 2015
378.5—dc23   2014044501

A catalogue record of the book is available from the British Library.

Design by Newgen Knowledge Works (P) Ltd., Chennai, India.

First edition: May 2015

10 9 8 7 6 5 4 3 2 1

Contents

List of Illustrations	ix
Series Editors' Introduction	xi
Acknowledgments	xiii
List of Acronyms and Abbreviations	xv

1 Introduction   1
   John N. Hawkins, Ka Ho Mok, and Deane Neubauer

Part I   Policy Implications for Shifting Research Capacity and Development

2 Developing Research Capacity in Education Schools and Faculties in Newer Universities: Seeking Research Excellence and Entrepreneurship   11
   Annette Gough

3 The Shifting Ecology of Research in Asian Pacific Higher Education: Imitation or Innovation   31
   John N. Hawkins

4 Time for Balanced Thinking: Reflections on Dichotomous Multiple Missions of Public Higher Education in the United States   51
   Stewart E. Sutin

5 Why the Asian Craze for Publication? An Examination from Academic Regime   61
   Po-fen Tai

6 National Policies in Chile Related to Research and Innovation: The Challenge of Cultural Change   81
   Mario F. Letelier and María J. Sandoval

Part II Entrepreneurship, Innovation, and Development in the Research Domain

7   Rethinking Innovation in a Higher Education Context   95
    Deane Neubauer

8   Questing for Entrepreneurship and Innovation
    for Enhancing Global Competitiveness in Hong Kong:
    Academic Reflections   115
    Ka Ho Mok

9   The Quest for Entrepreneurial University in Taiwan:
    Policies and Practices in Industry-Academy Cooperation   135
    Sheng-Ju Chan and Ka Ho Mok

10 The University-Community Compact: Innovation
    in Community Engagement   155
    Robert W. Franco

11 Management of Research, Development, and Innovation:
    A Case Study of Universiti Sains Malaysia   177
    Chang Da Wan and Molly N. N. Lee

12 Dynamics and Challenges of Public and Private Partnership
    in Thai Higher Education Institutions in Promoting
    a Creative Society: Implications for Research   199
    Prompilai Buasuwan and Bordin Rassameethes

13 Subjectivity, Indigenous Perspectives, and the New Qing
    History: The Role and Potential of Local Dimensions in
    Enhancing Research and Development in a Globalized Setting   215
    William Yat Wai Lo

14 Research, Development, and Academic Culture in Chinese
    Universities: A Historical Reflection   225
    Su-Yan Pan

15 Conclusion: Research Trends in Higher Education in
    Asia Pacific   245
    John N. Hawkins and Ka Ho Mok

Contributors Biographies   253
Index   259

Illustrations

Figures

5.1	Volume of publications compared to 1991 in selected Asian countries	62
5.2	The relative citation impact in selected countries, 2006–2010	62
5.3	The dynamics of an academic regime	65
5.4	The expenditure on R&D and its share to GDP	69
5.5	The growth of teaching staff from 2000 to 2010	73
5.6	The increase of manpower in R&D compared to 1996	74
5.7	The average expenditure per researcher from 1996 to 2009	75
5.8	The average volume of publications per researcher from 1996 to 2009	75
9.1	Increasing performance of IAC, 2003–2012	144
9.2	The dynamics of IAC	150
13.1	A common differentiated academic system	217
13.2	The differentiated academic system integrating the international and local dimensions	218

Tables

2.1	Comparison of recommendations for the future structuring of universities	15
2.2	ERA 2012—RMIT top-ten contributors to FoR codes from School of Education	21
2.3	Ranges of expected research performance at RMIT	24
2.4	Ranges of aspirational research performance at RMIT	25
6.1	Chilean export and produce compositions for 2013	83

7.1	Change typology transformation exercise within HE innovation	102
9.1	Ranking on the ease of doing business	138
9.2	Entrepreneurial attitudes and perceptions in selected countries, 2012	138
9.3	Top ten categories of incubation centers in Taiwan, 2013	146
11.1	Typology for knowledge and skills required for effective leadership and management of RDI	181
11.2	Major changes to the organizational structure of RDI management in USM between 2012 and 2013	184
11.3	Three evolutionary phases of RDI management at the institutional level in USM	194
11.4	Continuum of RDI management at the group level in USM	196
12.1	PPP in Thai HEIs	208
15.1	Number of student enrollments in HEIs in South Korea (1996–2010)	247
15.2	Number of new entrants in HEIs in Japan (1996–2010)	247

Series Editors' Introduction

We are pleased to introduce another volume in the Palgrave Macmillan International and Development Education book series. In conceptualizing this series we took into account the extraordinary increase in the scope and depth of research on education in a global and international context. The range of topics and issues being addressed by scholars worldwide is enormous and clearly reflects the growing expansion and quality of research being conducted on comparative, international, and development education (CIDE) topics. Our goal is to cast a wide net for the most innovative and novel manuscripts, both single-authored and edited volumes, without constraints as to the level of education, geographic region, or methodology (whether disciplinary or interdisciplinary). In the process, we have also developed two subseries as part of the main series: one is cosponsored by the East-West Center in Honolulu, Hawaii, drawing from their distinguished programs, the International Forum on Education 2020 (IFE 2020) and the Asian Pacific Higher Education Research Partnership (APHERP); and the other is a publication partnership with the Higher Education Special Interest Group of the Comparative and International Education Society that highlights trends and themes on international higher education.

The issues that will be highlighted in this series are those focused on capacity, access, and equity, three interrelated topics that are central to educational transformation as it appears today around the world. There are many paradoxes and asymmetries surrounding these issues, which include problems of both excess capacity and deficits, wide access to facilities as well as severe restrictions, and all the complexities that are included in the equity debate. Closely related to this critical triumvirate is the overarching concern with quality assurance, accountability, and assessment. As educational systems have expanded, so have the needs and demands for quality assessment, with implications for accreditation and accountability. Intergroup relations, multiculturalism, and gender issues comprise another cluster of concerns facing most educational systems in differential ways when one looks at the change in educational systems in an international context. Diversified notions of the structure of knowledge and curriculum development occupy another important niche in educational change at both the precollegiate and collegiate levels. Finally, how systems are managed and governed are key policy issues for educational policy makers worldwide. These and other key elements of the education and social change environment have guided this series and have been reflected in the books that have already appeared and those that will appear in the future. We welcome proposals on these and other topics from as wide a range of scholars and practitioners as possible. We believe that the world of educational change is dynamic, and our goal is to reflect the very best work being done in these and other areas. This volume edited by John N. Hawkins and Ka Ho Mok, on the topic Research, Development, and Innovation in Asia Pacific Higher Education clearly meets the standards and goals of this series and we are proud to add it to our list of publications.

JOHN N. HAWKINS
University of California, Los Angeles

W. JAMES JACOB
University of Pittsburgh

Acknowledgments

The editors thank the APHERP and the East-West Center in support of the present publication through organizing a senior seminar at the Hong Kong Institute of Education to facilitate discussions and debates concerning the research theme. Part of the findings discussed in this volume are based upon the research project conducted by Ka Ho Mok with funding support from the Research Grant Council of the Hong Kong Special Administrative Region (HKSAR) government. Ka Ho Mok, one of the coeditors of the present volume, thanks the Research Grant Council of the HKSAR government for providing funding support to conduct the fieldwork and survey in East Asia with the funded project HKIEd GRF 750210, "Fostering Entrepreneurship and Innovation: A Comparative Study of Changing Roles of Universities in East Asia." Particular thanks go to the colleagues of the Department of Asian and Policy Studies and Centre for Greater China Studies of the Hong Kong Institute of Education in hosting the senior seminar with support from colleagues from East-West Center, US. Other portions of research in this volume were supported by the Tomomi Takagi Memorial Fund at the University of California, Los Angeles (UCLA), Graduate School of Education and Information Studies, with much appreciation from John N. Hawkins, professor emeritus at UCLA. We would also like to acknowledge Ms. Ellen Waldrop, who with great dedication provided superb editorial skills in preparing this volume for publication. W. James Jacob and his team were essential in the final stages of editing for this volume, many thanks to them. And as always, the editors at Palgrave Macmillan, Ms. Sarah Nathan and Mara Berkoff guided us throughout the process with seriousness and good humor; we thank them and the Palgrave Macmillan team for all of their support and professionalism.

Acronyms and Abbreviations

AAC&U	Association of American Colleges and Universities
AACC	American Association of Community Colleges
ABET	Accreditation Board for Engineering and Technology
ACECQA	Australian Children's Education and Care Quality Authority
ACT	American College Testing
AIG	Australian Industry Group
AITSL	Australian Institute for Teaching and School Leadership
APAS	Automotive Parts and Accessory Systems R&D Center
APEX	Accelerated Program for Education Excellence
APHERP	Asia Pacific Higher Education Research Partnership
ARC	Australian Research Council
ASTRI	Applied Science and Technology Research Institute
ASTS	Academic Staff Training Scheme
AUQA	Australian Universities Quality Agency
BK21	Brain Korea 21
CAS	Chinese Academy of Sciences
CCSSE	Community College Survey of Student Engagement
CDR	Center of Drug Research
CICES	Center for Research in Creativity and Higher Education
CIDE	Comparative, international, and development education
CINTEC	Center for Innovation and Technology
CNIC	National Council for Innovation and Competitiveness
COE	Centers of excellence
COIN	CUHK Open Innovation Network
CONICYT	National Commission for Scientific and Technological Research
CORE	China Open Resources for Education
CORFO	Corporation for Development
CPC	Communist Party of China
CRC	Cooperative Research Centre
CRF	Collaborative Research Fund

CRIs	Centers for Research Initiative
CSU	California State University
CUHK	Chinese University of Hong Kong
DCMS	Department for Culture, Media, and Sport
DEEWR	Department of Education, Employment, and Workplace Relations
DTVE	Department of Technological and Vocational Education
DVC A&I	Deputy vice chancellor of academic and internationalization
DVC ICN	Deputy vice chancellor of industry and community network
DVC R&I	Deputy vice chancellor of research and innovation
EGM	Emerging global model
EPSCoR	Experimental Program to Stimulate Competitive Research
ERA	Excellence in Research for Australia
FoR	Field of Research
GDP	Gross domestic product
GERD	Gross Expenditure on Research and Development
GRF	General Research Fund
GRIs	Government research institutes
HBS	Harvard Business School
HE	Higher education
HEIs	Higher education institutions
HERDC	Higher Education Research Data Collection
HICOEs	Higher Institution Centers of Excellence
HKBAN	Hong Kong Business Angel Network
HKIEd	Hong Kong Institute of Education
HKRITA	Hong Kong Research Institute of Textiles and Apparel
HKSAR	Hong Kong Special Administrative Region
HKU	University of Hong Kong
HKUST	Hong Kong University of Science and Technology
HUST	Huazhong University of Sciences and Technology
IAC	Industry-academy cooperation
ICO	Innovation and Commercialization Office
ICT	Information and communications technologies
IEMs	Institutional Effectiveness Measures
INFORMM	Institute for Research in Molecular Medicine
IP	Intellectual property
IPPTN	National Higher Education Research Institute
IPS	Institute of Postgraduate Studies
ISO	International Organization for Standardization
IT	Information technology

ITC	Innovation and Technology Commission
ITF	Innovation and Technology Fund
KCC	Kapiolani Community College
KELA	Kapiolani Engagement, Learning, and Achievement
KMT	Kuomintang
KNIT	Knowledge Network Institute of Thailand
KPIs	Key Performance Indicators
LED-FPD	Light Emitting Diode and the Flat-Panel Display
LSCM	Hong Kong R&D Center for Logistics and Supply Chain Management Enabling
MIT	Massachusetts Institute of Technology
MOE	Ministry of Education
MOEA	Ministry of Economic Affairs
MOHE	Ministry of Higher Education
MOOC	Massive open online courses
MOOEs	Massive Open Online Experiments (Courses)
MOORs	Massive Open Online Research(s)
MTR	Mass Transit Railway
NaHERI	National Higher Education Research Institute
NAMI	Nano and Advanced Materials Institute
NCGP	National Competitive Grants Program
NCHE	National Council on Higher Education
NCSE	National Center for Science and Civic Engagement
NGO	Nongovernmental organization
NHESP	National Higher Education Strategic Plan
NHMRC	National Health and Medical Research Council
NIEs	Newly industrialized economies
NRCT	National Research Council of Thailand
NSC	National Science Council
NSF	National Science Foundation
NSSE	National Survey of Student Engagement
NUS	National University of Singapore
OECD	Organization for Economic Co-operation and Development
OFIE	Office for Institutional Effectiveness
OHEC	Office of Higher Education Commission
OLT	Office of Learning and Teaching
PASS	Postgraduate Academic Support Services
PPD	Personal and Professional Development
PPP	Public-private partnership
PRC	People's Republic of China
QS	Quacquarelli Symonds
R&D	Research and development

RCMO	Research, Creativity, and Management Office
RDI	Research, development, and innovation
REF	Research Endowment Fund
RGC	Research Grant Council
RMIT	Royal Melbourne Institute of Technology
ROC	Republic of China
RTDs	Research, technology, and development networks
RU	Research University
S&T	Science and technology
SCI	Science Citation Index
SENCER	Science Education for New Civic Engagements and Responsibilities
SET	Stock Exchange of Thailand
SL	Service learning
SLLT	SL Leadership Team
SLOs	Student Learning Outcomes
SMEs	Small- and medium-sized enterprises
SNU	Seoul National University
SSCI	Social Science Citation Index
STEM	Science, technology, engineering, and mathematics
TCOBS	Thailand Consortium of Business Schools Technologies
TEQSA	Tertiary Education Quality and Standards Agency
THU	Tsinghua University
UCLA	University of California, Los Angeles
UGC	University Grant Committee
UHM	University of Hawai'i, Manoa
UKM	Universiti Kebangsaan Malaysia
UM	Universiti Malaya
UMC	University Management Committee
UPM	Universiti Putera Malaysia
USM	Universiti Sains Malaysia
USR	University Social Responsibility
UT	University of Texas
UTM	Universiti Teknologi Malaysia
VTC	Vocational Training Council
WASC	Western Association of Schools and Colleges
WCU	World-class university
WPI	World Premier International Research Center Initiative
WTO	World Trade Organization

Chapter 1

Introduction

*John N. Hawkins, Ka Ho Mok,
and Deane Neubauer*

Research and development (R&D) have long been key components of what have generally been called "research universities." There is also recognition that in order to stay on the cutting edge of R&D, higher education institutions (HEIs) must increasingly strive for innovative R&D; this has important implications for the structure and governance of higher education (HE) as well as numerous other factors of HE change and transformation. Furthermore, in a manner that may be unprecedented in the period of the so-called modern university, innovation has been thrust upon the university almost as a form of social responsibility. Interestingly and overwhelmingly, due to the role the university is performing within the emergent knowledge society, innovation in the "knowledge-transfer" functions of the university—the teaching role foremost among them—has assumed increasingly greater importance (Neubauer 2011). In this book we would like to focus our attention on several of these factors including, but not limited to, the following suggestions.

There is a fundamental issue of the location of R&D in the academy structure. It is widely acknowledged that in many settings, including most members of the Organization for Economic Co-operation and Development (OECD), R&D typically resides in recognized research HEIs. Yet, in many cases, as massification has occurred and as hierarchical relationships have resulted in differential funding and prestige levels, there has been what is sometimes referred to as "mission creep." An example in the United States is the California Master Plan, which was designed to define a clearly delineated structure that focused R&D on the University of California segment, teaching and some research on the California State University (CSU) segment, and teaching and open access on the Community College segment. For a variety of socioeconomic reasons (not the least of which is the opportunity of overhead funding from external research grants), faculty in the CSU segment have been "creeping" toward replicating the R&D functions of the University of California segment, thus blurring the boundaries between the research functions of the system. Similar forces are present in newer systems in Japan, China, Hong Kong, Taiwan, and Korea to name just five Asia Pacific settings. These forces have a significant impact on the organization, planning, and governance of HE with respect to R&D and the emphasis on innovation (Hawkins and Jacob 2011).

A related issue of "location" relates to the so-called triple helix of university, industry, and government relations. In recent years, a number of concepts have been proposed for modeling the transformation processes of this three-way interaction. Adding the notion of innovation requires the blurring of boundaries between them and suggests different modes for the production of new knowledge. Knowledge flows are recursive rather than linear, and suggest many new and novel ways to think about R&D and the knowledge revolution. While typically discussed with respect to the sciences, this model has equal relevance for all areas of knowledge production including the social sciences and humanities (e.g., the nature and impacts of health policy) even though these have been much less self-consciously studied as such. Some of the chapters in this volume attempt to revisit the triple helix model in conceptualizing state-enterprise-university relations. Chan and Mok's chapter critically reviews how universities in Taiwan have engaged with the industry and enterprises for promoting innovation and knowledge-transfer activities. When exploring deeper university-enterprise cooperation, Chan and Mok have found that the existing triple helix model has actually missed one important dimension—the growing importance of the civil society or local community in promoting innovation, community-based business, and community development when deepening their cooperation with universities (see Chan and Mok in this volume). Meanwhile, scholars and researchers gathered at the University of Hawaii, Manoa, in July 2014 to discuss social policy responses and social innovation focusing on Asia, with one of the prominent themes being "bringing the society" back. When reflecting upon the changing role of the state in social-welfare provision and social policy design, especially in the state-alone mode, many Asian governments have found it difficult to sustain the growing expenditure on social welfare/social policy. It is in this context that social enterprises and community-based enterprises are strongly encouraged to work with the university sector for translating local knowledge into commercialized products in the market place.

Another fundamental issue has to do with the historical distribution of R&D in HE, with Europe and North America having a head start and HEIs in other emerging economies developing capacity later and forging links in a variety of ways with leading universities in those settings. There are various implications for this, especially in the increasingly globalized environment, in areas such as cross-border research and the migration of intellectual talent (the so-called brain-train); massification of academic research, basic research, academic research, and new public management; rise of private funding; internationalization of academic research; new social contracts for research; the role of new developments in technology; emerging "new giants" such as India and China (as members of the BRICs); the role of regionalization in R&D and innovation (e.g., the Bologna process in Europe and various new Asian and Pacific regional organizations); the link between R&D and innovation and the burgeoning quality assurance and accreditation movements especially on the international level; the financing of R&D; and the increasingly blurred role between the public and private sectors and their impact on R&D and innovation. The entire landscape of HE, with its various institutional structures and functions has been enormously impacted by the role of emergent private sector HEIs, many of them acting cross-nationally, some of which are enrolling hundreds of thousands at a time, gaining significant returns on capital, and impacting in major ways the status of traditional HEIs within their accustomed national settings (Hawkins 2011).

These issues represent broad, regional, and global concerns. Focusing on the HEIs and their responses to these broader forces leads to more specific concerns such as the purpose and functions of R&D and innovation in the academy and how dramatically changed funding patterns have impacted the organization of R&D and innovation. In many recognized research institutions, there has been a decreasing reliance on state/government funding for R&D and an increase in the role of private funding from the corporate sector in order to mount the kind of research necessary to remain competitive. This has implications for the basic research and applied research shares of the R&D effort, as well as academic autonomy and innovation. There are additional implications for the social returns to HE from this changed research landscape such as the relationship between employment and R&D investment that underpins the "high skills" strategy of many governments and HEIs in the Asian Pacific region. It is here that the innovative aspects of private sector (often proprietary) HE are being most experienced. At the institutional level this impacts the relationship between the postgraduate education experience and training and the labor market—the classic "alignment" issue.

The broad area of internationalization and the role of globalization in HE within the context of competition and rankings have contributed to an environment in which R&D and innovation are inextricably linked between institutions within the Asia Pacific region and between it and other global settings. These linkages are increasingly being recognized by HE leaders in the United States and Asia as well as Europe, even as others seek to critique and clarify such concepts as globalization and internationalization. It is now clear that breakthrough discoveries will also occur in many parts of the Asia Pacific region and many HEIs in the United States and elsewhere are seeking active partnerships and collaborative arrangements in order to participate in these new ventures. One aspect of this development may be a rethinking of how intellectual property regimes within countries are distributed between HEIs and other sources of knowledge innovation. Overall, how these linkages develop and enhance R&D and innovation in cross-regional settings is a critical question that we hope some of the chapters in this volume will address.

The quest for new approaches to R&D, entrepreneurship, and innovation has also had a significant impact on HE governance. In the Asian Pacific region and in the United States, HEIs have long incorporated offices and centers for R&D within their governing structures. More recently there have been more proactive efforts to establish new administrative units to focus on innovation as it relates to more traditional R&D. Chief Innovation Officers have been appointed in many HEIs in the region, usually attached to schools and colleges where R&D is typically performed (e.g., Science, Technology, Engineering, and Mathematics [STEM] areas, medical schools, engineering schools, etc.). This represents a new administrative input into the governance architecture of HE and one that has been little studied regarding its impact and effectiveness. As for the transnational mass-scale proprietary HEIs, the governance relationship has been fundamentally restructured as a result of "unbundling" traditional faculty relationships and roles while transforming the faculty role within the institution to that of a focused, specialized, contract employee. Decisions typically made within traditional HEI structures as part of the governance structure are increasingly made within a corporate management framework.

There is a realization that dependence on state sources of funding and support are not likely to meet the pressing demands from students and parents in Asia for high-quality education. Therefore, it is not surprising to see that Asian governments have adopted policies to encourage the private sector to get involved in developing an education market, and public universities are being strongly encouraged to engage with industry and business for deep cooperation. In this way, states want to see more synergy between the university and enterprise for promoting innovation, knowledge-transfer, and entrepreneurial activities of different kinds (Mok 2013a; 2015; Chan and Mok in this volume). Mok's recent comparative study related to university-enterprise cooperation in selected East Asian economies such as Singapore, Taiwan, South Korea, and Hong Kong has clearly shown a growing regional trend in Asia to foster stronger and closer relationships between the university sector and industry and business. The development of these linkages has not only diversified economic activities providing a strong impetus to the development of new economic pillars in South Korea and Singapore along with an integrated pattern of innovation and creativity but has also affected the way university is managed and its performance measured (Mok 2012). Surveys and field interviews were conducted by Mok in examining how academics assess and evaluate the call for deeper university-enterprise cooperation in East Asia and how this has clearly revealed the diverse views and opinions expressed by faculty members from different academic disciplines. Predictably engineering and business sectors show more support for these efforts, while humanities and social sciences colleagues have criticized HE for being run as commercial companies in which education ideals are jeopardized (Mok 2013b; Mok and Nelson 2013). The call for closer relationship between university-industry-business has no doubt made academics more critical of the imposed forms of privatization, marketization, and commercialization of HE (Turner and Huuseyin 2014).

Thus we see the following topics, among others, addressed by contributors to the book, seeing them primarily as hypotheses to be sharpened and/or revised.

- Massification of HE has resulted in a problem as to where R&D and its innovative mission should reside in HE systems. Systems in the past have sought to lodge R&D in discrete kinds of institutions and restrict it from others (e.g., the California Master Plan) but this approach has eroded as non-research-oriented HEIs have sought to move up, resulting in a form of mission creep.
- Government policies that promote research and innovation are (a) on the increase, (b) extend to and invite new relationships especially among private sector actors (but not exclusively), (c) are occasioning new ways of linking HEIs to the research and innovation activities of society, with (d) increasingly novel ways of both financing and recovering the benefits of research and innovation (including intellectual property rights).

- University responses to university-industry-business cooperation are becoming more common among HEIs in all Asian countries (if highly differentiated) with strong implications for university governance structures and relations. Overall, research is being repositioned within university structures with a range of impacts that include re-statusing of faculty and reconsideration of the kinds of skills and capabilities that both undergraduates and graduates should possess. As a general rule the HEIs are subject to a wide range of pressures to assure that graduates have skills deemed necessary by national, regional, and global economies.
- Regarding the mission of the university, Asian university perspectives are essential here. As HEIs continue to develop across the broad range of demographic, societal, and economic transitions characteristic of Asian societies, universities are being looked upon as focused sources of retention and articulation of those elements within such societies that "make them Asian." This extends to the understanding of the university itself as an institution and its mission to embody and to continue developing Asian perspectives.
- University strategies in enhancing research capacity are becoming both more intense and more comprehensive as the range of university-related research grows. Such efforts extend from developing and sustaining research activities within HEIs, previously known almost exclusively for their teaching role, to developing curricula that align the university with major issues within the world at large (e.g., population growth and entailments, societal aging, technology transformations, climate change, global financial issues, globalization, etc.).
- Within this environment of intense concentration on R&D and innovation, impacts on university governance are large as new activities come to be pursued within universities that require novel approaches and tend to "privilege" other parts of the institution than those that gave rise historically to governance structures.

All of the above constitute what has been called a dominant paradigm in HE. However, with a new emphasis on innovation and change, there is movement in some new directions that hold much promise for the future (Hawkins 2007). The book contains two large clusters of chapters. One focused on "policy implications for shifting research capacity and development," and the other on "entrepreneurship, innovation, and development in the research domain." Taken together the chapters that make up these two parts do so in an eclectic manner utilizing multidisciplinary approaches, case study examples, policy analysis, and the historical context in which such changes are taking place. It is our hope that the diversity in approaches to these large and challenging issues will stimulate further discussion of the future development of HE's major mission: R&D and innovation.

References

Hawkins, J. N. 2007. "The Intractable Dominant Educational Paradigm." In *Changing Education: Leadership, Innovation, and Development in a Globalizing Asia Pacific*, edited by P. D. Hershock, M. Mason, and J. N. Hawkins, 137–162. Hong Kong: Springer Press.

———. 2011. "The Transformation of Research in the Knowledge Society: The U.S. Experience." In *The Emergent Knowledge Society and the Future of Higher Education: Asian Perspectives*, edited by D. N. Neubauer, 26–41. London: Routledge.

Hawkins, J. N., and W. James Jacob. 2011. *Policy Debates in Comparative, International and Development Education*. New York: Palgrave MacMillan.

Mok, K. H. 2012. "The Quest for Innovation and Entrepreneurship: The Changing Role of University in East Asia." *Globalization, Education & Society* 10 (3) September: 317–336.

———. 2013a. *The Quest for Entrepreneurial Universities in East Asia*. New York: Palgrave Macmillan.

———. 2013b. "The Quest for an Entrepreneurial University in East Asia: Impact on Academics and Administrators in Higher Education." *Asia Pacific Education Review* 14 (1): 11–22.

———. 2015. "The Quest for Global Competitiveness: Promotion of Innovation and Entrepreneurial Universities in Singapore." *Higher Education Policy* 28 (1): 91–106.

Mok, K. H., and A. Nelson. 2013. "The Changing Roles of Academics and Administrators in Times of Uncertainty." *Asia Pacific Education Review* 14 (1): 1–9.

Neubauer, D. N. 2011. *The Emergent Knowledge Society and the Future of Higher Education: Asian Perspectives*. London: Routledge.

Turner, A., and Y. Huuseyin, eds. 2014. *Neo-liberal Educational Reforms: A Critical Analysis*. London: Routledge.

Part I

Policy Implications for Shifting Research Capacity and Development

Chapter 2

Developing Research Capacity in Education Schools and Faculties in Newer Universities
Seeking Research Excellence and Entrepreneurship[*]

Annette Gough

Introduction

All forms of formal education in Australia—from early childhood through the formal years of schooling to tertiary education—are increasingly under the microscope in Australia, and internationally, with all sectors under pressure to transform their practices by better engaging students, improving student outcomes, and teaching smarter, as well as addressing a range of social and political imperatives.

This pressure includes the following initiatives that build on decades of inquiries into education and teacher education by state and federal (Australian) governments and parliaments:

- The Australian government's Better Schools Plan that begins in 2014. This is a plan to improve results of all schools and all students by introducing education reforms that evidence shows improve results with the aim of taking Australian schools into the top five in the

world by 2025. The plan is based on reforms in the following five core areas (Department of Education, Employment, and Workplace Relations [DEEWR] 2013a):
  ○ Quality teaching
  ○ Quality learning
  ○ Empowered school leadership
  ○ Meeting student need
  ○ Greater transparency and accountability
- An Early Years Quality Fund to support quality outcomes for children by assisting early childhood services to attract and retain qualified hard working professionals (DEEWR 2013b).
- A separate Australian government program to ensure improvement in the quality of teaching in Australian schools, which will focus on improving the quality of teachers in the workforce, including professional standards for teachers, collection of teacher workforce information, awards for quality teaching and school leadership, and recruitment of professionals to teaching careers (DEEWR 2013c).
- A plan for improving the quality of teacher education in Australia covering the following (Garrett and Bowen 2013):
  ○ More rigorous and targeted admissions into university courses, potentially including interviews, demonstrated values and aptitude, and a written statement.
  ○ A new literacy and numeracy test, building on the National Plan for School Improvement, that each teaching student will have to pass before they can graduate.
  ○ A national approach to teacher practicum to ensure new teachers have the skills, personal capacity, and practical experience they need to do well.
  ○ A review of all teaching courses by the Tertiary Education Quality and Standards Agency (TEQSA).
- The Office of the Chief Scientist's reports on Science, Technology, Engineering & Mathematics in the National Interest (Office of the Chief Scientist 2012; 2013) and the associated funding for improving mathematics and science teacher education.
- An Australian Parliament Senate Committee Inquiry on Teaching and Learning (maximizing our investment in Australian schools), which is due to report later in 2013 (Parliament of Australia 2012).

Each of these initiatives will impact on teacher education and thus on the teaching activities of schools and Faculties of Education[1] in universities. Ideally they should also impact their research activities but this is not so clearly enunciated in the government policies to change teacher education, teachers, schools, and early childhood settings.

One result of the frequent reviewing of teacher education programs, the introduction of professional standards for teachers, and the changes to the five yearly accreditation of primary and secondary teacher education programs by the Australian Institute for Teaching and School Leadership (AITSL 2011) (through the relevant state authorities) and early childhood teacher education programs by the Australian Children's Education and Care Quality Authority (ACECQA 2012), as well as the changes mooted above (Garrett and Bowen 2013), is an increase in the administrative workload of academics in Faculties in compliance and regulation, and revisions to courses that are taught in the teacher education programs.

Despite these pressures, research is important for the Education academics—it is part of their job descriptions as academics and it is monitored through the annual Higher Education Research Data Collection (HERDC), which measures annual research publications and research income, and the Excellence in Research for Australia (ERA) evaluation, which rates the universities' research performances (Australian Research Council [ARC] 2012b). This paper discusses strategies for enhancing research capacity and developing and sustaining research activities in Education academics.

Changing Conceptions of Universities

Faculties are not alone in experiencing increasing pressures on their work; universities as a whole are also being interrogated and directed, both in general and on their research activities in particular. It is important to analyze these directions as their flow affects Faculties.

Future directions for universities have been the focus of two recent reports—one Australian (Ernst and Young 2013) and the other from the UK Institute for Public Policy Research (Barber et al. 2013)—which are currently being examined within universities. Both reports come from outside universities but they could be influential on government policies as there is much evidence already from the Australian government's initiatives listed above that there is a common belief that "deep, radical, and urgent transformation is required in higher education as much as it is in school systems" (Barber et al. 2013, 3).

There is convergence between these reports and Universities Australia's "A Smarter Australia: An Agenda for Australian Higher Education 2013–2016" (2013a) and "A Smarter Australia: Policy Advise for an Incoming

Government" (2013b) that described four trends driving change in Australia and in Australian higher education (HE).

- The digital economy and technology that are transforming HE will require universities to change their teaching, research, structures, and business models.
- The global education market, where half or more of Australia's universities are currently highly ranked, "however, they face increased competition as many countries develop and expand their own world-class capacity in domestic and international higher education" (2013b).
- The need for universities to respond to the economy's changing needs for skilled workers in order to sustain long-term economic and social progress.
- Australia's need to improve its productivity and, while "universities make an important contribution to national innovation and productivity,... universities themselves must become more productive in the face of fiscal pressures" (2013b, 2).

These are very similar to the (Australian) Ernst and Young (2013, 6) drivers of change that are identified for transforming the HE sector:

- Democratization of knowledge and access
- Contestability of markets and funding
- Digital technologies
- Global mobility
- Integration with industry

All three reports make suggestions for the future role of universities. The Barber et al. (2013) and Ernst and Young (2013) reports addressed options for the future structuring of universities (see Table 2.1), whereas Universities Australia (2013b, 1) ignored the structuring of universities (leaving it to the discretion of the individual universities to decide their future structuring, perhaps informed by these and other reports) and made recommendations to the incoming Australian government within the context that "universities are critical pillars that support Australia's economic and industrial transformation and growth" These recommendations were as follows:

- Increasing Australians' participation at universities
- Expanding the global engagement of universities
- Supporting Australia's research effort
- Ensuring sustainable and targeted investment
- Reducing red tape

Table 2.1 Comparison of recommendations for the future structuring of universities

Barber et al. (2013)	Ernst and Young (2013)
Model 1: The elite university	Model 1: Streamlined status quo university
Model 2: The mass university	Model 2: Niche dominators
Model 3: The niche university	Model 3: Transformers
Model 4: The local university	Other models are also possible: lifelong learning, global alliance, multidisciplinary, and hybrid.
Model 5: The lifelong learning mechanism	

Interestingly, although Education students comprise around 10 percent of undergraduate students in Australian universities, the Ernst and Young (2013) report does not include Education as a choice among the disciplines to be offered in any of the their three elaborated alternative models, instead choosing to list arts, engineering, science, business, medicine/health, law, information technology (IT), design, and other. Frequently, there is silence on the topic of Education in such discussions, even though potential students would not reach university studies without primary and secondary teachers. Teacher education is an area where universities can easily grow their undergraduate enrollments because there is always demand from potential students in teacher education programs, although the students are sometimes below the academic standard demanded by some of the recent government plans (e.g., AITSL 2011; 2013; Garrett and Bowen, 2013).

Although further discussion of models for the future of universities is beyond the scope of this chapter, the models do need to be considered as, given the silences around Education as a discipline, some university councils may well decide in the future that Education does not fit their intentions to be streamlined, elite, or niche. For example, being a niche dominator is a bit difficult when, currently, nearly every university in Australia offers teacher education programs (AITSL 2013)—although the University of Melbourne and the University of Western Australia are attempting to be niche providers of graduate only teacher education.

While future structures for and governance of universities are important topics, there are a number of governmental regulatory and quality assurance requirements that currently affect academic activities in both teaching and research. At the university level the most obvious is the TEQSA, established in 2011, which replaced the Australian Universities Quality Agency (AUQA) and conducted audits on universities between 2002 and 2011.

The purpose of TEQSA is "to ensure that the quality of Australian higher education providers through quality assurance and nationally consistent regulation" (TEQSA 2011, 3). TEQSA registers HE providers, accredits courses of study, conducts compliance and quality assessments, and monitors compliance with the Higher Education Standards Framework.

As noted previously, Faculties have another layer of regulation affecting their activities due to the external accreditation of teacher education programs by the AITSL and the ACECQA and their professional standards and procedures. AITSL recently released its first "Initial Teacher Education Data Report" (2013), launched as an annual publication contributing to the evidence base of information relating to initial teacher education.

The Australian government (2013, 1) also has announced strategic research priorities aimed at addressing societal challenges to "drive investment in areas that are of immediate and critical importance to Australia and its place in the world. They will catalyze focused investments in areas for which Australia must maintain a strong research and innovation capability." The five societal challenges to be addressed are

- living in a changing environment (research outcomes will identify strategies to develop resilient natural and human environments);
- promoting population health and well-being (research outcomes will help build resilient communities and achieve a state of physical, mental, and social well-being);
- managing our food and water assets (research outcomes will identify new food production practices and systems that can accommodate competing demands for soil and water while ensuring long-term sustainability of these assets);
- securing Australia's place in a changing world (research outcomes will identify ways to improve Australia's capacity to deliver national security); and
- lifting productivity and economic growth (research outcomes will identify the challenges and opportunities in a changing world economy).

These five new priority areas identified by the Australian government cover themes similar to the previous four National Research Priority areas (ARC 2002) that they replace (listed below), with the addition of lifting productivity and economic growth in the new priorities:

- An environmentally sustainable Australia
- Frontier technologies for building and transforming Australian industries

- Promoting and maintaining good health
- Safeguarding Australia

It is very likely, subject to confirmation by the incoming Australian government, that these new research priorities will be reflected in ARC's funding selection criteria and in research funding opportunities from government agencies. In recent years ARC has reported the number of proposals and success rates by the National Research Priority areas (ARC 2012a; 2012c). There will be creative challenges for Education-discipline researchers to align their research interests with these priorities.

One potential positive for science and mathematics education researchers lies in the reports from the Office of the Chief Scientist (2012; 2013) in the prioritizing of science, technology, engineering, and mathematics (STEM) education in schools and the need for inspirational teaching, inspired school leadership, different teaching techniques in these subjects, and the allocation of funding for research, as well as curriculum development projects and teacher education program changes. These reports are consistent with documents from elsewhere as "STEM is a central preoccupation of policy makers across the world" (Marginson et al. 2013, 13). This includes Europe (Rocard et al. 2007), Canada (Science, Technology, and Innovation Council 2013), and the United States (Committee on STEM Education, National Science, and Technology Council 2013), as well as many Asian countries (reviewed in Marginson et al. 2013). The Office of the Chief Scientist's recommendations are also being supported by the Australian Industry Group (AIG 2013) who recommend that universities and industry should collaborate on business-related research projects, that business and industry develop a project bank of real-work-based research projects for use by undergraduate and postgraduate students, and that there should be a national framework and strategies to promote and implement school-industry STEM skills initiatives within Australian primary and secondary schools. Each of these initiatives has research potential for Education academics.

Sources of Research Funding for Education

In an Australian context, in addition to consultancy and commercialization income, there are four recognized sources of research income for ERA purposes—Australian competitive grants research income, other public sector research income, industry and other research income, and Cooperative Research Centre (CRC) research income.

Category 1: Australian Competitive Grants Research Income

Prestigious Category 1 funding for educational research comes from three sources: ARC, the National Health and Medical Research Council (NHMRC), and, since only very recently, the Office of Learning and Teaching (OLT). Category 1 funding is theoretically available from NHMRC but this rarely goes to Faculties as their four research pillars are basic science, clinical medicine and science, health services research, and public health (NHMRC 2013).

The main sources of ARC funding are Discovery Projects and Linkage Projects, but there is also National Competitive Grants Program (NCGP) funding for centers (with none of this funding currently going to Education areas) (ARC 2013), Australian Laureate Fellowships, Future Fellowships, and Discovery Early Career Researcher Awards.

The success rates for funding in Education are very low, as can be seen from funding in 2012 for funding commencing in 2013 (the most recent period for which data is available):

- There were 732 Discovery Projects funded, of which 15 went to Education Field of Research (FoR) codes (ARC 2012a). This is a 2.0 percent success rate when the overall success rate was 21.37 percent.
- There were 306 Linkage Projects funded, of which 15 went to Education FoR codes (ARC 2012c). This is a 4.9 percent success rate when the overall success rate was 39.0 percent.
- There were 200 Discovery Early Career Researcher Award grants funded, of which 2 went to Education FoR codes (ARC 2012e). This is a 1.0 percent success rate.

Thus, ARC funding is not easy to get in Education. This feeling is compounded by there being only 1 ARC Future Fellow in Education out of 209 granted for funding in 2012 (ARC 2011) and of 81 Australian Laureate Fellowships awarded funding between 2009 and 2013, only 1 has gone to Education (ARC 2012d).

The OLT funding for academics and professional staff to investigate, develop, and implement innovations in learning and teaching (OLT 2013) has recently been classified as Category 1 research income and this has been good for Education. However, as the funds are for projects in learning and teaching across all HE providers, successful applications come from all discipline areas. Also while the OLT has A$58.65 million in program funding over four years, in 2012 funding for ARC Discovery Projects totaled A$253,982,000 and for ARC Linkage Projects it totaled A$101,809,345—so, the OLT is a relatively small funding source.

A total of A$8.77 billion research funding was submitted to ERA 2012 (ARC 2012b, 28)—of this around A$200 million was for Education FoR code 13. Breaking this down further, a total of A$3.75 billion of Category 1 Australian competitive grants research income was submitted to ERA 2012, but only 1–2 percent of this was for Education—the majority of the funding went to medical and health sciences, biological sciences, engineering, and agricultural and veterinary sciences (ARC 2012b, 29).

Category 2: Other Public Sector Research Income

Faculties are slightly more successful in gaining research funding from tendering for government research contracts and in obtaining public sector partners for ARC Linkage Projects, with 3–4 percent of this category of funding submitted to ERA 2012 coded for Education (ARC 2012b, 30). Thus from a total of A$2.38 billion of other public sector research income submitted to ERA 2012 around A$90 million went to Education. As with Category 1 funding, the majority goes to medical and health sciences, biological sciences, and engineering.

Category 3: Industry and Other Research Income

Faculties have middling success in attaining research funding by tendering for industry and other research contracts and in obtaining industry partners for ARC Linkage Projects, with 2–3 percent of this category of funding submitted to ERA 2012 coded for Education (ARC 2012b, 31). A total of A$2.26 billion of industry and other research income was submitted to ERA 2012 and around A$60 million of this went to Education. As with Category 1 and 2 funding, the majority again goes to medical and health sciences, biological sciences, and engineering.

Category 4: CRC Research Income

Although there are no CRCs focused on Education, the CRCs do have some Education-related research income (<1%) with engineering, agricultural and veterinary sciences, and environmental sciences dominating the income submitted to ERA 2012 (ARC 2012b, 32). A total of A$372 million of CRC research income was submitted to ERA 2012; of this, around

A$2 million went to Education. This dominance by engineering, agricultural and veterinary sciences, and environmental sciences clearly matches the National Research Priority areas (ARC 2012c) discussed earlier.

Commercial Research and Consultancy

Commercial research and consultancy work is an important source of funding for Education academics. This work is often small scale but it does generate income to fund conference attendance and to provide a respite from teaching to focus on research. It is also difficult to estimate a total for an institution as it is not measured as part of the HERDC on research annual income.

Research Productivity

Although Education does not rank well on research income, Education academics are relatively more productive than the other 15 FoR code areas in research outputs (ARC 2012b, 26), exceeded only by the highly funded areas of medical and health sciences; engineering; and biological sciences, and newer areas such as information and computing sciences; commerce; management; tourism and services; and studies in human society—all of which receive more total funding across Categories 1–4 than Education.

This data supports the contention that Education academics are able to produce publications without research funding, more so than other areas. This is an important strength.

Research Quality

A final consideration is the quality of the research performance of those contributing to Education FoR code 13.

At Royal Melbourne Institute of Technology (RMIT) University, and I am sure elsewhere, Education academics were not the only contributors to the research outputs and income considered as part of the ERA evaluations. Indeed, as can be seen from Table 2.2, academics from outside the School of Education dominated the top-ten contributors to two of the three FoR codes submitted for consideration in ERA 2012. FoR codes 1301 and 1303 both show academics from inside the School of Education make up less than 50 percent of the top-ten contributors.

That this is the case needs to be taken into consideration when considering the ERA 2012 data for Education FoR code 13 in all universities, but this is not publicly available information.

Another measure of research quality in Education in Australia is the number of universities whose performance in Education FoR code 13 was

Table 2.2 ERA 2012—RMIT top-ten contributors to FoR codes from School of Education

FoR code	RMIT top-ten contributors to FoR score (volume) from School of Education (%)	RMIT top-ten contributors to FoR score (peer review) from School of Education (%)
1301: Education Systems	30% (but now 20% as one staff member has gone elsewhere)	40% (but now 20% as one staff member has gone elsewhere—only top-five were listed)
1302: Curriculum and Pedagogy	60% (but now 40% as one staff member has gone elsewhere and another has retired)	60% (but now 50% as one staff member has gone elsewhere)
1303: Specialist Studies in Education	20% (but now 10% as one staff member has retired)	30% (but now 10% as one staff member has gone elsewhere and another has retired)

rated at or above world performance and this number is then compared with other disciplines (ARC 2012b, 13). This data is quite enlightening as Education is in the lowest quartile with only 16 of the 38 universities submitted for rating rated at or above world performance and only 1 was rated 5 (1 of only 2 FoR codes and only 1 university rated 5, all other codes had 2 or more universities rated 5). These ratings beg the question as to whether academics in some fields are harder judges of their peers or whether research performance in these lower-rated fields is actually lower than world standard.

Developing Research Capacity in a Faculty or School of Education

Developing research capacity in schools and Faculties is thus a challenge with very little in the way of external funding available to support research—and where such funding does exist it tends to go to the established universities, but not always so. Of the 30 Education FoR code 13 ARC Discovery and Linkage Projects proposals funded to commence in 2013 (ARC 2012a; 2012c), 11 went to the universities rated 4 or 5 in ERA 2012 (Melbourne, Sydney, Queensland University of Technology,

Monash, and Queensland), but 1 went to a university rated 1 in Education FoR code 13 in ERA 2012, and 6 went to universities rated 2, like RMIT (ARC 2012b). So it is possible and important to look at the actions of these successful universities to develop their research capacity.

Size of the faculty is a factor—the successful universities tend to have large academic staff but this is not universal. The University of Queensland only has 35 academic staff in its School of Education, yet it is rated best in Australia in ERA 2012. Of these 35 academics, 24 are associated with at least 1 funded research project, including 5 of the 6 professors and 6 of the 7 associate professors being associated with at least 1 ARC Discovery or Linkage project.

Developing research concentrations is important. Although only rated two in ERA 2012, the University of Tasmania was awarded one ARC Discovery and one ARC Linkage grant in 2012, both in the area of mathematics education but involving different staff. Some universities, particularly in the sciences, buy whole research teams from other universities to build their profile in a particular area—this has happened in two universities where I have worked.

Building a research culture within a school or Faculty sounds amorphous but it is important to create a research space and celebrate it, perhaps well summed up on the University of Queensland's School of Education (2013) website:

> Known as one of the top research schools of education in Australia, the School of Education attracts distinguished educators from Australia and around the world. The School is widely involved in school-based and community development, professional associations, and editorial projects. With a vibrant postgraduate culture, scholars, and researchers of national and international status generate over one hundred books, monographs, and articles each year.

This is, of course, easier said than done—and one needs to believe one's own publicity in the work in progress, where Deakin University (2013) is an example:

> The School of Education (SoE) at Deakin University is widely recognized for researchers who make innovative contributions to the growth of knowledge in education. Our researchers are active contributors to the educational debate in academic and policy settings both locally and internationally. They are successful in gaining research grants and consultancies and collaborate with local and international academic and industry partners. They publish with prestigious book publishers and in high quality journals. A number of staff are editors of refereed journals and sit on international editorial boards.

Some universities offer research fellowships to experienced and early-career researchers who have the potential to develop as research leaders and initiate new research teams. For example, at RMIT, the vice chancellor's Senior Research Fellowships offer a 4-year employment contract with A$50,000 over 4 years to support the achievement of individual research goals. None of these fellowships have yet been awarded to applicants in Education.

Creating research centers is also a strategy used by schools and Faculties in most universities. Of the top-5 Education FoR code 13 universities, the University of Melbourne's Graduate School of Education, for example, is home to 10 research centers; the Faculty of Education and Social Work at the University of Sydney hosts 3 universities' centers and 6 research networks; the Faculty of Education at Queensland University of Technology has 2 research centers; Monash University has 14 Faculty Research Groups; and the University of Queensland does not have a research center but it has 8 research-only staff.

Diversifying sources of research income is an important success factor. Given the data above on how difficult it is to get ARC research funding, other Category 2 and 3 research funding is critical for ERA considerations as is consultancy funding for enabling staff to engage in other research activities and teaching relief. The University of Queensland School of Education academics, while currently completing 20 ARC Discovery and Linkage projects having 2 ARC Future Fellows and 1 ARC Early Career Researcher Award recipient, also have projects funded by the OLT, NHMRC, the Commonwealth and State Departments of Education, AusAID, Uniquest, Pathfinder, the Queensland College of Teachers, and Healthways WA.

Collaborating across institutions is also a characteristic of successful schools of Education. Queensland University, for example, has ARC Discovery Projects and the OLT projects with other universities, and the ARC Linkage grants have a wide range of partners including BHP Billiton Mitsubishi Alliance, Youth Affairs Network of Queensland, the Endeavour Foundation, SA Department of Education and Children's Services, and the expected Education Queensland. The successful ARC Linkage proposals in Education FoR code 13 for funding in 2013 are with a wide range of partners, not just state departments of education or Catholic education offices (ARC 2012c).

Strategic recruitment of staff is also important. Most universities now expect lecturing staff to hold a PhD before appointment and selection panels look for research activity; but some are even including publication and research income targets in their selection criteria. For example, in 2003 the University of Melbourne's selection criteria for a professor of curriculum studies included an expectation of research income of half a million Australian dollars a year; two applicants who were highly regarded in the field as scholars but had no research income were not shortlisted for interview (personal communication).

It is also significant that the Education academic workforce is more aged than university averages with over 60 percent of Education academics aged over 50 in 2006, compared with the 46 percent of all university academics (Hugo 2008, 20), and many can be expected to retire soon. Motivating many of these older academics to be research active when they are happy to just teach is a challenge.

Support for new staff and early-career researchers is provided in many universities with a positive affect in schools and Faculties. The Queensland University of Technology had a new-staff start-up grant scheme for several years with which it used to build the research capability of new appointees; the University of Queensland, the University of Sydney, Victoria University, and Charles Sturt University still have such a scheme. Other universities provide specific support for early-career researchers to provide them with time release to work on grant applications or enable them to travel to conferences.

Creating and reinforcing research expectations and aspirations is also a common strategy and meeting the expectations is often used as a criteria for academic staff to be able to access conference funding and other research support. At RMIT, the expectations and aspirations that are part of the College of Design and Social Context academic workload allocation model for 2014 (RMIT University College of Design and Social Context 2013, 32) are shown in Tables 2.3 and 2.4.

Table 2.3   Ranges of expected research performance at RMIT

Indicator	Level A	Level B	Level C	Level D	Level E
	Assoc. lecturer	Lecturer	Senior lecturer	Assoc. professor	Professor
ERA outputs[a]	1	1–2	2–3	3–5	3–10
Income (A$)[b]	0–20K	0–30K	20–100K	40–100K	50–250K
HDR completions[c]	0	0.5	0.75	1.0	1.5

Notes:
[a] Eligible ERA outputs include research books, book chapters, journal articles, conference publications, creative works, and commissioned reports averaged across a three-year period. HERDC weightings (one significant book is equivalent to five journal articles) have been taken into account. Both the quality and quantity of the outputs have been taken into account, with improvement in research output quality being an important target. The ranges above provide the opportunity to balance these considerations.
[b] The total annual HERDC reportable research income divided by the number of chief investigators, averaged across a three-year period.
[c] Number of HDR candidate completions either as senior/joint senior supervisor or associate supervisor in a three-year period.

Table 2.4 Ranges of aspirational research performance at RMIT

Indicator	Level A	Level B	Level C	Level D	Level E
	Assoc. lecturer	Lecturer	Senior lecturer	Assoc. professor	Professor
ERA outputs[a]	1–3	2–4	3–7	3–13	3–15
Income ($)[b]	20–60K	30–150K	40–250K	50–480K	100–530K
HDR completions[c]	0	0.75	1.0	1.5	2.0

Notes:
[a] Eligible ERA outputs include research books, book chapters, journal articles, conference publications, creative works, and commissioned reports averaged across a three-year period. HERDC weightings (one significant book is equivalent to five journal articles) have been taken into account. Both the quality and quantity of the outputs have been taken into account, with improvement in research output quality being an important target. The ranges above provide the opportunity to balance these considerations.
[b] The total annual HERDC reportable research income divided by the number of chief investigators, averaged across a three-year period.
[c] Number of HDR candidate completions either as senior/joint senior supervisor or associate supervisor in a three-year period.

Moving Forward

According to the Ernst and Young (2013, 24) report, in order to build a successful university of the future, five challenges will need to be addressed:

- Quality and academic excellence
- Academic talent and workforce structure
- Commercial skills
- Change management and speed to market
- Relationship with government

While these challenges are intended for the universities' governing bodies, they are equally relevant for Faculties seeking to build the research capacity of the academic staff.

- The outcomes of the research activities of the academics must be of high quality and academic excellence otherwise the Faculty will lose market share and relevance.
- Given the aged workforce in Faculties, they need to attract new talent and build new workforce structures that can deliver increased research productivity and support new business models.
- Education academics need to enhance their commercial skills and capability to seek new research partners.

- Education academics have been traditionally resistant to change but they will need to find new ways to be true to the mission and maintain academic integrity and independence while changing their business models and increasing their speed to market, especially with research programs.
- Government funding for Education FoR code 13 is declining in Category 1, Category 2 and 3 funding is hard to get (and there is less of it for Education under Liberal governments), and Faculties are increasingly losing out to private providers on government research contracts. Education researchers need to find new ways of working with industry and government so they are seen as key partners.

This will not be easy in a climate of declining funding to universities by governments and the global financial crisis. Change is needed if Education is to be seen as a research strength in the newer universities, and not just a teaching-only part of the university, and if academics in Faculties are to entrepreneurial and achieve research excellence.

Notes

* Please note that this chapter was written in the week that followed the Australian federal election that resulted in a change of government (September 7, 2013). The government policies discussed here are those of the former Labor government (2007–2013), as the incoming coalition government had no election policies on higher education or research funding. The only indication of the principles and policy directions the coalition will follow comes from a speech by the new prime minister to Universities Australia earlier this year where he stated, "In a constrained budget environment, to avoid further cuts rather than to win higher funding is often the best outcome that particular sectors can hope for" (Abbott 2013). In the same speech he also stated, "We will encourage universities and institutes to ensure that their research work is world class, effectively delivered and well-targeted" and that the regulatory and compliance burden on universities would be reduced.

1. Hereafter, "Faculties of Education" will be referred to as "Faculties" for simplicity and discipline of education capitalized as "Education."

References

Abbott, T. 2013. "Address to Universities Australia Higher Education Conference." Canberra, February 28. Available online at: www.liberal.org.au/latest-news/2013/02/28/tony-abbotts-address-universities-australia-higher-education-conference.

Australian Children's Education and Care Quality Authority (ACECQA). 2012. *National Quality Framework*. Sydney: ACECQA. Available online at: www.acecqa.gov.au/national-quality-framework.

Australian Government. 2013. *Strategic Research Priorities*. Canberra: Australian Government. Available online at: http://www.industry.gov.au/research/Documents/SRP_fact_sheet_web.PDF.

Australian Industry Group (AIG). 2013. *Lifting our Science, Technology, Engineering and Maths (STEM) Skills*. Melbourne: AIG. Available online at: www.aigroup.com.au/portal/binary/com.epicentric.contentmanagement.servlet.ContentDeliveryServlet/LIVE_CONTENT/Publications/Reports/2013/Ai_Group_Skills_Survey_2012-STEM_FINAL_PRINTED.pdf.

Australian Institute for Teaching and School Leadership (AITSL). 2011. *Accreditation of Initial Teacher Education Programs in Australia: Standards and Procedures*. April. Melbourne: AITSL. Available online at: http://www.aitsl.edu.au/docs/default-source/initial-teacher-education-resources/accreditation_of_initial_teacher_education_file.pdf.

———. 2013. *Initial Teacher Education Data Report. May 2013*. Melbourne: AITSL. Available online at: http://www.aitsl.edu.au/docs/default-source/aitsl-research/insights/re00057_initial_teacher_education_data_report_2013_aitsl_may_2013.pdf?sfvrsn=4.

Australian Research Council (ARC). 2002. *National Research Priorities and Their Associated Priority Goals*. Canberra: ARC, Australian Government. Available online at: http://www.cepal.org/iyd/noticias/pais/3/31523/Australia_doc_1.pdf.

———. 2011. *Number of Successful Proposals for ARC Future Fellowships for Funding Commencing in 2012 by Primary FoR Division*. Canberra: ARC, Australian Government. Available online at: www.arc.gov.au/pdf/FT12/FT12_Listing_by_FOR_code.pdf.

———. 2012a. *Discovery Projects. Selection Report for Funding Commencing in 2013*. Canberra: ARC, Australian Government. Available online at: www.arc.gov.au/ncgp/dp/DP13_selrpt.htm.

———. 2012b. *ERA 2012 National Report*. Canberra: ARC, Australian Government. Available online at: www.arc.gov.au/era/era_2012/outcomes_2012.htm.

———. 2012c. *Linkage Projects. Selection Report for Funding Commencing in 2013*. Canberra: ARC, Australian Government. Available online at: www.arc.gov.au/ncgp/lp/LP13_selrpt.htm.

———. 2012d. *Australian Laureate Fellowships Funding Outcomes*. Canberra: ARC, Australian Government. Available online at: www.arc.gov.au/ncgp/laureate/laureate_outcomes.htm.

———. 2012e. *Number of Successful Discovery Early Career Researcher Award Proposals for Funding Commencing in 2013 by Primary FoR Division*. Canberra: ARC, Australian Government. Available online at: www.arc.gov.au/pdf/DECRA13/DE13_Successful_Outcomes_by_FoR_Code.pdf.

———. 2013. *National Competitive Grants Program (NCGP)*. Canberra: ARC, Australian Government. Available online at: www.arc.gov.au/ncgp/default.htm.

Barber, M., K. Donelly, and S. Rizvi. 2013. *An Avalanche Is Coming: Higher Education and the Revolution Ahead*. London: Institute for Public Policy Research. Available online at: www.ippr.org/publication/55/10432/an-avalanche-is-coming-higher-education-and-the-revolution-ahead.

Committee on STEM Education, National Science, and Technology Council. 2013. *Federal Science, Technology, Engineering and Mathematics (STEM) Education: 5-Year Strategic Plan*. Washington, DC: Committee on STEM Education, National Science, and Technology Council. Available online at: www.whitehouse.gov/sites/default/files/microsites/ostp/stem_stratplan_2013.pdf.

Deakin University. 2013. *School Research*. Melbourne: Deakin University. Available online at: http://www.deakin.edu.au/education/research.

Department of Education, Employment, and Workplace Relations (DEEWR). 2013a. *National Plan for School Improvement*. Canberra: DEEWR, Australian Government. Available online at: http://www.budget.gov.au/2013-14/content/glossy/gonski_policy/download/NPSI.pdf.

———. 2013b. *The National Quality Agenda—Early Years Quality Fund*. Canberra: DEEWR, Australian Government. Available online at: https://www.childcarensw.com.au/images/stories/early_years_quality_fund_fact_sheet.pdf.

———. 2013c. *Quality Teaching*. Canberra: DEEWR, Australian Government. Available online at: http://education.gov.au/quality-teaching.

Ernst and Young. 2013. *University of the Future: A Thousand Year Old Industry on the Cusp of Profound Change*. Australia, Melbourne: Ernst and Young. Available online at: www.ey.com/Publication/vwLUAssets/University_of_the_future/$FILE/University_of_the_future_2012.pdf.

Garrett, P., and C. Bowen. 2013. "Higher Standards for Teacher Training Courses." Press Release. Available online at: http://www.chrisbowen.net/media-centre/allNews.do?newsId=6577.

Hugo, G. 2008. *The Demographic Outlook for Australian Universities' Academic Staff*. CHASS Occasional Papers. Canberra: Council for Humanities, Arts and Social Sciences (CHASS). Available online at: www.chass.org.au/papers/pdf/PAP20081101GH.pdf.

Marginson, S., R. Tytler, B. Freeman, and K. Roberts. 2013. "STEM: Country Comparisons." Report for the Australian Council of Learned Academies. Available online at: http://www.acola.org.au/PDF/SAF02Consultants/SAF02_STEM_%20FINAL.pdf.

National Health and Medical Research Council (NHMRC). 2013. *Research Funding Statistics and Data*. Canberra: NHMRC, Australian Government. Available online at: www.nhmrc.gov.au/grants/research-funding-statistics-and-data.

Office of the Chief Scientist. 2012. *Mathematics, Engineering and Science in the National Interest*. Canberra: Australian Government. Available online at: www.chiefscientist.gov.au/wp-content/uploads/Office-of-the-Chief-Scientist-MES-Report-8-May-2012.pdf.

———. 2013. *Science, Technology, Engineering and Mathematics in the National Interest: A Strategic Approach*. Canberra: Australian Government.

Available online at: www.chiefscientist.gov.au/wp-content/uploads/STEMstrategy290713FINALweb.pdf.
Office of Learning and Teaching (OLT). 2013. *Grants and Projects.* Canberra: OLT, Australian Government. Available online at: www.olt.gov.au/grants-and-projects.
Parliament of Australia. 2012. *Senate Education, Employment and Workplace Relations Committee Inquiry into Teaching and Learning—Maximizing Our Investment in Australian Schools.* Canberra: Senate Printing Unit, Parliament House. Available online at: http://www.aph.gov.au/Parliamentary_Business/Committees/Senate/Education_Employment_and_Workplace_Relations/Completed_inquiries/2010-13/teachinglearning/report/~/media/wopapub/senate/committee/eet_ctte/completed_inquiries/2010-13/teaching_learning/report/report.ashx.
RMIT University College of Design and Social Context. 2013. *Academic Workload Allocation Model 2014.* Melbourne: RMIT University. Available online at: http://mams.rmit.edu.au/ixt980i46hs.pdf.
Rocard, M., P. Csermely, D. Jorde, D. Lenzen, H. Walberg-Henriksson, and V. Hemmo. 2007. *Science Education NOW: A Renewed Pedagogy for the Future of Europe.* Brussels: European Commission Directorate-General for Research. Available online at: http://ec.europa.eu/research/science-society/document_library/pdf_06/report-rocard-on-science-education_en.pdf.
Science, Technology, and Innovation Council. 2013. *Canada's Science, Technology and Innovation System: Aspiring to Global Leadership.* The 2012 State of the Nation Report. Ottawa: Science, Technology and Innovation Council. Available online at: www.stic-csti.ca/eic/site/stic-csti.nsf/vwapj/StateOfTheNation2012-may16-eng.pdf/$file/StateOfTheNation2012-may16-eng.pdf.
Tertiary Education Quality and Standards Agency (TEQSA). 2011. *Strategic Plan 2011–2014.* Canberra: TEQSA, Australian Government. Available online at: www.teqsa.gov.au/sites/default/files/TEQSAStrategicPlan2011-2014.pdf.
Universities Australia. 2013a. *A Smarter Australia: An Agenda for Australian Higher Education 2013–2016.* Canberra: Universities Australia. Available online at: http://apo.org.au/files/Resource/universitiesaustralia_asmarteraustralia_2013.pdf.
———. 2013b. *A Smarter Australia: Policy Advice for an Incoming Government 2013–2016.* Canberra: Universities Australia. Available online at: http://universitiesaustralia.s3.amazonaws.com/wp-content/uploads/2013/02/A-Smarter-Australia-Policy-advice-for-an-incoming-government.pdf.
University of Queensland, School of Education. 2013. *Academic Staff.* Brisbane: University of Queensland, School of Education. Available online at: www.uq.edu.au/education/academic-staff.

Chapter 3

The Shifting Ecology of Research in Asian Pacific Higher Education
Imitation or Innovation
John N. Hawkins

In an earlier essay I referred to research and scholarship as comprising a critical, if not the most critical part, of the "holy trinity" of higher education (HE), alongside teaching and service (Hawkins 2012). This remains true today even as the nature of research changes and what I refer to here as the ecology of research is such that it remains in a state of transformation and shifting alliances. As was noted earlier, the predominant place of research and pervasive expansion of this mission into most levels of HE was not always the case. John Henry Newman's view in the mid-1800s remains relevant and in some respects is being restated in current critiques of the role of research in HE: "A university... is a place of teaching universal knowledge. This implies that its object is... the diffusion and extension of knowledge rather than its advancement. If its object were scientific and philosophical discovery, I do not see why a university should have students" (1996, 22). The relationship between teaching, learning, research, and service is finding new expression in the Asia Pacific region and the dominant paradigm of continual expansion at all levels is being tempered by the race to establish "research universities," world-class universities, and higher rankings along with the attendant contradictions and predicaments that this race entails. All of this is linked increasingly to a quest not just for excellence in these areas but also innovation, an opaque if somewhat slippery concept.

In this chapter, I will present a brief summary of the dominant paradigm of the role of research and scholarship in the modern university, the current push for innovation in a changing research environment that challenges this paradigm, explore some examples of how this is being expressed in the Asia Pacific region (as well as the United States), and propose that the role and definition of what constitutes research developed largely in the United States and Europe may not be the best exemplars for other settings (countries, regions, territories, cultures) in the Asia Pacific region. There is a changing culture of research in this region that will have powerful implications for the future transformation of HE and the role of research and scholarship. Whether this changing culture will be imitative or innovative is at issue.

Research and the Modern University: Some Observations

We have seen the continual global expansion of what has become known as the research university; even in "non-research universities" and smaller liberal arts colleges, formerly thought of as "teaching colleges," faculty are expanding their research interests and in some cases being pressured by their leadership to engage in publishable scholarship. The literature on the nature of research in HE has typically focused on one or more of the following issues: research capacity, research productivity (linked to rankings and league tables), research excellence, and research relevance or utility among others (Vessuri and Teichler 2008). There are other ways to slice the research in the HE pie including more recent concerns such as university-industry linkages, universities serving as research extensions of the state, new market conditions as they relate to HE innovation, the research capacity gap between rich and poor nations and institutions, gender equity, colonial legacies, political-economic stability or instability, the role of international agencies, and so on.

When one speaks of research in HE, the focus is generally on the so-called research university although increasingly, research is finding its way into other segments of HE as well. To take the case of the United States as an example, of the over 4,000 higher education institutions (HEIs), only 261 are classified as research institutions and there is enormous diversity within that group (Bienenstock 2008). It is generally agreed that "high-quality" research universities share some essential characteristics as follows (ibid.):

- The existence of high-quality faculty committed to research
- The recruitment of high-quality graduate students

- A supportive intellectual climate
- High quality facilities to support research
- Sufficient funding to remain competitive and up-to-date
- A research infrastructure
- Supportive leadership with a vision

Trow (1974) noted long ago that as HE moved from elite to mass education, its social role changed as well, especially the role of research and the expansion of knowledge. New subdisciplines emerged, new research agendas were proposed, and everything downstream from an expanded research program changed as well. The classic model of the research university in the immediate post-WWII period in the United States was summed up by Lyman Glenny (1959) as a period of "happy anarchy," by which he meant that faculty functioned in an environment of freedom to teach and conduct research on topics of their choice, weaving together teaching and research, and funded generously by both their own sources (either state/public funds or endowments) and the US federal government. In addition, US HEIs practiced an "open door" policy for international scholars who were recruited as faculty and visiting scholars. There had been an early postwar buy-in to supporting research by the federal government that combined with a tradition of individual philanthropy and a broad and deep commitment to public service created a free and supportive environment for individual and team research in all disciplines, but especially in the sciences and social sciences (Vest 2007).

Central to the creation of this research and scholarly environment, and also to the research infrastructure that we see today, was the report issued in 1945 titled "Science—the Endless Frontier," commissioned by President Roosevelt and authored by Vannevar Bush, the head of the Office of Scientific Research and Development. The purpose of the report was to ascertain how the members of scientific community, especially those in HEIs, could serve US interests in the postwar era. The follow-up to the report came from Roosevelt's policy adviser, William Golden, whose influence was central to the founding of the National Science Foundation (NSF), which served as a model for other national agencies (e.g., National Institute for Health, National Endowment for the Humanities, and independent nonprofit organizations such as the Social Science Research Council, etc.). All of this contributed to the development of the basic research and development (R&D) architecture for the United States where US private and public HEIs became the national R&D infrastructure paid for in large part by US federal funding. As others have pointed out, this federal concern for, and investment in, the future of research and innovation in the United States has been responsible for stimulating over half of the nation's economic growth in the twentieth century as well as bolstering national security (Courant et al. 2010). This partnership between the federal government and HEIs forever changed US HE and its research mission and capacity not just financially but also through the introduction of practices such as indirect costs, staff differentiation, staff benefits, funding for utilities, staff travel, and a variety of other support activities that came to characterize the impact of research (much of it financial) on the university. It also put "big science" at the top of the research and scholarship hierarchy and influenced research methodologies, institutional support, funding, and faculty evaluation policies in the United States as well as HE in other emerging economies. This is often referred to as the Golden Era of research in HE, which lasted up to about 1980 when this laissez-faire attitude was challenged in many ways by Japanese production techniques, concerns over national security, and the rise of neoliberalism.

A shift also began to occur about this time toward the broader commercialization of R&D and a redefinition of the role of research (Vest 2007). One policy response to these shifts was the Bayh-Dole Act of 1980 that provided US universities the right to commercialize employees' inventions made while engaged in government-funded research. While this act was beneficial to both the HEIs and private industry, it marked a further turning point toward the marketization of HE and research and has not gone without criticism (Kennedy and Patton 2009).

However, during this initial transitional period, and indeed well before it, the terms "knowledge society" and "knowledge economy" began to be used to describe the context in which HE was operating. The former, developed by sociologists, and the latter, by economists, often confronted each other as scholars sought to make sense out of this new environment. It is likely that both terms date back to Hayek (1937) who noted the importance of knowledge for economic growth with the market as the guiding mechanism and market logic as the point of departure for political and educational policy. Various waves of this intellectual trend included the relationship between information theory and economic development, what became known as the Chicago school of economics, and the rise of neoliberalism, all of which focused on the market as the guiding principle (Valimaa and Hoffman 2008). This development, in the broader political economy, began to have a transformational impact on the traditional research paradigm.

The conventional research HE paradigm then was a fairly clear model of large endowment support for the private universities, large investments by state governments for the public universities, increasing federal/central government support for both sectors so that a convergence of both public and private sectors toward increasing reliance on the federal sector of research support became the norm (Vest 2007). Federal support for research in HE grew substantially in the post-WWII era and still remains the dominant source for funding basic scientific research although this is rapidly changing as the private sector increasingly becomes a partner in more applied research. Since the early 1970s the federal share of research support in the United States has been declining while industry's share has grown rapidly. While the shares remain disproportionate, the trend is instructive (National Science Board 2007).

It is in this context of the transformation of research that the term "triple helix" began to be used to describe the new research, knowledge production paradigm (Valimaa and Hoffman 2008). It is loosely defined at this time as a state in which the university becomes a node between industry and government in the knowledge production and innovation system. There has been a remarkable amount of discussion of how this model emerged, developed, and is being adopted and transformed globally in a recursive manner. In some settings, it is referred to in the language of "networks"—research, technology, and development networks (RTDs) (Gulbrandsen and Etzkowitz 1999). In others, there has been a debate as to whether or not it is really a metaphor, a model, or a reality, for example, generally thought of as involving public sector universities, government, and industry, it may ignore the role played by nongovernmental organizations (NGOs). There is also the issue of global versus local linkages, where the setting is important, and the emergence of this model can result in a continuous disorganization of existing institutional boundaries. We see in some settings (particularly universities) that it involves the internal institutional transfer of resources from one function to another to accommodate the model (Leydesdorff and Van den Besselaar 1994). To further complicate the discussion there are multiple models of the triple helix, and increasingly they are all bound up in a renewed focus on innovation. The model transforms the ecology of research as the three components interact and change the very environment in which they live—thus, the innovative component (Birrer and Tobias 2003).

The university research culture (largely in the sciences) has obviously been affected by the emergence and expansion of these linkages. However, the same can be said for industry, at least in the United States. In an historical context as Varma (2000) has noted in her study of corporate R&D laboratories in the United States, "A new culture of dependence with a mission-oriented approach is replacing the cherished culture of independence with a result-oriented approach" (395). Much of this is attributed to the global challenges facing the United States from Asia, decline of the US share of global GNP, recognition of the global complexity of the connection between research and innovation based largely on the Vannevar

Bush model of 1945, and the rise of neoliberalism. A new research culture has developed both in industry and HE reflecting other knowledge production changes such as decentralized funding, business-driven research, customization of research, increasing involvement of non-R&D staff, results-based research (shift from fundamental to applied R&D), shift of academic research to service industry, and outsourcing research globally (Slaughter and Rhoades 1996; Varma 2000; 2006; Rhoades and Slaughter 2006).

Currently, some variant of this model is in use in most Asian Pacific settings. When speaking of "research," what is most-often meant is the "research university" as exemplified by those in the United States and Europe. What is suggested here is that the ecology of knowledge production is in a state of change and that it is useful to entertain the idea that this model, briefly summarized above, which originated largely in the West and more specifically in the United States, may not be entirely appropriate for the variety of HEIs and national settings that themselves are being transformed. In fact, the imitative urge may serve as a barrier to scholarly innovation.

Some Asian National Settings

Here we will look at a small sample of national settings that have launched major HE reforms designed to attempt to imitate this model and have succeeded to some degree. The comments below are focused on the elite, research universities in these settings, since that is where the example of what constitutes scholarship and research is most-often defined as it was in the United States. It is suggested that even for this level of HEIs, let alone the mass of HEIs in Asia, the research model historically developed in the United States and Europe may not be the most appropriate for the twenty-first century and for developing innovative universities, colleges, and scholarship.

In China roughly 150 universities have been selected through either the 211 project or 985 project and billions of Yuan invested to raise the overall quality of these institutions, especially their research endeavors. In the Chinese Academy of Sciences (CAS) institutes, equally large investments have been made in mathematics, physics, chemistry, chemical engineering, biological sciences, earth sciences, and technological sciences to bring these fields up to world-class status. Without doubt, these efforts have yielded impressive results as measured by publication rates, patent rights, and other metrics (Salmi 2009). When looked at more carefully, there remains much to be done. Evaluations of both the quantity and quality of R&D show that while HEIs, especially those benefitting from the two programs mentioned above, are now contributing around 80 percent of internationally recognized publications and that China in 2007 had a higher share of scientific publications than other East Asian nations, the quantitative output has not been matched by a similar level of qualitative improvement (NSF 2007; Simon and Cao 2009). The reasons cited for this lack in quality are several but those focused on lack of creativity and reluctance for risk taking in innovation rank high (Simon and Cao 2009).

China has also moved quickly in the direction of facilitating university-industry linkages, away from basic research and toward applied research so that a national pattern has emerged reflecting an increasing share of university-affiliated enterprises in science and technology (S&T) dominated by those HEIs in the 985 project (Zhu and Liu 2009). Nevertheless, the research gap between China's best HEIs (those in the 211 and 985 projects) and world-class universities remains large, as does the research gap between all HEIs that are not part of these two projects and those that are, thus leaving the system with a large contradiction whereby a small elite group receiving large investments from the central authorities determines the definition of what constitutes "quality" research while, at the same time, not meeting this standard itself when compared with world-class universities elsewhere. A 2006 evaluation of the 985 project asks the question of how much more investment would it take to successfully imitate the top research universities in the West: "It is uncertain for the Chinese government how much total financial support would be enough for helping the top Chinese universities reach the goal of a world-class university" (Chen 2006, 22).

Japan has taken a similar route to boost their research efforts through the so-called Toyoma Plan (Shinohara 2002), launched in 2002, and Japan's Top 30 Program (Centers of Excellence for 21st Century Plan) impacting the research directions and priorities of 31 research universities at about US$150 million/year over 5-year periods. A related program (2007) on Global Centers of Excellence funded an additional 50–75 HEIs in five new fields every five years (Salmi 2009). As might be expected, most of these efforts were in the sciences although literature and some social sciences were also impacted. In general, this centrally directed effort to raise the quantity and quality of research in Japanese HEIs and institutes had several objectives as follows (Shinohara 2002):

- Invite world-class-level researchers to join faculty in select HEIs
- Involve doctoral-level students in research teams
- Financially support young researchers such as research assistants and postdoctoral scholars

- Increase international collaborative linkages with world-class universities
- Conduct international symposia and workshops
- Upgrade research equipment
- Increase research space
- Establish laboratories overseas
- Generally take measures to promote R&D

In 2007 the Ministry of Education, Culture, Sports, Science, and Technology (MEXT) launched the World Premier International Research Center Initiative (WPI) as a further effort to meet world research standards and "position Japan within the global flow of intellectual mobility." The stated goal for this research improvement effort was to

> provide concentrated support for projects to establish and operate research centers that have at their core a group of very high-level investigators [in S&T]. These centers are to create a research environment of a sufficiently higher standard to give them a highly visible presence within the global scientific community—that is, to create a vibrant environment that will be of strong incentive to front-line researchers around the world to want to come and work at these centers. (MEXT 2007)

These are just the most prominent of Japan's efforts to increase research quality in a global context. Again the question remains as to the success of these efforts and whether they have also had an effect on innovation rather than simply imitating a research model that is perhaps inappropriate for the Japanese system as a whole. Various evaluations have been conducted by MEXT as well as other agencies or companies (such as the Mitsubishi Research Institute). As has been the case in other Asian settings, the results of such evaluations have been mixed. On the one hand, the funds expended to launch and maintain these programs have produced positive results for some of the centers but on the other hand, results are questionable for others. The general critique has been that there is a lack of information about programs such as WPI and that less than half of the "internationally leading scientists" are aware of the program (Mitsubishi 2009). As to quality of the research that can be tracked to the centers of excellence (COEs) and WPI initiatives, it is mixed as well, with much room for improvement (ibid.). A final evaluation of these programs will be conducted in 2017, but it is noted that it is questionable as to whether the expenditures can be justified given the results so far. The research gap between those few HEIs who received the funds and those who did not remains and has widened. There appears to be little discussion about the nature of research and the need for alternative models for the range and diversity of HE in Japan (Mori 2013).

In the Republic of Korea a broad program called Brain Korea 21 (BK21) was launched in 1999 to upgrade Korea's research profile for the twenty-first century. This effort focused not only on the top research universities but also singled out selective regional HEIs, thereby impacting about 50 HEIs overall. The Korea case is instructive because it demonstrates what a middle-income nation can accomplish while seeking to raise their research standards to approximate those of the leading world-class universities. The principal vehicle for this effort was BK21. With over US$1.2 billion invested over 7 years, BK21 focused on raising the quality of graduate students rather than a direct investment in faculty research per se. Nevertheless, this investment had a significant impact on the research environment in Korea's top universities. The role of the national government in funding research was central: in 2003, 76 percent of all R&D funds came from the government. Seoul National University (SNU), as the flagship HEI in the country, led the way; it has been plainly said, "Most universities in Korea are aspiring to become flagship universities like SNU, a Korean Harvard, or Korean 'Todai' [Tokyo University]" (Kim 2007, 125). So the imitative urge is well represented in Korean HE, including the tenure and promotion system, reward structure, and publish or perish policies. Kim provides an interesting discussion of the limits of this structure, the over-reliance on the Science Citation Index (SCI) and Social Science Citation Index (SSCI) in evaluating research, and comparisons between Korea and Harvard, the University of Tokyo, and the University of California at Los Angeles demonstrating how SNU has come close to matching the prowess of these three comparison institutions. However, Kim notes the limits of these quantitative approaches to measuring the quality of research and little is said about whether or not an "innovative" or creative outcome has been achieved.

Varieties of evaluations on the impact of BK21 on Korean HE research quality and capacity have been completed or are in progress (Seong et. al. 2008; Shin 2009a; 2009b). There is general agreement that according to a variety of metrics, Korean research productivity has increased since the implementation of BK21 (as measured by the number of scholarly research articles, books, and other research outputs) but, at the most, these increases basically kept pace with other developed economies and in some cases (as compared to China) fell behind. There was no narrowing of the research gap between Korean HEIs and those of the West, particularly the United States. The RAND study critiqued most of the other evaluations as well as structural impediments in Korean HE to increasing research innovation and capacity. This report proposes a new evaluation model in order to determine the effectiveness and impact of BK21 on Korean HE. At the most, one could suggest that BK21 was very effective in bumping Korean R&D in selected HEIs to a new level; but given the investment and the continuing gap that exists with other advanced systems, one can wonder if it was worth the investment or if the program was too narrowly constructed toward the goal of achieving world-class university (WCU) status. The elite nature of the effort did not positively impact the bulk of Korean four-year HEIs other than to set up a research goal not likely to be achieved by most of them (Shin 2009b).

Other HEIs in the region have focused on carving out a particular niche in which to excel and be innovative. Recognizing that it is unrealistic to be "good at everything," University of Hong Kong (HKU), the Hong Kong University of Science and Technology (HKUST), and National University of Singapore (NUS) have deployed strategies to excel in selected areas. Recruiting the best faculty both locally and from abroad as HKU and NSU have done has resulted in a faculty mix that is very diverse and who "think in different ways," according to Barry Halliwell, deputy president of NUS (Thomas 2013). Building a research niche that is related to local circumstances is another such strategy. HKUST has achieved high marks from the Quacquarelli Symonds (QS) rankings because of its research program that focuses on under-researched areas in the local region, its relatively new history as a university (established 1991), and "a hunger to be better" (Thomas 2013). These institutions appear to be pursuing strategies that are both imitative (but in highly selective ways) and innovative.

A final look at the research environment in India demonstrates the limits of the imitative model of HE with respect to research and perhaps makes the case for finding new approaches to what constitutes research allowing for some success in building an innovative university. India's colonial legacy has left it with a system of research best described by Jayaram as "retailing knowledge" (Jayaram 2007). This has left India with a research system far behind other advanced countries both in quality and in quantity of research productivity. There is a hard distinction between teaching and research, which disconnects graduate students from the research world, and provides disincentives for faculty to maintain a research program beyond their dissertation. Research remains the purview of institutes, which are decoupled from universities and thus disconnected from graduate students. So while India does not imitate the dominant model of research it has not developed any real alternative either. On the one hand, India in some respects illustrates the difficulty of linking research appropriately with HE with the intent of creating new and innovative approaches to HE and relevant research. On the other hand, India has an opportunity to try new approaches to this linkage rather than be trapped in the race to develop "world-class" HE based on the dominant model. Indiresan in some respects makes the same point by suggesting that if India has the "will" (a big if) to establish an innovative research university, it can do so "without having to face opposition from entrenched vested interests" (2007, 118). While China, Japan, and Korea are clearly on a path to imitate the dominant model of the research university, India may offer a surprise by developing a new and innovative research university.

These few examples focus on HEIs that are considered as research universities and even here, despite the investment of large sums of money from central governments, the results in terms of quality and quantity have been less than desired. In these settings, what possibility do the bulk of HEIs have of reaching these international standards through imitation?

Challenges to the Conventional Paradigm

While the scholarship and research model briefly described above continues to have great resilience and serves as a goal for most HEIs in the Asian Pacific region, there has been a growing debate about the value and feasibility of such modeling. Alternative ways are being discussed that challenge and critique this model and suggest other more creative ways to look at the role of R&D and scholarship in HE. Here we will outline some of the features of that debate to pose the possibility of new and alternative ways of thinking about the role of scholarship and R&D in the twenty-first-century university.

It has been difficult for HEIs in the region to avoid the temptation to be imitative rather than innovative. That is, the strategy of imitation (largely of US and Western European HE) has in some respects limited the opportunities for innovation inasmuch as imitation is costly, based on "ladder climbing," and is often driven by rankings rather than by new ideas. Striving for WCU status, high rankings, the desire to strive toward the "emerging global model" (EGM), and other policy goals that rely on what Deem et al. (2008) call "copying" are typical of these strategies. This is especially true of research and scholarship, which in the United States carries with it a somewhat unique history. After WWII, the predominant role of government-funded research through large competitive contracts was first inaugurated by Harvard; subsequent emulation by MIT and Cal Tech firmly established this model, which was then followed by other HEIs across the United States. It was heavily science and discovery based; while playing a positive role in those disciplines, it also generated funding for other disciplines (social science and humanities), as well as setting the standard for evaluation of faculty, departments, centers, programs, institutes, and the university itself. The question here is, is this model appropriate or even feasible for HEIs in other national settings?

As the research mission of HE began to gradually increase in dominance and stature, it also impacted the reward structure of most HEIs so that faculty began to turn away from the teaching mission of the university and focused their attention on grant writing, raising funds for their research, publications, and other research-related activities; while this first reached its maturity in the sciences it was not long before this became the evaluative model for all disciplines. Are university faculty naturally drawn toward research and away from teaching and are there implications for HEIs in the Asian Pacific region? Some studies support this assertion, while others show the opposite. Is it possible to truly strike a balance between teaching and research in the modern university or is the "research model" so prevalent in the United States and elsewhere being blindly imitated globally?

One of the contradictions in imitating this research model is that in most settings in the Asia Pacific region, as has been shown elsewhere, HEIs are expanding capacity and admitting increasing numbers of students while at the same time seeking to meet high expectations for research, fund-raising, and publication prowess. As faculty are drawn away from teaching, increasing numbers of students are left without benefiting from the presence of the very faculty they came to encounter; they are often left with junior faculty or part-time faculty teaching the basic courses. As faculty are sorted along the research axis (those who are successful and those who are not), another divide appears as those faculty less able as researchers pick up the teaching load or are simply let go through the tenure process. This increases the number of failure points in the system. Again, this model may not be the most productive for many universities and may in fact limit the possibilities of becoming an "innovative" university. A faculty reward structure that hinges on faculty's articles being published in the "best journals" increasingly leaves many behind in the race to become a faculty in a top-ranked university especially as this becomes a global race where there is an increased number of faculty seeking this status with a fairly stable limited number of elite journals. Another divide thus appears if this becomes the imitative model, still dominated by the West. If the US experience is of any relevance, following this model also decreases the number of faculty who are hired on the tenure track, which now in the United States is below 30 percent in the major research universities.

Knowledge Production

Finally, the intensity of the pressure to publish, and not just publish for the sake of publishing (although there is clearly a danger here for institutions that will never be able to imitate the elite research universities) but to publish works of significance, one of a kind research, has presented the bulk of HEIs in the Asian Pacific region (as well as the United States) with an impossible knowledge production task. While superior teaching can be found almost anywhere, the best research must go through a complex process of blind peer review to be published in the limited number of first-rate journals or by book publishers. This can lead scholars at the less-than-elite institutions to believe that it is quantity rather than quality that matters and end up producing and publishing work in lesser journals, which according to Derek Bok are of "dubious worth" (Christensen and Eyring 2011, 359). In short, the world of scholarship today is far different from the era when most of today's WCUs were evolving. Research is in general far more expensive, scholars seeking to publish far more numerous, credible outlets for publication remain narrow and confined, and the entire ecology more competitive. This does not auger well for bright new scholars seeking to make a career in HEIs that are not part of the elite research university club. This is true for HEIs both in the West and in Asia, that is, as long as the reward system seeks to imitate rather than innovate.

What would a more innovative knowledge production approach look like? Over 20 years ago, HE luminaries such as Ernest Boyer suggested adding new categories to the definition of what constitutes scholarship: integration, application, and teaching (1990). Boyer also suggested broadening the definition of what constitutes peer review, creativity, and the pace of publication, as well as recognizing the value of popular writing and textbook publication. His suggestion was that adding the categories of integration, application, and teaching to the academic personnel and reward structure might expand the idea of what constitutes scholarship. Some of his suggestions have caught on in the United States but, generally, research universities and those that aspire to join this club still adhere to the more narrow definition of scholarship and reward tenure and other promotions based on the imitative definition. How would the emerging HE community in Asia receive such a suggestion? In California the well-known California Master Plan sought to differentiate HEIs by mission with a three-tier system of research universities (the University of California), state universities (the California State University system [CSU]), and community colleges. However, recently, there have been instances of "mission creep" there as well, as some CSU campuses have sought to be more recognized as research universities offering PhD degrees and seeking research funds among other changes and the plan has lost some of its sense of mission (Douglass 2010).

More recently, the Carnegie Foundation added a new category to address these same issues titled "Community Engagement Classification." The intent was to shift the focus of scholarship to the community environment in which the HEI resides. The foundation stated,

> One of the major strengths of the institutions that were classified as engaged with their communities was a compelling alignment of mission, marketing, leadership, traditions, recognitions, budgetary support, infrastructure, faculty development, and strategic plans—foundational indicators of community engagement. (Carnegie Foundation 2014)

A question arises as to what degree such a modular scholarship classification system would be useful in the Asian region and help break the cycle of imitation and enhance innovation in the area of scholarship and research. Some revised form of the California Master Plan might also be of interest in the region. This combined with more diverse paths to tenure and promotion and an incentive system that rewards teaching and alternative types of scholarship will go a long way toward creating a truly diverse and innovative system of HE.

Imitation or Innovation in Asia? What about Massification?

In the Asian Pacific region there have been notable efforts to raise the research quality and environment to that of other world-class research universities and an argument can be made that in some of these cases the imitative effort has been worth the investment (Asia will in the next decade likely be a major leader with respect to spending on R&D projects [Wheeler 2012]), but one could still question whether there have been any innovative breakthroughs. A World Bank evaluation of research and innovation in the Asian region notes some successes in the elite institutions but concludes that efforts to imitate successfully the WCU research model has been weak and that most nations in the region including the power houses of China and the Four Tigers are underdeveloped despite large expenditures on research. It questions the capacity for innovation given the current research model and the weak position of HE (World Bank 2012).

The logic of this dilemma is as follows:

- Research universities ala the Harvard model have defined what constitutes "real" research.
- In the United States this model came to be imitated by most HEIs with little regard for whether or not the model was feasible and would lead to innovation.
- Innovations such as the California Master Plan sought to resolve this dilemma with some success but have recently experienced mission creep.
- The rise of Asian elite HEIs has also sought to imitate this model with high-profile and expensive programs such as 211 project, 985 project, Toyoma Plan, BK21, and so on with limited success.
- Massification of HE in Asia has resulted in a plethora of HEIs ill equipped to compete on one size fits all model and are thus left to struggle with even less success with an appropriate research mission.
- There is a need for alternative ways of approaching the research mission of HE not just in Asia but in the United States as well if the goal of innovation is to be taken seriously.
- There are some innovative research features that are emerging in the United States and Asia that are worthy of further study:
  - Innovative use of regional and international research networks to promote joint research—has implications for mobility and migration of faculty
  - Increased collaborative research
  - Recognizing the value of interdisciplinary research models/centers/approaches to research
  - Aligning research locally with the world of work
  - Increasing student involvement that links teaching and research especially focused on "local" needs
  - Development of new reward structures for faculty and students with respect to innovative research approaches
  - Revision of the "publish or perish" trap modeled on the top research universities
  - Experimentation with differentiated systems and mission goals perhaps inspired by innovations such as the California Master Plan
  - Recognize more than one form of scholarly contribution
  - Diversity of tenure paths and faculty contracts and alternative ways in which professors are produced—only this is likely to change the structure of academic knowledge production

- This diversity of tenure paths has been experimented with in many US HEIs but produces a class system of haves and have not's (i.e., University of California, Los Angeles [UCLA] has different scales based on competitive market place incomes, e.g., law, management, medicine, education, etc.)
- Need for customized contracts with equitable rewards related to discovery, integration, application, and teaching; Harvard Business School (HBS) course development experience, case studies, course development track to tenure, and so on—scholarship based on development of teaching and learning is valued at HBS while many other business schools like Anderson follow the traditional model
- Regarding tenure, the problem is with the process and not the outcome—the publication-focused, lengthy, uncertain process does not square well with the diversity model of different paths to tenure and scholarship; improvement suggestions include abolishing rank—everyone to be a professor, no rank based on research productivity, use of new incentive models based on diversity, have a probationary status that then moves to continuing status, have clearly stated objectives, reviews, and incentives to innovate, and less emphasis on measures such as SCI, SSCI, and the like (Reed 1995)
- Consulting can help establish contact with the outside world and also help define scholarship in new ways, particularly if it helps connect students to the world and if the scholarship performed advances knowledge; the HEI must allow such work without requiring that it be "discovery," one of a kind scholarship, or imitative of the research university model.

Altbach has clearly stated that developing and maintaining WCUs and their centrally important research programs is extremely difficult and not likely to be successfully imitated in most nations. It requires the coming together of a constellation of factors that pose many challenges: sufficient funds, a history of large-scale public funding, excellent scholars, institutional autonomy, academic freedom, excellent research facilities, and so on (Altbach and Balan 2007). It is not likely that the HEIs that are less than flagship can reach these goals—there are questions about whether they can even do it. And, these are imitative goals, based on the experiences of the elite HEIs largely in the West, with Harvard at the apex of the imitated HEIs. What about the mass of HEIs that are not flagship? Surely there needs to be an effort to reconsider the research goals, objectives, rewards, uses, and innovations that might come from the bulk of HEIs in the Asia Pacific region that have arisen as a result of massification and could provide a feasible model for both teaching and research, for appropriate research projects with appropriate publication outlets and appropriate standards. This is the challenge for a new ecology of research for Asia and most likely other national and cultural settings as well.

REFERENCES

Altbach, P. G., and J. Balan, eds. 2007. *Transforming Research Universities in Asia and Latin America: World Class Worldwide*. Baltimore, MD: Johns Hopkins University Press.

Bienenstock, A. 2008. "Essential Characteristics of Research Universities." In *Universities as Centers of Research and Knowledge Creation: An Endangered Species?*, edited by H. Vessuri and U. Teichler, 33–40. Rotterdam: Sense Publishers.

Birrer, F., and S. Tobias. 2003. "Linking Science and Business: Examples of Educational Innovation." Paper presented at Leiden Institute of Advanced Computer Science, Rotterdam, The Netherlands, August 26–29.

Boyer, E. L. 1990. *Scholarship Reconsidered: The Priorities of the Professoriate*. Princeton, NJ: Carnegie Foundation for the Advancement of Teaching.

Bush, V. 1945. *Science—the Endless Frontier*. Washington, DC: United States Government Printing Office. Available online at: http://www.nsf.gov/od/lpa/nsf50/vbush1945.htm.

Carnegie Foundation. 2014. "About Carnegie Classification." Available online at: http://carnegieclassifications.iu.edu/.

Chen, X. 2006. "Ideal Orientation Policy-Making: Analysis of the 985 Process." *Peking University Education Review* 4 (1) January: 28–45.

Christensen, C. M., and H. J. Eyring. 2011. *The Innovative University*. San Francisco: Josey Bass.

Courant, P. N., J. J. Duderstadt, and E. N. Goldenberg. 2010. "Needed: A National Strategy to Preserve Public Research Universities." *Chronicle of Higher Education*, January 3.

Deem, R., K. H. Mok, and L. Lucas. 2008. "Transforming Higher Education in Whose Image? Exploring the Concept of the 'World Class' University in Europe and Asia." *Higher Education Policy* 21:83–97.

Douglass, J. A. 2010. "From Chaos to Order and Back." *Center for Studies in Higher Education*, Research and Occasional Paper Series 7 (10): 1–20.

Glenny, L. 1959. *The Autonomy of Public Colleges: The Challenge of Coordination*. New York: McGraw-Hill.

Gulbrandsen, M., and H. Etzkowitz. 1999. "The Convergence between Europe and America: The Transition from Industrial to Innovation Policy." *Journal of Technology Transfer* 24:223–233.

Hawkins, J. N. 2012. "The Transformation of Research in the Knowledge Society: The U.S. Experience." In *The Emergent Knowledge Society and the Future of Higher Education*, edited by D. E. Neubauer, 26–41. London: Routledge.

Hayek, F. 1937. "Economics and Knowledge." *Economica* 4:33–54.

Indiresan, P. V. 2007. "Prospects for World-Class Research Universities in India." In *Transforming Research Universities in Asia and Latin America*, edited by P. G. Altbach and J. Balan, 95–122. Baltimore, MD: Johns Hopkins University Press.

Jayaram, N. 2007. "Beyond Retailing Knowledge." In *Transforming Research Universities in Asia and Latin America*, edited by P. G. Altbach and J. Balan, 70–95. Baltimore, MD: Johns Hopkins University Press.

Kennedy, M., and D. Patton. 2009. "Reconsidering the Bayh-Dole Act and the Current Invention Ownership Model." *Research Policy*. Available online at: doi: http://hcd.ucdavis.edu/faculty/webpages/kenney/articles_files/09%20research%20policy.pdf.

Kim, K. S. 2007. "The Making of a World-Class University at the Periphery." In *Transforming Research Universities in Asia and Latin America*, edited by P. G. Altbach and J. Balan, 122–143. Baltimore, MD: Johns Hopkins University Press.

Leydesdorff, L., and P. Van den Besselaar, eds. 1994. *Evolutionary Economics and Chaos Theory: New Directions in Technology Studies*. London: Pinter. Available online at: www.carnegiefoundation.org.

MEXT. 2007. "World Premier International Research Center (WPI) Initiative." Available online at: www.mext.go.jp/english/research_promotion/1303822.htm.

Mitsubishi. 2009. *Report on the Results of the Questionnaire of WPI Initiative*. Tokyo: Mitsubishi Corporation.

Mori, R. 2013. Correspondence with Professor Rie Mori, National Institute for Academic Degrees and University Evaluation.

National Science Board (NSB). 2007. *Science and Engineering Indicators 2006*. Washington, DC: National Science Foundation.

National Science Foundation (NSF). 2007. *Asia's Rising Science and Technology Strength: Comparative Indicators for Asia, the European Union and the United States*. Arlington, VA: National Science Foundation, Division of Science Resources Statistics.

Newman, J. H. 1996. *The Idea of the University*. New Haven, CT: Yale University Press.

Reed, K. 1995. "Citation Analysis of Faculty Publication: Beyond Science Citation Index and Social Science Citation Index." *Bulletin of the Medical Library Association* 83 (4): 503–508.

Rhoades, G., and S. Slaughter. 2006. "Academic Capitalism in the New Economy: Challenges and Choices." *American Academic*. Available online at: http://firgoa.usc.es/drupal/files/Rhoades.qxp.pdf.

Salmi, J. 2009. *The Challenge of Establishing World-Class Universities*. Washington, DC: World Bank.

Seong, S., S. Popper, C. Goldman, and D. Evans. 2008. *Brain Korea 21, Phase II A New Evaluation Model*. Santa Monica, CA: RAND Education.

Shin, J. C. 2009a. "Building World-Class Research University: The Brain Korea 21 Project." *Higher Education* 58:669–688.

———. 2009b. "Classifying Research Universities in Korea: A Performance Based Approach." *Higher Education* 57:247–266.

Shinohara, K. 2002. "Toyoma Plan—Center of Excellence Program for the 21st Century." In *National Science Foundation Tokyo Regional Office*. Tokyo: Japan.

Simon, D., and C. Cao. 2009. *China's Emerging Technological Edge: Assessing the Role of High-End Talent*. Cambridge, UK: Cambridge University Press.

Slaughter, S., and G. Rhoades. 1996. "The Emergence of a Competitiveness Research and Development Policy Coalition and the Commercialization of Academic Science and Technology." *Science, Technology, and Human Values* 21:303–339.

Thomas, K. 2013. "Scientific Research: How Asia Carved Its Niche." *Guardian*, January 17.

Trow, M. 1974. "Problems in the Transition from Elite to Mass Higher Education." In *OECD Policies for Higher Education*. Paris: OECD.

Valimaa, J., and D. Hoffman. 2008. "Knowledge Society Discourse and Higher Education." *Higher Education* 56:265–285.

Varma, R. 2000. "Changing Research Cultures in US Industry." *Science, Technology, and Human Values* 25:395–416.

———. 2006. *Managing Industrial Research Effectively*. Hyderabad: ICFAI University Press, 1–202.

Vessuri, H., and U. Teichler, eds. 2008. *Universities as Centers of Research and Knowledge Creation: An Endangered Species?* Rotterdam: Sense Publishers.

Vest, C. M. 2007. *The American Research University from World War II to World Wide Web*. Berkeley: University of California Press.

Wheeler, D. 2012. "Asia Will Power Growth in Research and Development This Year." *The Chronicle of Higher Education*, January 4, 2012, 1–3.

World Bank. 2012. *Putting Higher Education to Work: Skills and Research for Growth in East Asia*. World Bank East Asia and Pacific Regional Report. Washington, DC: World Bank.

Zhu, W., and N. C. Liu. 2009. "Research Performance of Chinese Research Universities: A Scientometric Study." *Journal of Higher Education* 30 (2): 30–35.

Chapter 4

Time for Balanced Thinking
Reflections on Dichotomous Multiple Missions of Public Higher Education in the United States

Stewart E. Sutin

Introductory Comments: Framing the Debate

Public higher education (HE) in the United States has evolved in different ways as societal needs have changed over time. Currently, concerns have arisen regarding affordability, access, accountability, quality of education, cost-effectiveness, campus security, and graduation and job placement of colleges and universities. Public HE functions in a context characterized by economic volatility, intense financial strains faced by most students and parents, a more diverse student population, breakthrough technologies, increasing reliance upon adjunct faculty and online education, and a troubled P-12 public education system that graduates far too many students who are not college ready. Institutions are called upon to operate at lower costs, while restraining tuition pricing and improving quality of education and student support services. At the same time, state funding is unpredictable and has not kept up with growth in enrollment and demands for more and better services. By 2012 state and local government funding of public HE had reached its lowest level in 25 years per full-time-equivalent student (State Higher Education Executive Officers 2013). These realities should cause leaders and faculties to reflect upon discretionary choices that include their institutional missions, research and teaching priorities, core curriculum, and the operating environments that support these missions. The complexity of these problems mandates strategic responses. While the choices are many, this chapter will examine contested ideas about "massification," defined herein as unsustainably broad institutional missions and murky curriculum. It postulates that lack of focused and realistic institutional missions and curriculums contribute to inefficient deployment of resources, higher costs, and inferior learning outcomes. The gloomy outlook for improved funding of public HE supports the case for fundamental reforms. In as much as the US experience continues to be of great interest to HE reformers in the Asia Pacific region, it is important to examine HE development in this particular setting.

The Public Debate: A Narrative of Contested Ideas

The public interest in HE has a broad constituency. It includes government officials, educational foundations, employers, parents, and students. Their frustrations stem from decades of tuition increases in multiples of inflation, lack of transparency, mounting levels of student debt, graduation and job placement rates deemed unacceptably low, and perceptions of attitudinal indifference within the academy. A shift by some states toward performance-based funding illustrates a growing conviction that colleges and universities are incapably managed. A growing body of presidential and gubernatorial commissions and foundation-funded studies articulate similar concerns (US Department of Education 2006; Delta Cost Project 2011; Pennsylvania Department of Education 2012). Tenured faculty are often depicted as being resistant to change. Their attention has focused on *institutional output*. Absent reform, some believe that the prognosis for HE is dismal. This was articulated in the US Department of Education report as follows: "History is littered with examples of industries that, at their peril, failed to respond to—or even notice—changes in the world around them" (US Department of Education 2006). Fairly or unfairly, perceptions matter.

The missions of public HE vary by sector and institution, as they serve between 75–80 percent of all students in HE. Research 1 universities are charged with broad responsibilities to support scholarship, create knowledge, and nurture talents that will serve students in their chosen professions and personal lives. Many offer an expansive delivery system. Community and technical colleges reside at the other end of the continuum and educate more than 40 percent of all students enrolled in HE. More than 1,100 2-year colleges serve educational and skill development needs in their respective regions. They do not support research agendas, and are dedicated to instruction and a comprehensive mission that includes a transfer function to four-year colleges, terminal associate degrees and certificates in workforce occupations, developmental education for students who are not college ready, and community education. Non-research 1 public universities, many of whom offer graduate degrees in select fields, serve still other perceived public needs. Many of these universities, especially in states such as Pennsylvania and New York were originally founded as "normal schools" to train teachers for local public school districts. Some non-research 1 public universities include research and scholarship within their mission. Inevitably, broader missions and expansive curriculum weigh upon cost of instruction as more courses, some with low enrollment, are added to plans of studies. Are institutions willing to contract their mission and/or curriculum so that financial and other resources are aligned with more clear and sustainable priorities? Do administrators and faculty accept the need to cease being *all things to all people?*

A balanced analysis of the public record does reflect responsiveness of public HE to meet broader societal and student expectations. The rapid growth of online education and use of instructional software offers one example of gradual change. The expanding array of student support services demonstrates sensitivity to the types of challenges facing many students. Globalization of curriculum and respect for diversity on campus offer further illustrations of change. The rapid growth of the community college system and expansion of its mission in response to local socio-economic needs is remarkable. Horrific acts of violence on campus have prompted institutions to develop emergency preparedness and response plans. These offer but a few examples of HE responsiveness. Yet the bar by which performance is judged by the public has risen while public funding for HE is constrained. Many influential leaders outside of HE singularly dwell upon perceived shortcomings.

Critics of colleges and universities concern themselves with improvement of output indicators, while many colleges and universities concern themselves with educational and service inputs. Within this contextual cauldron, emotions often compromise objectivity and sound judgment. Examples of bad behavior include the sudden dismissal, then rehiring, of the University of Virginia president, Florida politicians call for eliminating anthropology from the curriculum, efforts by the Texas Board of Regents to control the president of University of Texas (UT) at Austin, and demands by the governor of Texas for public universities to deliver a 4-year college degree for US$10,000 without increasing public funding.

A *New York Times* Op-Ed written by Frank Bruni quotes Hunter Rawlings, president of the Association of American Universities, with reference to the conflict between the governor's Board of Regents and the president of UT, Austin, as "the epicenter of the public debate about the function of higher education" (Bruni 2013). Messages are clear. Adverse consequences await those who fail to contain tuition costs and improve upon measurable outcomes. Traditional respect for institutional autonomy and academic freedom of public HE is at risk. Public colleges and universities must recognize how high the risk quotient has risen and mitigate massification while developing a more comprehensive strategy.

Institutional Mission, Academic Purposes, and Massification

A clear and sustainable mission and curriculum are foundational elements of a highly effective institution. Lack of clarity, focus, coherence, and sustainability inevitably undermine sound decision making applied to allocation of human, financial, technological, and facilities resources. Aspirational or vague mission statements muddle decision-making processes and detract from requisite operational efficiencies. Non-research 1 colleges and universities who embrace research as a central component of their institutional mission may cause unsustainable financial strains on annual budgets by reducing faculty course loads or by setting research productivity expectations likely to compromise quality of instruction. An empirical study to examine the pervasiveness of mission massification and its budgetary consequences will contribute to our understanding of this phenomenon. For example, while the state system of public HE in California seemingly embraces research, it is important to quantify the implications for instructional cost and quality. In contrast, Framingham State University, Massachusetts, has adopted a limited institutional mission by placing quality of instruction at its core. Further research of mission statements of non-research 1 public universities will help measure the extent to which massification of institutional mission is problematic.

Research 1 universities must address their general education goals and their alignment with curriculum and pedagogy. Massification of curriculum, according to some authorities, comes at a cost of adding courses to meet faculty interests more than student needs. Derek Bok, former president of Harvard, has written, "A closer look at the record...shows that colleges and universities, for all the benefits they bring, accomplish far less for their students than they should" (2008). Bok further opines that too often general education goals and curriculum are "incoherent." Frank Rhodes, former president of Cornell, cautions that the traditional university is apt to change over the years due to "new learning technology, harsh financial constraints, and changing public demand...but must keep student learning at the heart of its mission" (2001). Curriculum supportive of articulated general education goals will improve learning outcomes for undergraduates, while lowering cost of instruction as low enrollment courses and those failing to support articulated learning outcomes are dropped from the course roster. To date, most gains in faculty productivity and cost of instruction result from hiring more adjunct faculty, increasing course loads and numbers of students per class section, and reliance upon online education. The above may pose adverse consequences to quality of education, while leaving massification of curriculum in place.

Community colleges, often called "the people's college," arguably face the most sensitive challenges for constraints on its mission. The birth of two-year colleges largely took the form of junior colleges, with a clear purpose of providing two years of liberal arts education for students intending to continue their education at four-year colleges. After World War II, many returning veterans sought career training at two-year colleges—leading directly to employment. This need was anticipated by the so-called Truman Commission in 1947 and the passage of the GI Bill. During the next 25 years, career and workforce education became a core component of the 2-year college mission. Many junior colleges were renamed community colleges, while newly founded schools were named community or technical colleges at the outset. Open enrollment, rather than competitive admissions, remains the norm. More recently, the mission of many comprehensive community colleges has evolved to include "developmental" education for high school graduates unprepared to undertake college studies and community education that serves a wide range of needs and interests of local populations. In the face of increasing student enrollment and declining state funding, more community colleges leaders are questioning the viability of comprehensive institutional missions. Developmental education offers an illustration of mission expansion to meet societal needs. American College Testing (ACT) reveals that a minority of high school graduates are college ready. According to data provided by American Association of Community Colleges, 60 percent of students attending community college require one or more developmental courses in reading, writing, and math. According to a recent study by ACT, "A large gap exists between how school teachers perceive college readiness of high school graduates and how college instructors perceive the readiness of incoming first year students" (ACT 2012). The question arises as to whether community colleges can function as the educational safety valve for students who are not college ready. Perhaps an improved solution can be found through changes of public policy and funding.

One example of effective responsiveness within HE comes to mind. Several community colleges have successfully hosted a "middle college" collaboration with school districts in which at-risk high school students are brought to community college environments for their class work. Students who attend were identified as being unlikely to graduate high school. Greater use of instructional technology and a shift from lecture to learning-centric environments have produced extraordinary results. Many of these models are portable. The Community College of Allegheny County, Pittsburgh, Pennsylvania, hosted a middle college that served an estimated two hundred at-risk high school students per annum from four school districts. All were identified as highly probable dropouts by the four high school partners in our consortium. On the average, 90 percent graduated on time with a normal high school diploma and 60 percent continued on to college. Why are state education budgets not built around proven models instead of limiting curriculum, emphasizing rote-based learning as the basis for statewide tests, and limiting important components of curriculum? A financial and educational model built around first-time success is far more cost effective than later, and largely failing, efforts at remediation. The private sector has learned that quality control on the front end yields superior, more reliable, and cost effective product. Public education has much to learn.

Collaborative intervention strategies between HE and school districts built upon more effective pedagogy and instructional software offer solutions that conventional and failing models of assembly line production/learning processes do not. Certain improvements in the educational and business models of some sectors of HE are best achieved through more thoughtful systemic reforms and more strategic changes of educational policy at the state level. Until that occurs, those who design state public HE policy are more part of problem than the solution. Should state education policy fail to facilitate collaboration intervention in support of at-risk high school students, community colleges may need to reluctantly reconsider the viability of offering developmental education courses due to lack of adequate financial resources.

Funding Outlook for Public HE

Those leaders and faculty in public HE who await material and sustainable improvement of public funding for HE are misinformed, given to wishful thinking, or both. Leaving aside prevailing budget deficits at the state and federal government levels, underfunded state pension liabilities are somewhere between US$1 and US$3 trillion—depending upon the actuarial assumptions. As pension outlays come due, the shortfalls will be funded by current state operating budgets. The financial consequences from unsustainable retirement and health care plans are upon us. Competition for state monies comes from P-12 education, Medicaid, and other forms of human resources support, the criminal justice system, a decaying transportation and water supply infrastructure, and wasteful spending practices. As a result, total state funding of public HE declined from 12.3 percent of aggregate annual budgets in 1987 to 10.3 percent in 2011 (National Association of State Budget Officers 2013).

Public HE in many states will do well to hold onto current budgetary allocations. Aggregate student debt is an unsustainable US$1 trillion, while other consumer debt also hovers around US$1 trillion. Average income of medium-income household has declined during the past ten years. The premise that students and/or their parents will assume still higher levels of debt to pay for the cost of a college education defies logic. Constrained access to public funding of HE is likely to persist.

Notwithstanding recent and relatively modest funding increases for public HE in some states, much of the damage has already occurred. Overall state funding of HE fell by 7.6 percent in FY 2011–2012 (Gallup 2013). According to data released by the Center on Budget and Policy Priorities, Arizona and California tuition had increased by 78.4 percent and 72 percent, respectively, from FY 2008 to FY 2013. During the same years, tuition increases of between 38 percent and 67.3 percent took place in Florida, Washington, Georgia, Alabama, Hawaii, Nevada, Colorado, and Louisiana (Center on Budget and Policy Priorities 2013). Gross federal debt is projected to exceed US$17 trillion by 2013 year end, compared to US$11.9 trillion in FY 2009 (US Government Debt 2013). The Pew Center on States calculates an aggregate US$1.38 trillion state funding deficit caused by underfunded pension and health care benefits for retirees (Pew Center on States 2012). Medicaid spending in the United States totaled US$413.9 billion in FY 2011 and average student loan debt came to US$24,300 in the first quarter of 2012, with 90-day+ delinquency rates moving steadily upward (Federal Reserve Bank of New York 2013). Declining purchasing power of middle- and lower-income families brought about reductions of funding college for their children from an average of US$7,000 in 2008–2009 to US$5,700 in school year 2012–2013 (Belkin 2013).

Awareness of a failing business model mounts within HE. A recent poll conducted of college and university business officers by Gallup for "Inside Higher Education" reported that only 27 percent strongly agree that the prevailing institutional business model is sustainable during the next 5 years, while 92 percent believe that student retention is key to revenues (Gallup 2013). Another survey consisting of four hundred presidents and chancellors of four-year colleges reports, "Now more than ever, finances dominate what college presidents think about on a daily basis" (*Chronicle of Higher Education* 2013). A survey conducted in 2013 by Gallup for "Inside Higher Education" reports that an estimated 60 percent of college and university presidents worry that "budget shortfalls and declining state support will be a challenge for their institution in the coming year" (Gallup 2013). Is it any wonder that *Economist* reported "many American universities are in financial trouble" in an article bylined "The College-Cost Calamity" (*Economist* 2012). These are among the many data points that raise serious questions about the sustainability of student debt and excessive reliance upon tuition and public funding as core elements of prevailing business models in HE. Financial realities suggest that public HE must acclimate itself to a culture of increasing financial self-reliance.

As times change, so too must the skill sets of leaders in public HE. Complex problems require comprehensive solutions. In this context, serious questions arise about the sustainability of massification of mission and curriculum within public HE.

Concluding Observations

To paraphrase Mohandas Gandhi, if we could only close the gap between what we are capable of doing and what we actually do, most of the world's problems can be solved. The good news is that only few problems facing public HE are beyond our capacity to influence—if not solve altogether. The base of a good-quality education exists and need not be created. Outstanding public research 1 universities, many of which are among the world's elite, are in place. A prodigious delivery system makes education physically accessible and is supplemented by a growing body of online degree programs. Much is already known about the kinds of changes needed and processes proven to work within HE. As HE develops skill sets to serve educational and business leaders for the future, why not apply that know-how to foment internal innovation, data-based planning and decision making, diagnosis of mission and curriculum, and metrics that define successful outcomes. Massification of mission and curriculum must be addressed as colleges and universities explore ways to improve educational quality, endeavor to improve learning outcomes for students, and make public HE more accessible, affordable, and accountable.

References

ACT. 2012. *National Curriculum Survey.* Iowa City, IA: ACT. Available online at: http://www.act.org/research-policy/national-curriculum-survey/.

Belkin, D. 2013. "Parents Shell out Less for Kids in College." *Wall Street Journal*, July 23. Available online at: http://online.wsj.com/news/articles/SB10001424127887324144304578622343932131354.

Bok, D. 2008. *Underachieving Colleges: A Candid Look at How Much Students Learn and Why They Should Be Learning More.* Princeton, NJ: Princeton University Press.

Bruni, F. 2013. "Frank Bruni's Blog." *New York Times*, April 12.

Center on Budget and Policy Priorities. 2013. "Media Briefing: Examining States' Dramatic Higher Education Cuts and Tuition Increases." Press Release, March 19.

Chronicle of Higher Education. 2013. *What President's Think: A 2013 Survey of Four-Year College Presidents.* Washington, DC: Pearson. Available online at: http://results.chronicle.com/PresSurveyP1?elid=CLP2013print.

Delta Cost Project. 2011. *Trends in College Spending 1999–2009.* Washington, DC: American Institutes for Research.

Economist. 2012. "Higher Education—The College-Cost Calamity." August 4.

Federal Reserve Bank of New York. 2013. *Student Loan Debt by Age Group.* New York: Federal Reserve Bank of New York. Available online at: http://www.newyorkfed.org/studentloandebt/index.html.

Gallup. 2013. *Gallup-Inside Higher Ed College and University Presidents Panel— 2013 Survey 3 Findings.* Washington, DC: Gallup. Available online at: http://www.gallup.com/services/176747/gallup-inside-higher-college-university-presidents-panel-2013-survey-findings.aspx.

National Association of State Budget Officers. 2013. *Fiscal Survey of States, Spring 2013.* Washington, DC: National Association of State Budget Officers. Available online at: http://www.nasbo.org/publications-data/fiscal-survey-states/fiscal-survey-states-spring-2013.

Pennsylvania Department of Education. 2012. *Governor's Advisory Commission on Postsecondary Education: Report and Recommendations.* Harrisburg, PA: Pennsylvania Department of Education. Available online at: http://teampa.com/wp-content/uploads/2012/11/ACPE-Final-Recommendations-11-14.pdf.

Pew Center on States. 2012. *The Widening Gap Update.* Report. Washington, DC: Pew Charitable Trusts, June 18. Available online at: http://www.pewtrusts.org/en/research-and-analysis/reports/0001/01/01/the-widening-gap-update.

Rhodes, F. 2001. *The Creation of the Future: The Role of the American University.* Ithaca, NY: Cornell University Press.

State Higher Education Executive Officers. 2013. *State Higher Education Finance, FY 12.* Boulder, CO: State Higher Education Executive Officers, The College Board. Available online at: http://www.sheeo.org/resources/publications/shef-%E2%80%94-state-higher-education-finance-fy12.

US Department of Education. 2006. *A Test of Leadership: Charting the Future of U.S. Higher Education.* A Report of the Commission Appointed by Secretary of Education Margaret Spellings. Washington, DC: US Department of Education. Available online at: http://files.eric.ed.gov/fulltext/ED493504.pdf.

US Government Debt. 2013. "Government Debt in the United States—Debt Clock." Available online at: http://www.usgovernmentdebt.us/.

Chapter 5

Why the Asian Craze for Publication?
An Examination from Academic Regime
Po-fen Tai

Introduction

Over the past two decades, Asian countries have been engaged in an academic competition for academic publishing, and this amazing growth of academic publications is found in Singapore, Japan, South Korea, Taiwan, and China where countries are regarded as newly industrialized economies (NIEs). According to the databases of Thomson Reuters, the volume of publications in the East Asian NIEs has exceeded that of the United States, which was the main contributor for academic publications between 2006 and 2010 (Taiwan Research Report 2011, 5). Taking 1991 as the baseline year where the index equals 100, South Korea, China, Singapore, and Taiwan all have experienced significant growth in the publication volume, more rapidly than the United States and Japan, the world's leading nations for innovation and technology (Figure 5.1).

However, the myth that progress is being made in terms of research productivity may be broken if relative citation impact is taken into account. During the 2006–2010 period, except for Singapore, the relative citation impact of academic research in Korea, Taiwan, and China was lower compared to the global average (see Figure 5.2). In the meanwhile,

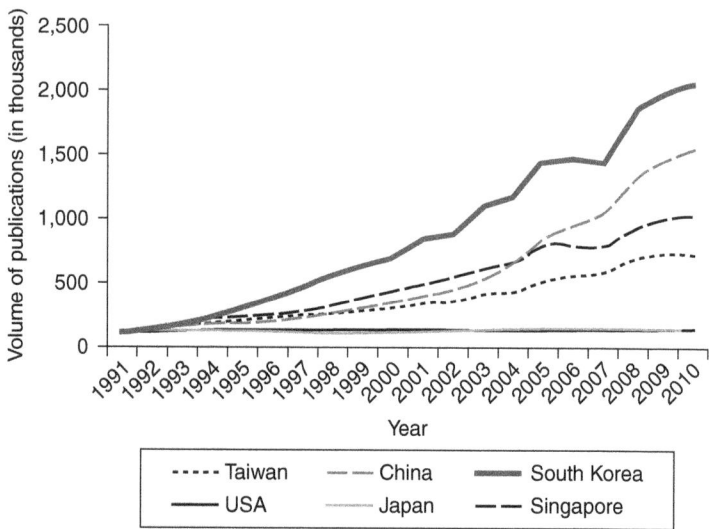

Figure 5.1 Volume of publications compared to 1991 (1991 = 100) in selected Asian countries.

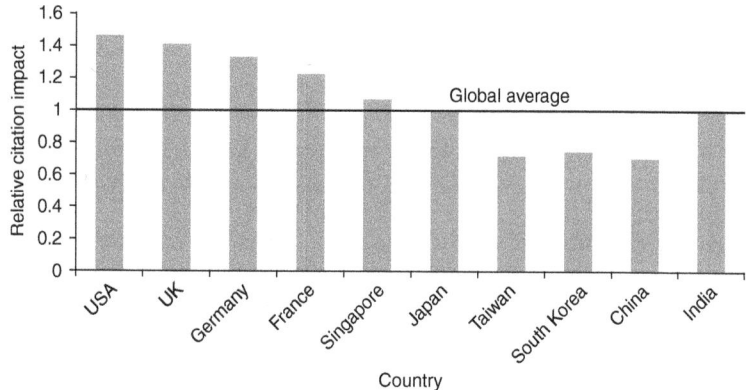

Figure 5.2 The relative citation impact in selected countries, 2006–2010 (global average = 1).

the share of the top 5 percent and top 1 percent highly cited articles shows that Singapore is the only country that has a high relative citation impact, higher than China, Taiwan, South Korea, and even Japan (Taiwan Research Report 2011, 8).

Ideally, the research community largely determines the research agenda, while the governments distribute the funds to maintain the capacity of economic knowledge and innovation and accept the responsibility for social and economic development. To understand the characteristics of academic development, Glänzel (2000) identified four basic patterns and research profiles: the Western model, the characteristic pattern of former socialist economies in transition, the bioenvironmental model, and the Japanese model. The Western model is categorized by a focus on clinical medicine and biomedical research as seen in European and North American countries. The characteristic pattern of former socialist economies in transition focuses on physics and chemistry, with China being a prime example. The bioenvironmental model is commonly seen in developing nations and countries that are heavily dependent on their natural resources such as Australia and South Africa, where there is a concentration on biology, earth sciences, and space sciences. The Japanese model is found in developed Asian economies, with a higher focus on engineering and chemistry.

Glänzel's classifications contribute to the characteristics of an academic production system. However, his model simplifies the Asian academic patterns and also insufficiently characterizes the change of academic development. There are different scenarios for different East Asian NIEs. Taiwan and China are well represented in agriculture, engineering, and mathematics. Japan is proficient in chemistry, space, immunology, botany, and geography. Singapore is excellent in a variety of natural fields such as chemistry, space, mathematics, immunology, botany and geography, biology and biochemistry, molecular biology and genetics, clinic material, economics, environment, botany, and agriculture. South Korea is proficient in material engineering, space, and botany (Taiwan Research Report 2011). With an increasing importance of science and innovation in economic development, the governments have been drawn into playing role in funding research and in deciding on overall research directions and priorities.

This chapter attempts to understand why academic publishing in the East Asian NIEs has been recently increasing. The explosion of the number of academic papers published included in this study is so unusual that it invokes some questions. Why and how are these East Asian NIEs involved in this academic competition? Why has South Korea, rather than China, produced relatively more journal articles? How can the academic performance of Singapore, a city-state, be better than the other Asian countries in both quality and quantity? What factors influence the growth in publishing?

Academic Regime: A Concept beyond Academic Market

Higher education (HE) serves important societal needs for scientific and technological innovation that benefits economic development. In the intellectual landscapes of the East Asian NIEs, one common characteristic is that the state plays a determinant role in leading research and HE systems. HE is highly regulated, while a fundamental difference is that HE has various patterns of academic regimes characterized by different educational policies and research and development (R&D) labor market regulations. All five NIEs are, in different ways, attempting to build world-class research universities at the top of the system and to contribute research and top-level training to knowledge economy. Drawing on the comparisons for the publication of journal articles, this chapter proposes the concept of the "academic regime" to explain academic development in the five NIEs.

According to Stephen D. Krasner (1983), the term "regime" within international relations is defined as "implicit or explicit principles, norms, rules, and decision-making procedures around which actors' expectations converge in a given area of international relations." Derived from the liberal tradition, regime is a form of government including a set of rules, cultural or social norms, that regulate the operation of government and that affect the behaviors of states, institutions, or social actors. However, the normative definition is not agreed upon by most analysts who question how the "norms" and "principles" of a given regime should be defined. The emphasis on consensus here is a bias in favor of seeing continuity and a stable order in an international regime. It begs the further question of how the consensus is made, as well as whose norms and whose rules? The different institutions are shaped and reshaped within the interaction of agencies and actors. This dynamic model has a strong implication for the interpretation of regime stability and change.

Borrowing from the concept of a regime, "academic regime" is defined as "institutions shaped by the interactions of state, market, and academic community and influenced by the agencies and actors in the academic fields." Academic regime can be regarded as a triple helix of the state, market, and academic community (see Figure 5.3). Academic regimes are developed by states' policies and public investment, and reshaped by the market as well as the academic community in the context of political, economic, and social change. A common characteristic in the NIEs is that states intend to develop their economies by promoting research and HE. Economic growth is ensured by regulating manpower and promoting specific research fields, especially technology research focused on the

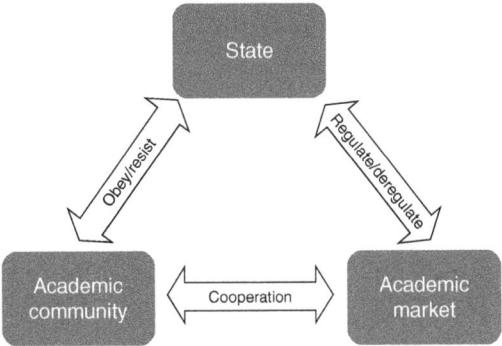

Figure 5.3 The dynamics of an academic regime.

economic-growth orientation. Based on the belief of "blue-sky research," which indicates the role of HE and research is to meet the social need for scientific and technological innovation (Altbach and Forest 2006), states should provide substantial educational finance and directly control the scope, scale, and direction of HE, including disciplines, courses, and professions.

In the last two decades, the demand for HE has grown in the East Asian NIEs accompanying the growth of economic development. HE is more affordable and accessible for the public because of the increase of GDP and household income. However, governments are reluctant to increase educational resources to meet the rising expenditure of the hallmarks of HE. In order to deal with the public finance crisis, the governments of Japan, Taiwan, South Korea, and China have to adopt an open policy for HE and allow the private sector more opportunities to meet the demands of people desiring to learn. Growing private institutions and new research agencies have forged a new relationship between university and enterprise, and in turn push the governments to deregulate and to increase the autonomy of university and institutions. These developments have enhanced capacity in research commercialization and in the transfer of university-generated inventions and discoveries to commercial sector.

Recently, the five Asian NIEs have been experiencing a change in the role of the state regarding research policy and HE development, a rise of private institutions, and enhanced university-industrial partnerships. Different stakeholders, such as academic communities and business groups, have now been demanding involvement in establishing research priorities and financial allocations. To respond to the pressures from a variety of stakeholders, governments have to restructure research funding by redefining universities' responsibility and competitive R&D funding mechanism based on performance and merit, according to the Organization for Economic Co-operation and Development (OECD) report (2003). These lead to universities and academic communities looking for more publications and innovations to obtain more research funding.

In contrast, the emergence of less-regulated academic labor markets in Asia and HE systems is consistent with the shift of the role of university, which is expected to develop a new cooperation with enterprise and be independent from the states' control. Especially in Taiwan and South Korea, universities play an important role in pushing the political transformation from authority to democracy. In response to the requirements for universities to be autonomous, the governance for HE has shifted from a states' regulation to a new system of oversight that introduces a new incentive mechanism. Furthermore, to attract the investment of private sectors in HE, some regulations on the work conditions of faculty, quotas for students, fees, and land use of campuses have been lifted. The academic community is partially allowed to participate in the decision about the development of disciplines, courses, and resource distribution.

However, continuous and satisfying employment of academic profession has become insecure because of the decline of the lifetime employment system and a growing number of academic staff that are excluded from regular employment. The academic communities' capacity to resist state control and to respond to market direction varies according to the degree of autonomy the university has as well as the identification and organization of the academic community. First, the state continues to play a role in promoting mass-oriented HE and establishing hierarchical university systems in the East Asian NIEs, although the growth and diversification of HE increases the autonomy in academic fields. Second, the degree of commercialization and privatization in the HE system also influences the role and status of academic profession. The boundaries between the market and academic community are blurred and reshaped by the new technology transfer laws. To obtain more research funding, the promotion of R&D has become the major mission for universities and research institutions. The academic communities have to deal with the decline of the "elite" status because of the increase in the number of faculty, sometimes in a relatively uncontrolled way. The pressure for international publication has been growing as an increasing competition within private labor market. The introduction of pay scales for the professional ranks makes the international publication not only the prestige of professional status but also salary, income, and employment opportunities. While research and publications have become the primary means for resource distribution and academic status, the increase of publication is at the expense of the quality of teaching and services activity (Boyer 1990).

Three Types of Academic Regimes

Just as there are significant variations in the details of economic and political development among the five NIEs, the interactions among state, academic enterprise, and academic community make it likely that the countries will proceed along slightly different academic paths. To characterize academic regimes in the East Asian NIEs, two dimensions of measurement are developed, one focusing on state policies for HE and strategies for promoting manpower in R&D as well as innovation, and another focusing on the employment system, between lifetime employment and contracted employment (sometimes combining with tenure track).

The first dimension mainly indicates the resource distribution under different forms of an HE system. The mission of the university in Asia, based on utilitarianism, is to meet the demands of national defense or economic and social development. In terms of manpower, states in the East Asian NIEs adopt two strategies. One is referred to as the elite orientation where states set goals of academic development through funding and resourcing. The other strategy is local popularization by expansion of knowledge and an increase in the manpower for R&D in private sectors. In the case of Singapore, the languages of the colonial powers remained and were enforced by the state, while in Taiwan and South Korea, and their colonizer Japan, the tradition of HE was transformed and replaced by the American university model, regarding HE as human capital investment while encouraging the expansion in private sectors. Singapore is a typical example of a country that uses the elite model where the state still controls quality by managing the manpower markets. The state intends to develop HE as a means of improving manpower and technological innovation, while it attracts global investment and regional R&D talents. In contrast, Japan, South Korea, and Taiwan adopt a dual HE strategy—keep a bureaucratic control on public universities and expand the manpower market through private sector and therefore create a new HE service industry for universal access. Developing from the elite to mass stage of HE, China provides another example of development toward the expansion of HE by the scale and scope of the manpower dedicated to this endeavor.

The second dimension focuses on the international and internal competiveness through academic employment and evaluation. As research and scholarships have increased in importance, so have various definitions of academic roles and responsibilities that reflect a major change in the roles of the profession. Associated with campus democracy, larger academic stakeholders and the business community have demanded involvement with establishing of research priorities and making decisions on financial allocations and the research direction of a university. International publication has been introduced as a tool for evaluating the performance of a faculty and deciding the funding distribution and the conditions of employment such as status, salary, and even the qualification for getting an employment. Accompanying an increased involvement in HE by the private sector, there has been an increase in the degree of commitment to research activities, emphasis on the role of research linking business firms, and contributions to particular disciplines such as engineering, medicine, and natural science.

In parallel to these developments, the employment of faculty has changed from lifetime employment to contracted employment, which is not necessarily combined with a tenure track. Japan and Taiwan represent a typical lifetime employment model, which is associated with senior-level faculty in public universities but is changing to a short-term and insecure employment for the new scholars in private universities. China, like Japan, adopts a lifetime employment model for meeting the rising demand for professionals. On the contrary, Singapore demonstrates the use of contracted global elites. South Korea has now adopted a contracted system combined with a tenure track where a person's prestige, salary, availability, research resources, and even the longevity of career is determined by an evaluation process.

Using this analytic framework (Figure 5.4), three ideal types of academic regimes are identified: state-led global elite competiveness (Singapore), a dual system—public elite and private universal access model (Japan, Taiwan, and South Korea), and state-directed mass model (China).

Type 1: State-Led Global Elite Model

Singaporean government develops HE as a new industry. To increase competitiveness, it expands the public investment and recruits international elites. The characteristics of Singaporean HE include (1) an increase in budget expenditures; (2) global elite immigration; (3) international publication market; (4) international educational market; (5) diversification and flexibility of faculty employment; and (6) low university autonomy.

Singapore is a unique case in Asia in that it has a single, international publication market and finds access to international networks without

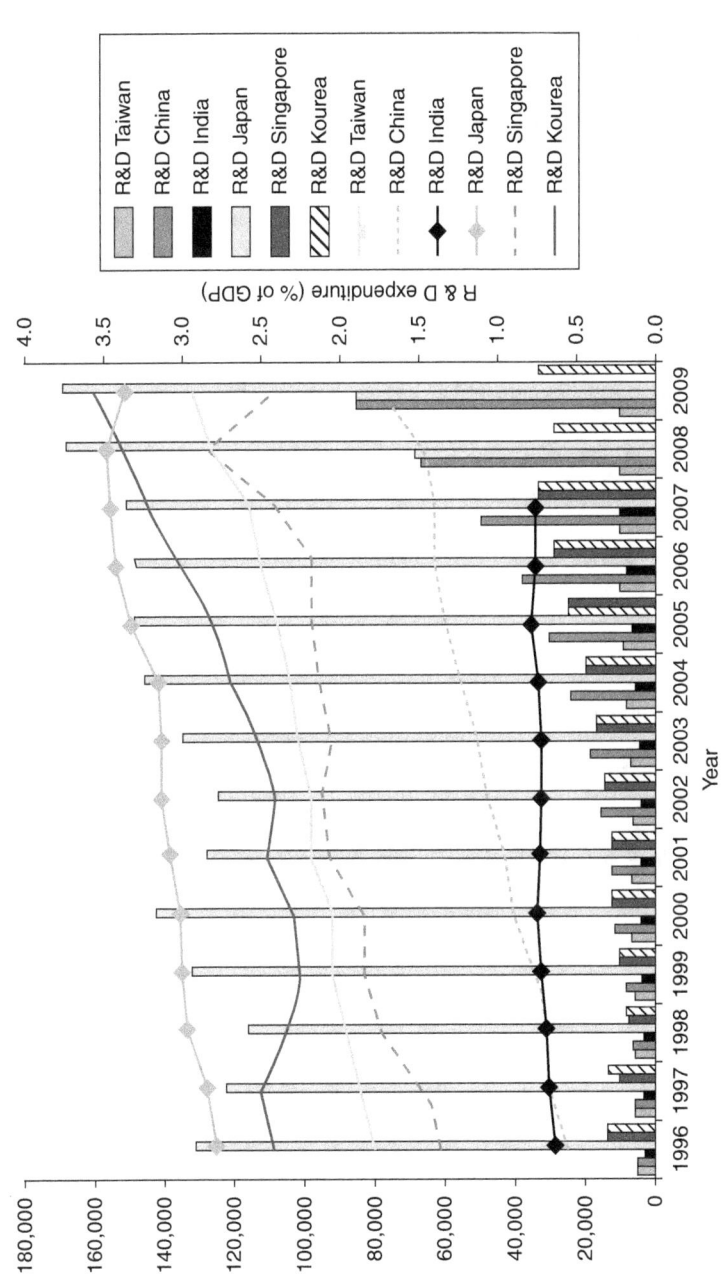

Figure 5.4 The expenditure on R&D and its share to GDP.

major difficulties. The role of language has to be taken into consideration when examining its connections in the international academic community. The policy to use English is considered as a way of enhancing Singapore's completive edge in the global market. Furthermore, Singaporean state adopts a strategy to develop a variety of fields by introduction of international expatriate staff. They comprise between 16 and 20 percent of the universities' academic staff (Selvaratnam 2007, 188). State control and interventionist policy over "borrowed manpower" increase the efficiency and output of publication, and thus promote the performance of Singapore's universities in the world university rankings.

Type 2: A Dual System Model

The HE in Japan, South Korea, and Taiwan has kept as both a public sector controlled by the government and, at the same time, an expanded sector by means of privatization. Their common characteristics include (1) an increase in private investment; (2) brain drain and limited local talents and immigration; (3) dual publication market; (4) internal educational market; (5) from lifetime to contracted employment; and (6) limited university autonomy.

Japan represents a case of stagnant academic development. Public institutions experienced financial shortfalls in the 1980s. The publication rate in Japan has failed to increase because of insufficient funding and uncertain employment. The growth rate of funding is 29.78 percent, while the growth rate of researchers was 5.81 percent. To stimulate academic publishing, the government has adopted diversification of employment based on faculty's achievement. In the 1980s, the fixed-term contract system was introduced for faculty and their status of employment was no longer ensured. Contracted and part-time employments have replaced the lifetime employment in private institutions. A young faculty must secure a series of qualifications, with the most valuable being the publication of research articles; but still a formal position is not guaranteed.

Taiwan and South Korea have shown a similar trend of the increases in funding and manpower. The growth rate of researchers in Taiwan and South Korea was 119 percent and 146 percent, respectively, while the growth rate of funding was 114 percent and 145 percent, respectively. As enrollments, which are uncontrolled by the states, have grown, the academic systems have become oversaturated and highly competitive within the expansion of the private sector. With little research funding, the members of the academic profession, especially in private sectors, engage in publication competition in order to sustain their academic careers. They are forced to produce more volumes to meet the evaluation requirements but not necessarily improvement the publication's quality. Furthermore, the HE in Japan, South Korea, and Taiwan all face a similar difficulty in the shortage of students owing to the transformation of population structure—aging population and a decrease in population due to very low fertility (Park 2006; Yonezawa 2006). International mobility is a new emerging phenomenon among the East Asian NIEs. As a consequence of the oversupply of graduates and researchers, the new talents are forced to look for new opportunities in neighboring countries. There is a significant movement from Japan, South Korea, and Taiwan to Singapore and China, the rising educational industry areas. The traditional industrialized economies are now facing the brain drain that may reduce their innovation and creativity occurring not only in the education sphere but also in other areas of technological and economic development.

Type 3: State-Directed Mass Model

China represents a model consistent with characteristics of a developing socialist country, including (1) a growth of public investment; (2) increasing local talents and constrained immigration; (3) dual publication market; (4) internal educational market; (5) public servant employment; and (6) low university autonomy.

Along with the dramatic expansion of HE, China has shown an amazing increase in global scholarly publications. During 1996–1999 period, the aid for research funding grew at a rate of 721 percent while the growth rate of manpower was only 112 percent. The numbers associated with HE were quite large, although it still enrolled 25 percent of the age cohort. The scale of population and manpower constitute the competitive edge China has regarding employing researchers in the future. The growth of the research profession is ensured by the Chinese government. China has the potential for the highest volume of research articles and the exponential growth of manpower.

Explanations for the Differences of International Publication

Why is Singapore more successful than the other four countries in international publications? Academic publishing is influenced by three factors: funding, manpower, and language. These factors should be considered within academic regimes, which are constructed and restructured through the interactions of state, academic market, and academic community. First, financial input for publishing is associated with publications. Based on the public investment hypothesis, more financial input will produce more academic papers. With a trend toward greater selectivity and competitiveness in limited resources and positions, both universities and faculty are increasingly evaluated and assessed by publications and innovations. The second factor is regarding the human resource hypothesis. The manpower is directly associated with the production of articles. Finally, as a universal and dominant language in the area of natural science, medicine, and engineering, English is direct access to knowledge and technology of advanced world economy.

First, the expansion of public investments in R&D stimulates the growth of publishing. In the past decades, public funding of university research is one of the major instruments used by the government to steer academic development. The governments input funds to develop "knowledge economy"—greater reliance on intellectual capabilities, specially innovations in high-technology and biomedicine. Figure 5.4 shows that the R&D funding steadily increased in Taiwan, China, India, Japan, and Singapore, but grew flexibly in South Korea. Japan was the country with the highest expenditures on R&D, at US$169,181 million in 2009, which is equal to 2 times the spending in China, 5 times that of Taiwan, 8 times that of India, 36 times that of Singapore, and 5 times that of South Korea. However, both the quality and quantity of publications in Japan were inconsistent with its funding. The publication rate in China exceeded Japan during the 2000–2006 period. Meanwhile, the quality of publications in Singapore also surpassed Japan.

From 1996 to 2009, in terms of the percentage of GDP expenditures, Japan shared the highest percentage of R&D to GDP, higher than Taiwan, Singapore, China, and India. However, in 2009, South Korea shared the highest percentage of R&D to GDP, even moving beyond Japan (3.36%) by reaching 3.56 percent. Taiwan and Singapore are the next highest in R&D expenditure of the states. At the same time, China continued to input more and more resources in R&D and showed the steepest growth rate from US$4,880 to US$84,850.

Japan, Taiwan, and South Korea are currently facing public fiscal stringency and the resulting trend toward significant underfunding in HE. Governments are empowering public universities and lifting administrative interventions that used to regulate budgets, fees, courses, and even quotas for students. In contrast, Singapore and China are two exceptions that continue to add public funding to boost HE. Singapore is a unique case in regard to the state-led global elite model because it views HE as a new international industry. China is another unique case because it represents the characteristic pattern of former socialist economies in transition, where states promote HE by both expenditure increases and the deregulation for private sectors.

The second explanation is from the human resource hypothesis. The increase of manpower directly contributes to the publication rate. There are two sources for academic manpower: one mainly comes from universities and the other comes from R&D, including researchers in public and private sectors.

Research is not a good business—it requires heavy investments with high risks; most of the time the knowledge gained from research findings is not profit making and may also be unexpected. Thus, the university is an important base for R&D and the training of researchers. Accompanying the expansion of HE, the increase in teaching staff constitutes the new engine for producing academic journal articles. Figure 5.5 shows that the academic staff grew amazingly in China, at 265.9 percent during the 2000–2010 period. Taiwan, Japan, Singapore, and South Korea all kept slighter growth rates during the same period. Figure 5.6 illustrates the details of the change of manpower in R&D. Except for Japan, the manpower growth increased greatly—manpower tripled in Singapore in 1996, while it doubled in China, South Korea, and Taiwan during the same period. Indeed, the increase of manpower in R&D compared to 1996

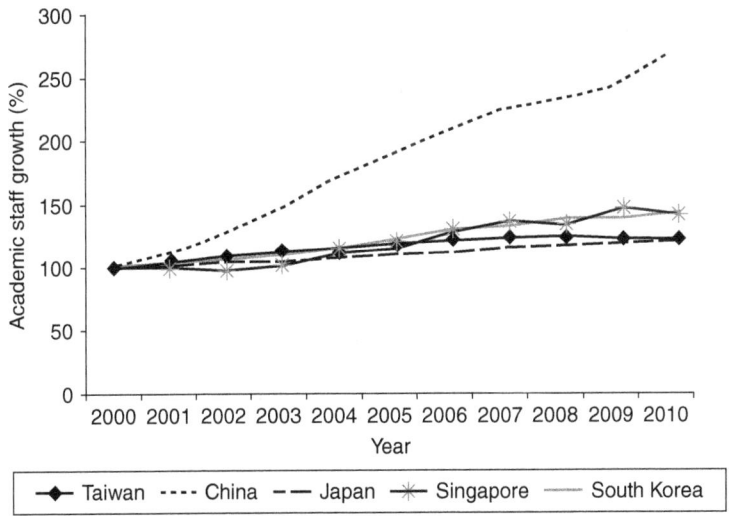

Figure 5.5 The growth of teaching staff from 2000 to 2010.

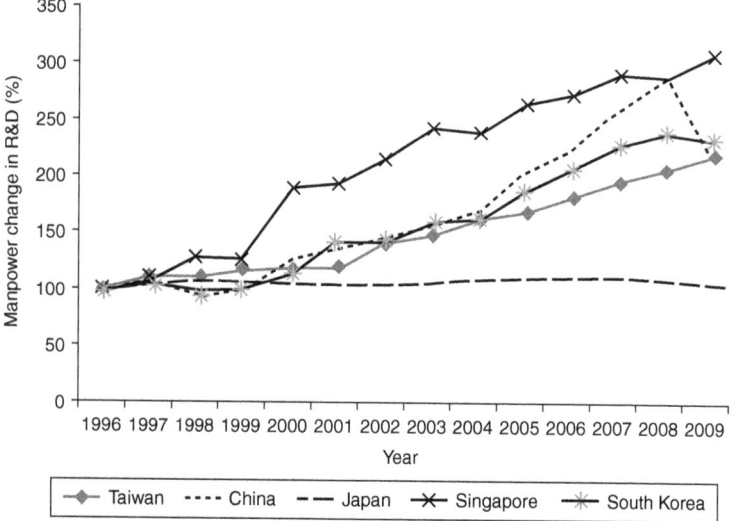

Figure 5.6 The increase of manpower in R&D compared to 1996 (1996 = 100).

grew rapidly in Taiwan, China, South Korea, at 219, 212, 230, and dramatically in Singapore, at 308, while that in Japan was only at 106.

In terms of the average funding pre researcher, from 1996 to 2009, a scholar in Singapore shared the highest research expenditure, from US$0.22 to US$0.30; with Japan, from US$0.11 to US$0.12; Taiwan, from US$0.06 to US$0.09; Korea, from US$0.08 to US$0.17; and China, from US $0.03 to US$ 0.11 (see Figure 5.7). Singaporean scholars shared the highest expenditure, at even more than US$1 million every year, about 4 times that of Japan, and 36 times that of China. Corresponding with funding, Singapore had the highest productivity, with an average of 0.25 volumes of publications per scholar, more than South Korea and Japan, at 0.12 and 0.11 volumes, respectively, as well as Taiwan and China, at 0.07 and 0.05 volumes, respectively (Figure 5.8).

The productivity of publication is considered under the various academic regimes. Under the academic regime of the Singaporean model, an abundance of funding and the recruitment of international talent has promoted academic publishing and vaulted Singapore beyond Japan and the other East Asian NIEs, recently, in respect to quality. The concentration of funding by the government, combined with low academic autonomy, has allowed universities to achieve their goals of economic and social development.

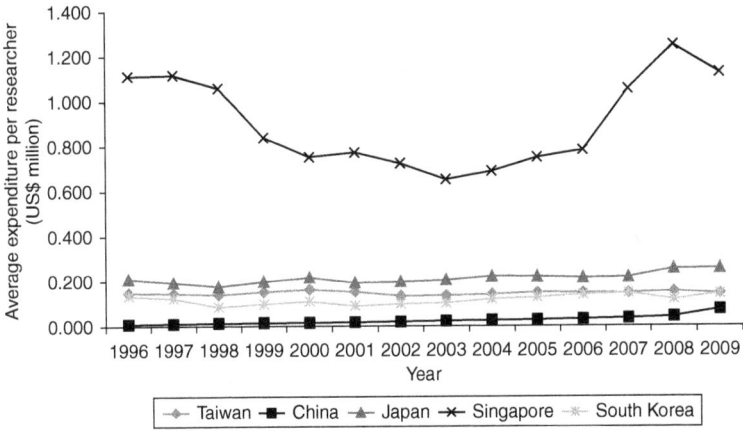

Figure 5.7 The average expenditure per researcher from 1996 to 2009.

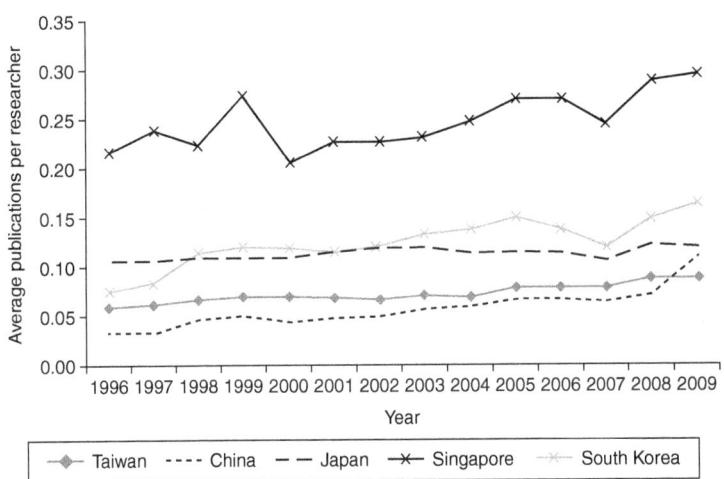

Figure 5.8 The average volume of publications per researcher from 1996 to 2009.

In contrast, Japan has shown a stagnated growth in HE, along with its "loss of two decades," after the collapse of asset price bubbles within the Japanese economy. The hierarchical structure of HE helps the university to remain as a screening device for limited elites who can obtain a status and permission for lifetime employment in large enterprises when they graduate from select universities. Lifetime employment ensured to certain senior faculty in the academic profession comes at the cost of uncertain employment and career for new faculty. The uneven allocation of resources is not decided by the government alone but also with the assistance of senior members of the academic community who are at the top of the higher education institution (HEI). Their aim is to create world-class research rather than to improve value addition of education to industry. The deficits in the Japanese academic regime may be a cause for its loss of leading position in Asia for academic publishing, and may further influence the innovation and creativity of manpower utilization.

Compared with Japan, significant progress in academic publishing in Taiwan and South Korea makes the case for manpower increase in R&D and HE transformation from elite to universal access. First, the difficulty that HE systems face at the turn of the millennium is the increase of manpower diluting government expenditures. The funding for an individual researcher is not stable, is unpredictable, and is highly competitive. The growth of numbers without a parallel increase in government financing threatens the quality of instruction and research. Second, scholarly publication has become the main criteria for evaluating professional performance and thus creates a competition of quantity of academic publications among academic faculty. Professionals are in danger of losing their positions and careers within the commercialized education system. The dictum "publish or perish," suggests that young faculties are forced to generate useless research and articles, while some leading professors focus less on their students in the pursuit of tenure. A more competitive academic market, but limited funding, leads to short-term, basic, quantitative research publications.

China represents a typical case of transformation of the post-socialist model, where HE plays an important role in reconnecting with an international milieu. A loan from the World Bank has helped China improve its academic and scientific standards in universities and research institutions since the reform of the socialist market economy in the late 1980s. To catch up with most other developed countries in the world, the Chinese government has adopted an open door and decentralization policy, which includes growth of a diversified HE system, an increase of university autonomy, a diversification of funding and resources for research and HE, the promotion of the faculty status, and a reorganization of the university. However, the dramatic increase in HE throughout the 1990s was accompanied by disproportional budget allocations between elite and nonelite, formal and nonformal, and public and private institutions (Hayhoe and Zha 2006).

Finally, with regard to the publication market, the role of language has to be taken into consideration when examining its connections in an international academic community. Singapore has a single, international publication market, while China, Taiwan, Japan, and South Korea have "two arenas"—international and local publications. The single market, like Singapore, finds access to international networks without major difficulties. The state provides public resources and supports an international commitment of their faculty to produce international publications. In contrast, the countries with two arenas are developing international cooperation and publications, although a home scientific community and publications in the respective countries' language still plays a major role, especially in the fields of social science and literature. Because of the language barrier and unique system of employment, HE in Japan has developed in isolation from the global HE community (Yonezawa 2006). Similarly, South Korea, Taiwan, and China also face the difficulties of language barrier for international publication.

Conclusion: The Limit of Growth under Various Academic Regimes

To compare the performance of academic publications, academic regime has been developed and defined as "the institutions shaped by the interactions of state, market, and the academic community and the influence these agencies and actors have in academic fields." An academic regime is not only a model of government but also a dynamic framework among state, market, and the academic community, which is embedded in a wider background of political, economic, and social development. By analyzing HE, funding distribution, and academic employment, three types of academic regimes have been identified: state-led global elite model (Singapore), dual system model—public elite and private universal access model (Japan, Taiwan, and South Korea)—and state-directed mass model (China).

The specific national academic regimes in the East Asian NIEs are experiencing a common evolution summarized by HE policies shifting from national oversight to institutional autonomy, from states' control to the market, and from local franchising to a growing international competition. Singapore is, clearly, developing better than the other East Asian NIEs in terms of international academic publishing. Singaporean government develops HE as an international industry by increasing national funding and recruiting international elites. With funding increase and recruitment of international elites, Singapore presents a successful integration of publication within state-controlled global competition. It exalts the quality and quantity of publication; it thereby promotes the rank of university and produces practice-oriented, high-level, and international manpower in selected fields. Through an incentive package, Singapore still attracts many expatriates without tenured positions, although they are alienated from local society. These have been combined with a highly competitive HE environment to fuel the drive for its intellectual publications.

In contrast, Japan, Taiwan, South Korea, and the new follower, China, are on their way toward deregulation, privatization, and commercialization of HE systems. However, they are witnessing credential inflation and an oversupply of HE systems with the shrinking of the population. They illustrate a state-led local elite model where the state plays an important role in distributing educational and research resources, ensuring that scientific research benefits both social and economic development. Leading national universities play an important role as a screening device for occupational and professional positions. The quality of academic publications has been maintained by the support of national funding and established academic communities, but at the expense of new staff's positions and careers. They are simultaneously facing decline of the professional status and educational devaluation. The governments of Taiwan and South Korea do not evenly increase their funding but concentrate their resources on a small number of universities in order to increase their competitiveness. Battling for survival, junior faculties are forced to produce more articles in this publication competition. The growth of competitiveness, especially in these two countries has stimulated the increase of the quantity rather than the quality of international publications.

China is still heading toward the expansion of the HE market under the direction of the state. Although China still falls behind the other East Asian NIEs in both funding and productivity, it is one of the fastest expanding areas in regard to the expansion of funding and manpower in both HE and research.

The growth of academic publications reflects a great transformation in the HE system and the professional employment structure. Academic market expansion or research capacity promotion cannot be treated as a simple phenomenon decided by public investment or human resource input. Instead, it raises important questions about the effectiveness of different combinations of state policies, enterprise involvement, faculty engagement, amounts and distributions of funding, characteristics of publication market, and structure of academic labor market. These discussions raise the question of the concept of the academic regime and its further application for evaluation of academic research and HE within the context of wider political, economic, and social developments in the East Asian NIEs. As universities and academic communities are more engaged in the game of international publication, the balance between basic and applied research may be distorted and the responsibilities for teaching and moral training may be ignored. Slaughter and Leslie (1997) criticize that senior academics often respond positively to opportunities for attracting funds from industry, and many junior academics have "difficulty conceiving of careers for themselves which merged academic capitalism and conventional academic endeavor." The results of this study provide evidence that the East Asian NIEs need to keep an eye on the growth rate of published papers in areas where growth is limited.

REFERENCES

Altbach, P. G., and J. J. F. Forest, eds. 2006. "Introduction." In *International Handbook of Higher Education*, edited by J. J. F. Forest and P. G. Altbach, 1–21. Dordrecht, The Netherlands: Springer.

Boyer, E. L. 1990. *Scholarship Reconsidered: Priorities of the Professoriate*. Princeton, NJ: Cambridge Foundation for the Advancement of Teaching.

Glänzel, W. 2000. "Science in Scandinavia: A Bibliometric Approach." *Scientometrics* 48 (2): 121–150.

Hayhoe, Ruth, and Qiang Zha. 2006. "Higher Education in China." In *International Handbook of Higher Education*, edited by J. J. F. Forest and P. G. Altbach, 667–691. Dordrecht, The Netherlands: Springer.

Krasner, S. 1983. "Structural Causes and Regime Consequences: Regimes as Intervening Variables." In *International Regimes*, edited by S. Krasner, 1–21. Ithaca, NY: Cornell University Press.

OECD. 2003. *Governance of Public Research: Toward Better Practices*. Paris: OECD. Available online at: http://www.oecd.org/science/sci-tech/governanceofpublicresearchtowardbetterpractices.htm.

Park, N. 2006. "Korea." In *International Handbook of Higher Education*, edited by J. J. F. Forest and P. G. Altbach, 867–879. Dordrecht, The Netherlands: Springer.

Selvaratnam, V. 2007. "Singapore: Universities Autonomy versus State Control: The Singapore Experience." In *Government and Higher Education Relationships across Three Continents: The Winds of Change*, edited by G. Neave and F. A. van Vught, 173–192. Oxford, UK; Tarrytown, NY: Published for the IAU Press, Pergamon.

Slaughter, S., and L. Leslie. 1997. *Academic Capitalism: Politics, Policies, and the Entrepreneurial University*. Baltimore, MD: John Hopkins Press, 173.

Taiwan Research Report. 2011. *Taiwan Research Report 2011*. New York: Thomson Reuters. Available online at: http://frontend.stpi.narl.org.tw/files/docs/2011%20Taiwan%20Research%20Report.pdf.

Yonezawa, A. 2006. "Japan." In *International Handbook of Higher Education*, edited by J. J. F. Forest and P. G. Altbach, 829–837. Dordrecht, The Netherlands: Springer.

Chapter 6

National Policies in Chile Related to Research and Innovation
The Challenge of Cultural Change

Mario F. Letelier and María J. Sandoval

Introduction

As knowledge, research, development, and innovation become increasingly valued resources for economic growth and social development, university culture becomes more and more the subject of scrutiny. These institutions provide professionals, researchers, and in general, an education that impacts on ways of thinking and acting, on national capacities, and on culture shaping.

In Chile, as in other countries, some national policies, as related to funding, quality assurance, and equity, have helped to shed light on the ways universities react to change. Maintaining economic growth occasionally requires facing the challenge of increasing export income, not only by expanding markets by increasing quality but also by increasing expressed value per unit. There are some reasons that make it possible to state that such a transition is not an easy one, even if most conditions seem favorable in theory. Some of the implicit difficulties postulated here are tightly associated with university culture, which seems to be becoming a source of resistance not well dimensioned (Letelier et al. 2012).

In this chapter, the challenge of national growth based upon research, development, and innovation (RDI) is analyzed from the university perspective. The main purpose of such analysis is to help highlight some possible directions for improving university impact on society's needs, and analyze university organization, governance, and mission. The Chilean experience of the last 20 years is mainly used as a reference.

By using a mathematical analogy, Chile's present situation, as seen from the authors' and many other nationals' perspective, can be considering as reaching a GDP asymptotic trend, in which the country's economy is seen as approaching an asymptotic growth. At present the per capita national income is US$19,000. For strong and continuous growth, as desired, it is necessary to reach an inflexion point or several relevant things have to happen simultaneously within a short period in order to increase the rate of growth. Such simple qualitative analogy hides a number of very complex problems, many of them related to cultural changes that, as said, have to concur in a hopefully relatively short period.

The main objective of this chapter is to highlight factors that condition change as related to RDI, which usually are, at most, cursorily addressed when designing and implementing policies.

Context

The Chilean population is 17.4 million at present and its continental surface is 757,000 square kilometers. The country is rich in minerals, mainly copper, in the desertic north. The coast contour is 6,400 kilometers long, and the country's length is 4,300 km. This geography supports a variety of marine resources, and climates and soils that are apt for many types of agropecuary production. The country's export and produce compositions for 2013 are shown in Table 6.1.

Through a continued policy of trade agreements, extending to most continents at this time, new markets are being opened or increased, so that economic growth has been steady. The average growth rate during last 10 years was 4 percent (Central Bank of Chile 2013).

Main destinations of national exports are China, European Union, the United States, and Japan. Recent economic swings in those countries have not greatly impacted Chile's in-country income. This trend can be tracked since the second half of the 1980s, which means close to 25 years of sustained development, excluding a few years of negative performance.

In the meantime, national policies related to RDI have led to an increase of funds aimed at supporting private and university initiatives with an explicit autonomous focus. In the case of research, quality is targeted, and in the case of innovation, business is the desired output. CONICYT

Table 6.1 Chilean export and produce compositions for 2013

Gross Chilean exports composition	
Exports	2013 (%)
Mining	58
Industry	38
Other	4

Industrial products composition	
Industry	2013 (%)
Food	29
Chemical	23
Cellulose	12
Equipment	11
Other	25

(National Commission for Scientific and Technological Research) is the government agency associated with research and CORFO (Corporation for Development) is the corresponding agency for innovation (CONICYT 2010; 2011; 2013a; 2013b; CORFO 2013a; 2013b). In 2013 their respective total budgets were US$531 million and US$157 million.

CONICYT has funded a significant number of scholarships for graduate studies in Chile and abroad, awarded through an assessment process that takes into account the prestige of the graduate programs and the program's relevance for the applicant's goals. This policy has not had explicit disciplinary or developmental directions.

National RDI spending was 0.5 percent of national GDP in 2010, far behind the Organization for Economic Co-operation and Development (OECD) overage of 2.4 percent. Universities spend 35.6 percent of the national total, and this figure has been decreasing over the years. The complement is spent by companies (National Budgets Direction 2013; World Bank 2013).

There is a shared opinion that RDI in industry has been a reactive one, following short-term demands, while in universities, research has mainly aligned itself to international academic trends. The government, correspondingly, has been recently (2008) devising RDI policies that would force some long-term directions through the work of the National Council for Innovation and Competitiveness (CNIC), which is an advisory body (CNIC 2010a; 2010b; 2013; Comisión asesora presidencial 2013).

In general, the three well-known relevant actors that contribute RDI worldwide, as already mentioned, are industry, government, and universities. In industry, innovation appears in several guises, such as high-tech start-ups and big industry advancements in new technologies, new products, and the like. These sources of innovation have their own experts and scientists, as well as some links with researchers or research centers in the country or abroad.

Governments usually fund research units such as centers, laboratories, and others that address innovation fields considered strategic for the respective country, among them being military, energy, industry-specific, environment, specific resource areas, food, health, and so on.

Universities seem to be, by and large, the main producers of scientific research, directed toward obtaining new knowledge. As scientific knowledge production has to adhere to protocols and follow some dynamics that in part are inherent to science and in part imposed by the leading scientists, its relation to innovation is not obvious.

A worldwide concern associated with RDI is the human capital required for this purpose. It is acknowledged that scientists and engineers are fundamental components of such capital. In the United States, a big effort in the educational front can be tracked, at least to the beginning of the 2000s, in which the Accreditation Board for Engineering and Technology (ABET) and the National Science Foundation (NSF) united efforts in order to foster an engineering education more attuned to the country's needs in RDI. A relevant feature of this enterprise has been the emphasis put on the learning outcomes expected from the educational process. Among those outcomes, the first specified is the capacity for applying knowledge of mathematics, science, and engineering. In this educational conception, no matter what the economic trends may be, it is assumed that RDI is closely tied to science and engineering.

Starting in 2013, the Chilean government opened a funding program for engineering colleges, with the objective of improving the quality of engineering education along the lines already described. In 2014 funds were allocated to five proposals that involved ten engineering colleges. This is an important step that reflects clearly the official involvement in RDI and its intention to transform ideas into concrete action.

Policies that consider universities as instruments for adding value to the national scenario face the challenge of cruising successfully through the academic culture, a subject that is central to this chapter.

The Three Cultures

National policies in RDI, as introduced above, plus other associated policies have led to the relative solidification of beliefs, values, and ways of thinking and acting, which may merit being called culture, associated to the following main sectors: government, companies, and universities. Such policies have purposely operated on the concept of laissez-faire. Some time in the past, people from all sectors became skeptical about the real possibility of fixing given industrial priorities. Trust was assigned to market forces on most fronts. This translated into internationally open trade markets, private higher education (HE) expansion, and shrinkage of government bureaucracy.

An effective national action oriented to strengthen RDI with long-term economic impact needs to systemically align the sectors that play important roles. Experience shows that such an endeavor may be much more difficult than expected. This chapter attempts to show the impact of about 30 years of laissez-faire policies intended to push RDI for economic growth.

The Center for Research in Creativity and Higher Education (CICES) has participated, in different roles, in the discussion, application, and evaluation of national policies related to research, HE quality assurance, university development, and related matters. From the authors' perspective, one main reason many policies fall short of their objectives is the existence of a set of beliefs or assumptions that the intervening parts have about each other's parts or their roles. Some of those beliefs need to be revised if the desired alignment is to be achieved soon.

In the following text, some critical beliefs held by each sector in relation to self/other sectors that need to be revised are listed, with a focus on the university sector. They reflect the authors' experience, and are not, so far, the result of any formal study.

1. Government
   a. Universities should be autonomous with the state providing some funds for specific development, such as RDI.
   b. Universities act as systems and have the basic capacities for planning, prioritizing, and evaluating courses of action.
   c. Companies are interested in having working links with universities.
   d. Companies are interested in RDI.
2. Companies
   a. Universities are not practically oriented.
   b. Business should grow, in the first place, by expansion.
   c. RDI means, in practice, buying better equipment abroad.
   d. It is not companies' duty to help educate professionals.
3. Universities
   a. Government should provide funds for almost everything.
   b. Government understands very little of university priorities.

c. Universities should be fully autonomous and allowed to freely choose their priorities.
   d. Companies work generally with low scientific standards.
   e. Scientific research, internationally visible, is the best prestige indicator.

All the above-listed beliefs can be backed up by many examples of evidence. They have been selected as a sample, apt to better characterize the challenge of aligning the corresponding proponents. All such beliefs should be seriously reconsidered in order to foster RDI in Chile. All of them imply resistance to change.

In particular government's second belief (1b) is very critical. Time and again, policies aimed at improving university efficacy have rested on such a belief. Still, most universities consider strategic planning as an externally imposed task of little practical use and one that is business contaminated. Bigger universities still have to show their capacity for acting as a system to implement institutional change. They have replicated laissez-faire philosophy; different schools are usually very autonomous and difficult to align as an institution in pursuit of a common goal.

New Roles and Capacities for RDI

One source of complexities is that the concept of RDI is polydimensional. Not only are there three main concepts combined in it but also all of them include several distinctions. Chilean innovation, at this time, is associated with any improvement that increases income or welfare. Its relation to scientific knowledge and to research is little discussed.

For the sake of conciseness, it may be accepted that the government is seriously aiming at fostering RDI as a critical resource for sustained economic growth and that the productive sector will embrace RDI when it is convinced that it is an unavoidable expansion factor. What remains not so clear is the role of the university in this scenario.

Chilean universities get their funding mainly from educational fees paid by students and from government funds. The traditional 25 institutions also get basic state funding. These sources of income relate vaguely to RDI. In part they relate to academic research, which is valued in fund assignment and is a relevant prestige factor. Academic research is defined here as research that is promoted through scientific advancement, the results of which are published in journals of varying impact factors and have loose links with the local economy. A leading force behind this activity is journal publication, which is decided by academic peers and editors, and is overwhelmingly associated with developed, English-speaking countries, which may not necessarily be interested in the connection between scientific advancement and the Chilean economy. Such decision bodies may be assumed to be concerned more either with their countries' interests or with some scientific trends.

A very arguable belief, implicit in the Chilean academic culture, is that "good science" will always influence the country's development at some time. This belief belies the fact that, given the extent of scientific knowledge in areas related to innovation, scientific expansion may take many different routes, which implicitly are established, by the editors of relevant academic journals who are believed to know Chile's social, political, and economic challenges.

All this taken together may explain why universities stick to traditional teaching, which provides educational income at relatively low cost, and to academic research that helps to improve the teaching and advance institutional positions in academic rankings. Many well-intentioned government policies for improving the quality of teaching have had little impact and seem to confirm Knight and Yorke's statement, "Mandated changes may produce compliance, but professionals (*academics*) have considerable scope for compliance-without-change, resistance, and subversion" (Knight and Yorke 2003; emphasis added).

To move universities to a position where they can contribute effectively within a new policy of national RDI requires us to look closely at two variables: autonomy and financial incentives.

Autonomy at this time in Chile means self-chosen institutional executives (rector, deans, and departmental heads) and freedom to fix priorities related to teaching, research, and societal links.

In the face of increasing external investment in RDI in Chile, and possible momentum increase in industry, university-generated innovation may or may not be relevant for the country in the future. However, the education of new professionals and researchers will always have a big impact on Chilean culture and its shift toward innovative mentality. This is only possible if faculties are engaged in RDI to some extent and their goals are really linked to that of local economy.

The role of the university and the desired level of cultural change needs to consider several variables or perspectives that also imply change in other sectors. The ideas advanced in the following text draw on many documents and available data.

University Roles

Beyond the classical definition of university roles or functions is the need for some typology of these institutions, according to their balance of teaching and research and their ownership. This topic lingers in the actual discussion, mainly in the National System of Higher Education Quality Assurance.

This is relevant for establishing standards of performance that depend on the type of university. As the prestige of research universities increases, these distinctions become more and more relevant.

A very critical variable for institutional change is the performance assessment system and its indicators. So far, main official indicators applied by the Ministry of Education, through different policies, are as follows:

- Teaching
  - Student retention rates
  - Student graduation rates
  - Admission standards
  - Faculty qualifications
  - Program and institutional accreditation
  - Employment data

- Research
  - Indexed publications
  - Impact factor of publication
  - External funds raised
  - Number of researchers
  - Graduate programs

These indicators operate inside universities for faculty assessment, promotion, salaries, and incentives and, it is safe to state, contrive strongly to shape university culture.

No matter how much successive governments preach for teaching quality improvement, applied research and innovation, and taking care of national problems, this seems unlikely unless incentives align effectively with those goals.

Government Definitions Policies

Official documents in RDI often assign different roles to universities but many times they are not coherent because they tend to ignore the dynamics of science, its relations to innovation, and valid dimensions of university culture.

During the same period in which HE evolved and developed to its present state, the government kept a tight surveillance on government staff expenditure. One of its continuous professed policies has been to keep state expenses as low as possible.

In the perspective of this analysis, this policy has led to a noticeable lack of expertise in matters critical to long-term development. Government culture may be as difficult to change as that of universities. As university lacks capacities for systemic change, so does the government in the area of RDI. CONICYT has little planning capacity, beyond its present role related to state fund distribution in terms of initiatives loosely framed and operating under the philosophy of laissez-faire. National commissions may be politically relevant but their expertise is limited and difficult to increase.

It is postulated here that, in order for the Chilean university system to align effectively to a national and aggressive policy on RDI, the government has to study and define several elements as follows (Letelier and Sandoval 2013).

1. *National expectation from scientific research*: The role of scientific research in scientific culture, teaching, and innovation.
2. *Types of research to be promoted, funded, and incentivized*: At least three types of research appear as relevant—basic scientific; applied exploratory; and applied, innovation led. Ways of assessing their products also need to be considered.
3. *Areas of RDI tied to national needs that go beyond business*: These areas of RDI include, among others, energy availability, water shortage, natural disasters (earthquakes, tsunamis, volcano activity, etc.), and potential use of nonexploited natural resources. These need special funding and facilities that may or may not be attached to universities.
4. *Universities' roles in RDI*: This needs to be defined in much more precise terms for university development. If this definition is not clear, universities are likely to continue the same roles and activities. They will not accept a role that is not consistent with their basic duties.
5. *University governance*: In Chile, due to a long, related political history, many quarters advocate the greatest possible autonomy and internal democracy for universities. Experience shows, those variables usually lead to minimum effort and maximum profit within the operating regulations. Any important change means extra effort and uncertain benefit. This is an almost taboo subject in educational political quarters; but unless it is realistically addressed, little change may occur. It is needed to create systemic innovation capacities requiring real leadership and the need for accounting to external constituents that the present system inhibits.

Some of the variables described seem difficult to manage. However, if they are not addressed, it is not inconceivable that the traditional HE system may be overcome by other institutions, internal or imported that will take the RDI challenge into their own hands, especially in profitable areas.

A very relevant concern about RDI is, as stated previously, the need to face long-term, structural national challenges that cannot be expected to be addressed by the business sector. In addition to the problems already cited, it is necessary to consider problems tied to climate change, infrastructure development, health, education, and many others that transcend government periods and, requiring big expenses, their return can be difficult to measure or collect.

In Chile especially, there is a need for significant improvement in education at all levels. Traditionally, over the last several decades, education has not been a profession that has attracted the best or even good students. In Chile, most schools admit applicants with very low academic credentials. This has led to the establishment of an educational culture that is not able to measure up to the new challenges the country is facing. A kind of reengineering of those schools is necessary in order to lay the foundations of new ways of thinking that are more in line with RDI.

Conclusions

Implicit in the above analysis is the idea that to align RDI means a focus on innovation as the leading force. Development and research have to be focused on innovation irrespective of whether it is well defined or is of exploratory or potential character. Innovation that adds significant value is usually related to novel uses of knowledge or to new knowledge that is expressed in one or another kind of technology.

This may or may not lead to scientific publications, which, in any case, are a secondary output of innovation. Therefore, an effective focus on knowledge-intensive innovation means new ways of defining and assessing results. In the university context, this is a culture-breaking issue that in Chile likely needs help from the government.

The Chilean state seems to require new capacities for addressing this problem. Some consensus about this is expressed in proposals for creating a ministry for RDI or at least some stable unit inside some extant ministry.

One important issue, seemingly one of the biggest complexities to be faced, is that RDI has to be related to education and to the productive sector, so no simple unit may be able to encompass all relevant sectors.

To the authors, design of RDI policies helps to highlight the fact that each development stage requires new political capacities. At this moment, such capacities need to be strengthened in Chile because the country may be lacking some amount of global or systemic thinking to model variables related to science, technology, education, country potentialities or problems, and sustained international trade. Such global thinking is necessary for devising and implementing complex policies.

According to the previous comments, this state of affairs is the outcome of several decades of laissez-faire policies related to RDI, university management, human capital growth, and business, among other areas. This philosophy of development seems to have been so far successful but, as normally happens, has also handicapped the country's capacities for implementing political changes in which the country needs to think and act as a whole, at least in the three main sectors recurrently cited herein. Very likely the required changes will occur, since the need is apparent and accepted across political sectors and competent human resources exist.

This chapter has no pretensions of presenting a full analysis of its main subject. Rather its modest intended contribution is focused on warning regarding the cultural variables that may determine great resistance to change in a moment when strong and fast change is required.

References

Central Bank of Chile. 2013. Available online at: http://www.bcentral.cl/index.asp.

Comisión asesora presidencial. 2013. *Comisión Asesora en Ciencia, Tecnología e Innovación entrega informe al Presidente*. Comisión asesora presidencial. Available online at: http://www.corfo.cl/sala-de-prensa/noticias/2013/mayo-2013/comision-asesora-en-ciencia-tecnologia-e-innovacion-entrega-informe-al-presidente.

Corporation for Development (CORFO). 2013a. *Comisión Asesora en Ciencia, Tecnología e Innovación entrega informe al Presidente*. Santiago: CORFO.

———. 2013b. *Program for "The New Engineering of 2030."* Santiago: Corfo-Chilean Economic Development Agency.

Knight, P., and M. Yorke. 2003. "Assessment, Learning, and Employability." In *The Society for Research into Higher Education and Open University Imprint*, 216. Berkshire, UK: Open University Press.

Letelier, M., C. Oliva, R. Carrasco, and L. López. 2012. "Higher Education in Chile: Culture, Assumptions, and the Challenge of Relevance and Effectiveness." In *Chile: Environmental, Political, and Social Issues*, edited by D. Rivera. Hauppauge, NY: Nova Science Publishers.

Letelier, M., and M. J. Sandoval. 2013. "Componentes de una agenda para el desarrollo de la ciencia, la tecnología y la innovación en Chile." Unpublished paper, contact author.

National Budgets Direction. 2013. *Dirección de Presupuestos.* Santiago: National Budgets Direction. Available online at: http://www.dipres.gob.cl/594/w3-propertyvalue-21754.html.

National Commission for Scientific and Technological Research (CONICYT). 2010. *Ciencia y tecnología en Chile: ¿Para qué?* Santiago: VERDE diseño. Available online at: http://www.conicyt.cl/documentos/CyTConicytparaque.pdf.

———. 2011. *Annual Memory.* Santiago: CONICYT. Available online at: http://www.conicyt.cl/wp-content/uploads/2012/07/Memoria_2011.pdf.

———. 2013a. *Comisión Nacional de Investigación Científica y Tecnológica.* Santiago: CONICYT. Available online at: http://www.conicyt.cl/.

———. 2013b. *Ciencia y Tecnología para Chile.* Santiago: CONICYT. Available online at: http://www.conicyt.cl/wp-content/uploads/2012/07/Conicyt_Brochure_2013_sp.pdf.

National Council for Innovation and Competitiveness (CNIC). 2010a. *Generation and Systematization of Support for Evaluating the National Innovation Strategy in the Area of Business Innovation.* Background Report. Santiago: CNIC. Available online at: http://www.cnic.cl/index.php/doc_details/4-orientaciones-para-el-presupuesto-publico-del-sistema-nacional-de-innovacion.html.

———. 2010b. *Evaluation Report National Innovation Strategy for Competitiveness. International Panel.* Santiago: CNIC. Available online at: http://www.cnic.cl/index.php/doc_details/2-evaluation-report-of-national-innovation-strategy-for-competitiveness-chile.html.

———. 2013. *Surfing towards the Future Chile on the 2025 Horizon. Strategic Orientations for Innovation.* Santiago: CNIC. Available online at: http://www.cnic.cl/index.php/orientaciones-estrategicas-para-la-innovacion.html.

World Bank. 2013. *Data: Chile Income Level.* Washington, DC: World Bank. Available online at: http://data.worldbank.org/country/chile.

Part II

Entrepreneurship, Innovation, and Development in the Research Domain

Chapter 7

Rethinking Innovation in a Higher Education Context
Deane Neubauer

Introduction

As a North American participant to this senior seminar I wish to put before us a phenomenon that to date is in some ways predominantly "American" but in other ways has become some combination of "international" and "global." In doing so I wish to problematize both the notion of higher education (HE) innovation and that of "boundary-ness" to the extent that this sense applies to varied phenomena within knowledge environments, including HE.

The particular innovation I wish to examine has attracted various labels, perhaps the most common of which is the "disrupting" movement, a term that came into use early in the new century to refer to a wide variety of phenomena developed as alternatives of one form or another to HE (and in some frameworks to all of education) as framed and conducted by commonly accepted conventional institutions, for example, universities (for a good summary of the state of matters relatively early on in what became a rapidly changing environment, see Christensen et al. 2011). As Christensen et al. put it,

> The theory of disruptive innovation has significant explanatory power in thinking through the challenges and changes confronting higher education. Disruptive innovation is the process by which a sector that has

previously served only a limited few because its products and services were complicated, expensive, and inaccessible, is transformed into one whose products and services are simple, affordable, and convenient and serves many no matter their wealth or expertise. The new innovation does so by redefining quality in a simple and often disparaged application at first and then gradually improves such that it takes more and more market share over time as it becomes able to tackle more complicated problems.

A year after this study by the Center for American Progress, the *New York Times* would be moved to declare 2012 the "Year of the MOOC [massive open online courses]," focusing on the explosive emergence of entities such as edX, Udacity, and Coursera and the soon to follow development of MOOCs in a wide variety of subject matters and taking multiple forms (Pappano 2012). Dazzled by the unanticipated success of Sebastian Thrun and Michael Sokolsky's course in "Introduction to Artificial Intelligence" offered by Stanford University in the fall of 2011, MOOCs captured the logic and technology of online education and transformed it fundamentally.

As many have pointed out (and as I will discuss further below), MOOCs are *complicated* at a variety of *levels* or *dimensions*. (See, e.g., the history and critique of MOOCs offered by Aaron Bady [2013] who has framed his discussion as "The MOOC Moment and the End of Reform.") As a phenomenon of *innovation*, however, they can serve as a vehicle for discussing the broader subject of innovation in and through HE, which is the intent of this chapter. I will proceed by framing innovation as a social process and then explore through MOOCs and a variety of other innovations how change is both occurring and proceeding throughout contemporary HE.

Innovation as a "Thing" and a "Process"

In an earlier work Christensen et al. suggest that there are two kinds of innovation: disruptive and sustaining. In the commercial realm sustaining innovations are "improvements to products that enhance performance in dimensions traditionally valued by consumers. They make existing products and services better." Disruptive innovations by contrast "change the value equation. Initially, disruptive innovations under-perform mainstream products, but offer some advantages of cost and ease of use. They cause fundamental changes in the marketplace" (Christensen et al. 2005). This frame of reference, which is widely shared, makes a fundamental assumption that innovation is a social and/or economic good. Clearly much of the role of innovation within environments of economic exchange *is* to produce at some point further market advantage, either through product improvement or cost/price gains for the innovator. This frame, in and of itself, tends to ignore or underestimate the tension between "change" viewed as a social process and innovation as a subcategory of change. In much of the literature on innovation, and certainly in common use within a marketplace frame of reference, innovation is normatively valued as "good" and the relative proof of its particular good can be determined by marketplace metrics, for example, placement, degrees, and dimensions of acceptance, effects on cost and price, and its role in stimulating further innovation. From such constructions arises a culture of innovation that breeds its own sociology with its embedded normative premises.

To make a broader sense of the notion of innovation in HE context, I think it is useful to focus on the four broad dimensions of functionality commonly associated with HE. It is widely held that HE over the centuries and across a vast array of societies and cultures performs at least four common and essential social functions: knowledge creation (the research function); knowledge transmission (the teaching function); knowledge conservation (the library and museum function); and (with some greater differentiation) contribution to the broader social good (the public value function). It seems sensible to undertake a discussion of the role of innovation in HE from the framework provided by these functions—to ask in effect at some point whether a given innovation increases or decreases the value embodied in each function.

To make such an assessment requires further conceptual leaps. One is the notion of value over time (which presumes that agreement might be reached over what might be reasonable periods for making such judgments). Another is the realization that outside the closed value framework of the market, many innovations might be judged to be of negative value; and indeed, our commonsense language reflects this in such terms as innovation for the sake of innovation, or more condemnatory, even "destructive" innovation. The second conceptual leap is to situate innovation within at least a modest differentiation of types of change. One typology suggests that within contemporary contexts (such as efforts to catalog and describe the kinds of changes being wrought by contemporary globalization) one can usefully discriminate changes as consisting of genuine novelty, combinatory elements, extinction, constituting predicaments, or as essentially elements of the existing status quo (explored further in Berry and Neubauer [2008]). These are briefly described as follows:

- *Novelty*: Genuine novelty often involves new ways of "experiencing the world," creating entirely new aspects of processes and institutions.

In this sense the Internet is a paradigmatic innovation that has profound implications for how we communicate, create, and retrieve information globally. Innovations such as these, along with their consequences, make it useful to ask how innovation of this form of novelty affects overall processes of change (Castells 2009).

- *Combinations*: Globalization also changes the world by combining older ways of behaving with what's new, sometimes combining two or more ways of doing things. Online banking and shopping, for instance, bind together traditional shopping and banking with 24-hour high-speed computer access from home or anywhere in the world. This new combination eliminates the need to travel to shop or bank, producing new ways to accomplish these traditional activities, ways that have considerable impact on individual time management, social organization, jobs, and consumption patterns.
- *Extinction*: While globalization brings some practices, values, or institutions into being, it also causes others to disappear. The notion of extinction becomes visible within the United States, for example, when WalMart and other "big box" retailers overwhelm and eliminate local retail stores.
- *Predicaments*: Predicaments in this context refer to complex situations in which it is difficult or impossible to come up with a predictable "solution" in responding to the novelty created by innovation. Conventional notions tend to see change either as essentially reductionist (how the part affects the whole) or as an essentially step-by-step, linear process (beset with significant, often catastrophic interruptions) that societies and institutions use to identify "problems" and in one way or another "solve" them, often with the presumptive innovation. Complexity theory and chaos theory, however, offer us new ways to view the world and this dynamic of innovation and change. These approaches examine how highly complex systems may generate single or simple "outcomes" and resist anything that might be called a solution to the consequences that ensue. Complexity theory, for example, investigates how flocks of birds naturally turn together in flight, and how schools of fish move in synchrony through the sea. It also examines how something happens when large numbers of individual units come together and interact with each other. The emerging knowledge society contains numerous examples of complex interactions that pose these kinds of predicaments (Hershock 2012).

To conclude this point, in my view, it is insufficient to identify innovations occurring either within HE or outside it, but which affect it, without taking the next step and seeking to either identify whether they may constitute a novel change dynamic or produce important probable effects. Not to take this step is to deny both scholars of HE or practitioners useful pathways to mark emerging changes and transformations in the structures and functions of HE as we currently know and understand them.

Having made these initial distinctions, I wish to proceed first to an examination of various perceived innovations with contemporary HE and by doing so suggest the range of dimensions they represent for the whole of the HE process. In the subsequent section, I wish to explore how some of the more "present" of these might be valued given some relatively commonplace expressions of value in HE and from this go on to suggest other innovations that may arise out of them and broader implications for the future(s) of HE.

Innovating in HE

In recent work undertaken through the Western Association of Schools and Colleges (WASC) in which I have previously provided some partial reporting (Neubauer 2012), an effort has been made to develop a catalog of sorts for what is being termed the "Changing Ecology of Higher Education." (A set of "concept" papers detailing some of this work can be found at WASC [2013].[1]) The notion of an ecology was selected for seeking to identify some of the many innovations characterizing current HE to self-consciously underscore the highly dynamic and interactive nature of these events. In pursuing this work, we have sought to be sensitive at all times that perhaps the key fact to present about this ecology is its intensely dynamic character—what one "knows" about it today, is not necessarily adequate for tomorrow.

Having made that point and seeking to keep notions of this constant contingency before us, one approach to this changing ecology suggests that at the very least it may be composed of and examined through the following dimensions expressed as a series of changes:

- *Changes in the characteristics of learners*: These can include the increasing diversity and demographic shifts of students (racial/ethnic, economic background, country of origin, age, disability, and, in the US, veterans); the extended life span of learners; increasing numbers of nondegree-seeking students; greater mobility within HE; degree of academic readiness; proficiency in knowledge and information fields

and skills; and increasing numbers of students working while simultaneously seeking degrees.
- *Changes in the roles and responsibility of faculty*: These include the unbundling of traditional faculty roles especially with respect to course design and execution; recasting instructors as guides to facilitate student learning; the increasing use of nonprofessorial faculty; and persistent questioning of "faculty authority" within conventional knowledge constructs.
- *Changes in methods of instruction and learning processes*: These include the vast increase in the variety and adoption of different instructional modes including the use of virtual, hybrid, blended, customizable, personalized, self-paced, and other modalities; the growth of cross-disciplinary, cross-institutional, and transnational teaching; efforts to incorporate into instruction and learning processes increasing knowledge of how people learn, including recent advances in neuroscience; the incorporation of differential learning styles and intelligences and other forms of research-based principles of learning; increased use of collaborative and collective learning both inside and outside the classroom; and the incorporation of mobile learning and social media.
- *Changes in the content and focus of instruction*: These include notions of greening of the curriculum; internationalizing and addressing global issues; expanding service learning (SL) and internships; increasing the emphasis on civic responsibility and civic engagement; promoting undergraduate research; incorporating digital literacy (visual information, new media, digital production, programming); and remixing, reusing, and repurposing information.
- *Changes in the political and economic environments of HE*: These include demands for evidence based on outcomes of student learning (that go beyond standard examinations); demands for affordability of HE; demands for efficiency and cost control; demands for portability of degrees and certificates; increased perception of HE by politicians and policy makers as a "failing or deficient" sector; changes in demands for external certification of quality and capability of HE providers; criticisms of the liberal arts as being increasingly irrelevant to the contemporary world; the growth of new economic relationships between HE and economic actors in society; the growth of historically noneducational entities into offering degrees, for example, hospitals, theater groups, think tanks, film production companies, publishers, and global Internet companies among others.

- *Changes in the frameworks of HE*: These include "Do It Yourself" (DIY) models of education including students/learners creating their own degree programs; MOOCs, competency-based instruction and certification; partnerships with industry for workplace training and lifetime learning; and charter universities with novel content and styles.
- *Changes in processes and values of certification, credentials, and accreditation*: These include the creation of badges as new models of competency and certification; creating common definitions of credentials that have recognition status; certification of prior learning; integrating informal and formal learning with accreditation and certification bodies; and developing common standards across regions and common practices of recognition and accreditation.
- *Changes in the policies that frame and govern HE and the metrics that are being developed to assess it*: These include new and increased focus on productivity, such as return on investment and return on value; focus on quality of life metrics; assessing impacts of private equality and for-profit education on the whole of HE systems and reviewing the policy structures that interface nonprofit and for-profit education; exploring shifts in cost burdens of education in terms of multiple beneficiaries (e.g., business as well as students); and promoting the public good as defined by increased value of HE to individuals and society.

As indicated, each of these can be viewed as a distinct dimension along which HE innovation is taking place. One first step toward converting a conceptual array such as this (or some other) into an assessment of transformation within HE framed in terms of innovation would be to apply the change typology presented above to this catalog. Such an exercise would perhaps look something like Table 7.1.

Populating this typology with empirical examples from different types of institutions (e.g., primarily teaching institutions; technical and other research universities; multicampus global universities) and from different countries would provide us with a base map from which a more formal enumerative catalog could be constructed. From this database one could both populate and analyze the table to observe both the range of innovations and their presumptive impact. At the very least, having some such categorizing tool coupled with a way of gaining an initial sense of impact would provide us with a quite new and different vocabulary for innovation, especially within the Asia Pacific region. Such an outcome could, potentially emerge as a useful HE *policy* tool for both national governments and regional HE cooperative efforts.

Table 7.1 Change typology transformation exercise within HE innovation

Dimension of change	Type of changes			
	Novelty	Combination	Predicament	Extinction
Nature of learners				
Roles and responsibilities of faculty				
Methods of instruction and learning process				
Content and focus of instruction				
Pressures on HE				
Frameworks in HE				
Certifications, etc.				
Policies and metrics				

Source: Author.

Back to MOOCs

The above schema, coupled with the catalog of items that constitutes this inventory of a changing ecology of HE (though stressing again that many other approaches to this changing ecology are, of course, possible), gives a sense of how one might approach the issue of assessing the innovative aspects present in the disrupting movement. MOOCs have gathered the most attention, not surprisingly, given the huge numbers of participants that have become engaged and the rapidity with which the phenomenon has spread. They have also gained significant attention because of their counterintuitive arrival on the HE scene of having been initiated in many cases by very high-statused institutions such as Stanford and MIT and in their early manifestations by their ideology that significant parts of HE should be available to anyone and without costs. In a world, especially in the United States, in which the costs of attaining education at the most prestigious institutions have become increasingly high, this is perhaps the most disruptive aspect of this phenomenon. Other forms of HE dissemination had also promoted the open-access aspect of courses, for example, the Khan Academy and iTunes U. What differentiated MOOCs from these earlier "low-wall access" approaches to HE was their entry into the field of higher education institutes (HEIs) of the highest status and the "massive" nature of such courses—the fact that the technologies of simultaneity could spotlight a distinguished faculty presentation within a context that engaged hundreds of thousands of participants simultaneously from around the world.

From the point of view of this chapter and being led by the logic of the above scheme, we are led to ask at least the following four fundamental questions about MOOCs as exemplars of the kind of innovation present within HE:

1. How extensive are the changes involved? As innovations, how significant are they in affecting the institutional patterns and behaviors that they are disrupting?
2. Are they, for example, truly novel in that they supplant previous forms of the phenomenon—in this case "traditional" HEIs—at least in some important respects? Are they comparable, say, to the historical example of Microsoft to WordPerfect, or are they more aptly characterized as combinatorial such that some genuinely synthetic "product" emerges from the innovation—in this case, the integration of MOOCs into the curricula of conventional institutions.[2]
3. To what extent are MOOCs themselves transitional? In the world of constant and continual innovation have MOOCs played a role in recasting strands of innovation within HE that may lead to even more far-reaching kinds of changes?
4. Casting back to some of the initial points made at the beginning of this chapter, what are the likely normative consequences of such changes with respect to our existing patterns of presenting HE throughout the world?

I do not intend to address these issues here but I do hold that in one form or another they are all latent and/or manifest in HE policy agendas and that by and large as "policy systems of HE" (if such a thing can be imagined) these issues are not being addressed enough. That is, innovation of these and related forms is actively being enacted and effected throughout our HE systems, largely outside the conventional policy frameworks. This, to continue this line, seems to be a guarantee that the conventional institutional systems of HE—the legacy systems if you will—are soon to be shocked by even more massive and far-reaching patterns of innovation and change with the inevitable consequence that many will not survive the challenges presented.

My argument is that at the policy level we need to institute a kind of future thinking that is sufficiently informed, robust, and institutionally situated by which we can identify these kinds of changes early and assess their possible/probable impacts on our existing institutions. Such an endeavor will provide us with a set of policy tools with which to begin a necessary assessment of the relevance and value of such innovations for the social functions historically associated with HE. At the margins of this imagined project we need to begin a broader assessment of how many of such functions are being performed by other institutions within the knowledge society.

Welcoming Big Data

I suggest in the foregoing that MOOCs and many of the other phenomena touched upon in the changing ecology of HE inventory presented above are themselves highly transitory.[3] MOOCs, as it were, grew out of the dramatic previous innovations of online education, which over two or more decades had become institutionalized both within traditional HEIs as well as served as platforms for entirely new ones. As many have suggested in relation to the changing dynamics of the information and knowledge society—and of contemporary globalization itself—change as a social phenomenon has both speeded up and changed (Harvey 1990). One consequence of this is that in many ways our institutional patterns of adaptation may become even more dysfunctional. This, I am suggesting, is in large part what is happening throughout the disruption movement. Our very institutions of HE, on the whole, are increasingly out of sync with the change patterns of information and knowledge transformation. As Ken Robinson puts it in his brilliant video on the changing paradigms of education, our institutions had their establishment in the historical enlightenment, gained much of their current form within the industrial revolution, and have been slow to change beyond the painful but necessary structural adaptations documented by Trow from elite to mass to universal institutions (Trow 1974; Robinson 2010).

MOOCs and much of the rest of the disrupting movement have grown out of this increasingly dysfunctional relationship between older institutional forms, emergent societal needs, and the intervening forces of knowledge society transformation. In some respects every major innovation in knowledge technology adds to the "transformational burden" of HE (see, e.g., Kim 2012).

Big Data presents a framework for an entirely new set of disruptions and innovations. Big Data—the ability to gather literally untold amounts of information and process it for increasingly fine and distinct tasks—has over the past few years moved out of the laboratory and demonstration stages in a variety of fields, from genetic engineering to data mining by the National Security Agency to Amazon.com. So prevalent has this approach to data become throughout society that in early September 2013, a new website, AbouttheData.com was announced with the specific purpose of permitting individuals to collate and view consumer relevant information that a host of social entities has gathered on *them* (Singer 2013). (AboutheData's tag line is, "Make the data work for you—know what data says about you and how it is used.") These movements in Big Data, I would suggest, are individualizing the focus of a variety of applications in genuinely novel ways—promising that individual characteristics can increasingly be accommodated within knowledge applications in ways that significantly increase the direct benefits to individuals, defined by their own unique qualifications and attributes.

One rapidly growing application of these activities is within a subfield being identified as "individual medicine"—an effort to utilize the vast increases in knowledge about the human genome and DNA to tailor medical applications for specific individuals. A recent book on the subject by Tim O'Reilly and his colleagues (2012) carries the title, *How Data Science is Transforming Health Care: Solving the Wanamaker Dilemma*. That dilemma, attributed to the early twentieth-century American department store magnate John Wanamaker, was summarized by him as, "I know that half my advertising doesn't work. The problem is I don't know what half." This has been the dilemma of modern medicine throughout the vast range of its applications, particularly in pharmaceutical and surgical intervention, wherein probabilistic distributions of many complicating factors operating simultaneously impede the effectiveness of such interventions. Big Data science is seeking to develop highly individualized data files for individuals that allow such interventions to be targeted for their specific conditions within the constraints of their own genetic structure and conditions and with gradations of appropriate interventions. Current research is focused on the rapid processing of such massive data coupled with analytical tools that can efficiently and accurately provide information both necessary and relevant to treatment (Rotella 2013; Schatz and Langmead 2013).

The analogy with education, at all levels, is lurking just around the corner and beginning to develop both a face and a search for relevant business models. In this frame "individualized medicine" becomes "individualized education." The educational version of Wanamaker's dilemma might be expressed as "I know what I am teaching, but I don't know what they are learning" despite our heroic efforts in developing evermore sophisticated assessment tools over the years. Parts of the construction of individualized education are already evident within the disruption movement from DIY education—face to face, online, and blended—provided at any number of institutions to the development of badges and competency-based education at the demonstration end (see, e.g., LeBlanc 2013). Another thread stretches from the early work of Gardner and his colleagues in differential intelligences to the virtual explosion of research over the past two decades on the neurological correlates of learning, especially when focused on language learning (McLaughlin et al. 2004) and more recently in efforts to extend plasticity theory to assess the impacts of digital devices on learning in young children (Carr 2011). Part of the analogous promise of Big Data as individualized learning lies in the ability to match individual learning styles and intelligences, as determined by evermore sophisticated techniques and there by maximize learning outcomes at the individual level.

The business models for Big Data in HE are already being experimented with by firms such as Educause (2012). It is not too far-fetched an idea to see that already existing web-based education structures such as iTunes U or firms that are becoming increasingly sophisticated in Big Data explorations will now come to view HE as an enormous market, still largely dominated by legacy institutions. When their capacity to produce, aggregate, transmit, and conserve knowledge is linked to the potential markets of HE *and* when it becomes tied to individualized Big Data, the already permeable and transformative paradigm of contemporary education may be shifted further. This has come to be reflected in recent large-scale efforts to deliver K-12 curricula digitally, which gives the delivery firms great sway over curricular style and content, but equally, because of the nature of Big Data gathering and analysis, a significant first step into individual student assessment and all that may flow from that (Rich 2014).

Conclusion: So What?

A fundamental question to be asked of these HE innovations is their degree of reach and their ultimate transformative effect. Like all of the innovations studied by Christensen and others, it is mindful to see that innovation within complex structures is a process. Some will succeed and many will fail. Our research task and the task within our own HEIs are to investigate and invest wisely without undue caution and to assess results with rigor. I argue that this task, common to responsible HE practitioners and administrators everywhere, has become increasingly difficult by significant degrees within the transformative dynamics of the knowledge economy and in the context of contemporary globalization. When seeking to generalize from any single national experience, it is prudent to ask whether the phenomenon under examination is likely to be a forerunner of events and practices in other locales or whether there are in effect outliers—interesting phenomena for the moment but in the larger sweeps of time and space, ultimately more epiphenomenal than central.

Certainly, the American examples alluded to above are due this test. However, I would argue that in radically new ways the boundaries of innovation diffusion are themselves under rapid transformation, as the explosive growth of MOOCs suggests. To a remarkable degree, signaled by data such as the rapid growth of new HEIs, including global universities, and the range of elements that can be inventoried within the changing ecology, coupled with the dramatic growth of cross-border education, the frames of reference for HE innovation are shifting. My plea is for the cooperative engagement of comparative research that can produce information and recommendations that assist all within the HE policy process to attend the challenges represented by such innovation.

Appendix

Bundles Characteristic of the Changing Ecology

Characteristics of Learners

- Increasing diversity and demographic shifts (racial/ethnic, economic, country of origin, age, disability, veteran, etc.)
- Extended life span of learners (lifelong learning)
- Increasing numbers of nondegree-seeking students
- Greater student mobility from college to college
- Academic readiness of students for college and university work
- High technological affinity/dependency of students
- Desire of students to have meaning and make a difference
- Increasing numbers of working students (with implications for availability of time on task)

Roles and Responsibilities of Faculty

- Unbundling traditional faculty roles of course design, instruction, grading, assessment, mentorship into separate discrete entities (e.g., the faculty member who teaches the course may not be the faculty member who designed the course)
- Recasting instructors as guides of student learning
- Increasing use of adjuncts, part-time, and contingent faculty
- Shifting power relationships between students and teachers
- Disruption of traditional role of faculty as authority, content provider, and distributor of knowledge

Methods of Instruction and the Learning Process

- Increasing variety of instructional methods including virtual, hybrid, blended, customizable, personalized, self-paced, and so on
- Growth of cross-disciplinary, cross-institutional, and transnational teaching

- Increasing knowledge of how people learn; advances in the neuroscience of learning
- Incorporation of differential learning styles
- Using research-based principles of learning in instruction (i.e., faculty members take into account students' prior knowledge of the subject matter; actively involve students in learning through engaged interactions and discourse; challenge students to meet high expectations; provide opportunities for practice, feedback, and review; and help students generalize, apply, and transfer what they have learned)
- Increasing use of collaborative, collective learning inside and outside the classroom
- Incorporation of mobile learning and social media

Content and Focus of Instruction

- Greening the curriculum (sustainability, environmental awareness, etc.)
- Internationalizing the curriculum and addressing global issues
- Expanding SL and internships
- Increasing the emphasis on civic responsibility and civic engagement
- Promoting undergraduate research
- Incorporating digital literacy (visual information, new media, digital production, programming)
- Remixing, reusing, and repurposing information

Pressures on HE

- Demand for evidence-based outcomes of student learning
- Demand for affordability
- Demand for efficiency and cost control
- Demand for portability of degrees and certificates
- Public and politician/policy maker's poor perception of HE
- Changes in federal regulations and federal reach into colleges and universities
- Criticisms of the liberal arts
- Growth of profit/nonprofit arrangements between universities and businesses—mergers, acquisitions, partnerships, and conversions
- Movement of historically noneducational entities to those offering degrees (hospitals, theater groups, think tanks, film production companies, publishers, global Internet companies, etc.)

Frameworks in HE

- DIY models of education (creating own degree programs)
- MOOCs
- Competency-based instruction
- Partnerships with industry for workplace training and lifetime learning
- Charter universities

Certification, Credentials, and Accreditation

- Badges
- Creating common definitions of a credential
- Certifying prior learning (e.g., Council on Adult and Experiential Learning)
- Integrating informal and formal learning within the accreditation process
- Developing common standards across regions and common processes of accreditation

Policies and Metrics

- Focus on productivity, return on investment, and return on value
- Focus on quality of life metrics
- Assess impacts of private equity and for-profit education; review policies that govern partnering between nonprofit and for-profit institutions
- Shift more of the cost burden of HE to business as education becomes more job market oriented
- Promote the public good (increased value of HE to individuals and society)

Notes

1. For full disclosure, I served as chair of a "Changing Ecology Task Force," the results of which triggered the organization of these concept papers and which accounted for much of the work that produced the dimensions of change used as an example within this section of the chapter.
2. Again, the rapidity with which MOOCs have "cycled through" parts of HE is stunning. On the one hand, they have been eagerly welcomed into the curricula

of some large-scale teaching institutions—San Jose State University, California, partnering with Udacity, for example—and they have been quickly judged in various instances to be "seeking to adopt too much too soon" by others. In this regard, see the URL, http://www.sjsu.edu/plus/, and Roscoria (2013). "As massively open online courses continue to gain traction, they're proving a disruptive force in HE. The traditional emphasis on in-person classes has brought universities to a price point that does not look sustainable," said Adrian Sannier, senior vice president of product for Pearson eCollege. "With mounting student debt, consumers are looking for a lower cost education that they can access in a time and place that works with their hectic lives. And they expect to leave the university with a degree that prepares them for work. But a general arts or science education is tough to transition into the work environment," said Stuart Bowness, cofounder and CEO of MediaCore. "Generally speaking, educational institutions of today are not training students for the environments in which they're being placed with work," Bowness said. "And what's really beginning to disrupt this is these massively open online courses." These courses allow working adults to learn new skills in small bites, equip them with skills they can use immediately and do not charge students. Bowness said that when someone can take a course at no charge, it makes a traditional college education a tough sell. "Where institutions are really being challenged is how they add value over and above what a student could learn from a massively open online course," he said.
3. One view of this issue may be gained from the presumption that as the current technology trajectory continues along its course, an increasing number of "crowd-involving" events will emerge within HE—for example, if MOOCs, then why not Massive Open Online Research(s) (MOORs) or Massive Open Online Experiments (Courses) (MOOEs)? Once the technology is available, its application is (merely) a matter of introducing it into academic environments and testing to see whether others subscribe to it (Neubauer 2013).

References

Bady, A. 2013. "The MOOC Moment and the End of Reform." May 15. Available online at: http://thenewinquiry.com/blogs/zunguzungu/the-mooc-moment-and-the-end-of-reform/; accessed on August 19, 2013.

Berry, P., and D. Neubauer. 2008. *Uncertain Steps: The Prospects for Contemporary Globalization*. Asia Pacific Higher Education Research Partnership. Available online at: http://apherp.files.wordpress.com/2013/11/uncertain-steps.pdf; accessed on March 4, 2015.

Carr, N. 2011. *The Shallows: What the Internet Is Doing to Our Brains*. New York: Norton.

Castells, M. 2009. *Communication Power*. Oxford: Oxford University Press.

Christensen, C. M., S. D. Anthony, and E. A. Roth. 2005. *Seeing What's Next: Using the Theories of Innovation to Predict Industry Change*. Boston, MA: Harvard Business School Publishing.

Christensen, C. M., M. B. Horn, L. Caldera, and L. Soares. 2011. *Disrupting College: How Disruptive Innovation Can Deliver Quality and Affordability to Postsecondary Education.* Washington, DC: Center for American Progress.

Educause. 2012. "Educause Live—The Rise of Big Data in Higher Education." March 22. Educause. Available online at: http://www.educause.edu/events/educause-live-rise-big-data-higher-education; accessed on September 13, 2013.

Harvey, D. 1990. *The Condition of Postmodernity.* Oxford, UK: Blackwell Publishing.

Hershock, P. 2012. "Information and Innovation in a Global Knowledge Society: Implications for Higher Education." In *The Emergent Knowledge Society and the Future of Higher Education: Asian Perspectives,* edited by D. Neubauer, 7–25. New York: Routledge.

LeBlanc, P. 2013. "Credit for What You Know, Not How Long You Sit." *New England Journal of Education,* September 10. Available online at: http://www.nebhe.org/thejournal/credit-for-what-you-know-not-how-long-you-sit/?utm_source=NEJHE+NewsBlast+9%2F11%2F13%3A+Competency!&utm_campaign=NEJHE%27s+New+Blast&utm_medium=email; accessed on September 13, 2013.

Kim, J. 2012. "6 Ways the I-Phone Changed Higher Ed." *Inside Higher Ed,* July 1. Available online at: http://www.insidehighered.com/blogs/technology-and-learning/6-ways-iphone-changed-higher-ed; accessed on May 13, 2013.

McLaughlin, J., L. Osterhout, and A. Kim. 2004. "Neural Correlates of Second Language Word Learning; Minimal Instruction Produces Rapid Change." *Nature Neuroscience* 7 (7): 703–704.

Neubauer, D. 2012. "The Changing Ecology of Higher Education." In *The Emergent Knowledge Society and the Future of Higher Education: Asian Perspectives,* edited by D. Neubauer, 209–216. New York: Routledge.

———. 2013. "Going Global: Cross-Border Mobility of Talent." Paper presented to the International Symposium on Talent Competition and Circulation in Asia: Education, Migration and Economy, National Taiwan Normal University, October 18–19.

O'Reilly, T., M. Loukides, J. Steele, and C. Hill. 2012. *How Data Science Is Transforming Health Care.* Strata Rx Conference. Kindle Edition. Available without cost through Amazon.com.

Pappano, L. 2012, "The Year of the MOOC." *New York Times,* November 2. Available online at: http://www.nytimes.com/2012/11/04/education/edlife/massive-open-online-courses-are-multiplying-at-a-rapid-pace.html?pagewanted=all&_r=0; accessed on August 19, 2013.

Rich, M. 2014. "New All-Digital Curriculums Hope to Ride High-Tech Push in Classrooms." *New York Times,* March 3.

Robinson, Sir K. 2010. "RSA Animate—Changing Education Paradigms." Available online at: http://www.youtube.com/watch?v=zDZFcDGpL4U&feature=youtu.be; accessed on August 28, 2013.

Roscoria, T. 2013. "Pressure Mounts as MOOCs Force Higher Ed to Rethink." Center for Digital Education. Available online at: http://www.centerdigitaled.

com/news/Pressure-MOOCs-Higher-Ed.html; accessed on September 10, 2013.
Rotella, C. 2013. "No Child Left Untableted: Rubert Murdoch's New Idea for How to Educate America." *New York Times Magazine*, September 15.
Schatz, M. C., and B. Langmead. 2013. "The DNA Data Deluge." June 27. Available online at: http://spectrum.ieee.org/biomedical/devices/the-dna-data-deluge; accessed on September 13, 2013.
Singer, N. 2013. "A Data Broker Offers a Peek behind the Curtain." *New York Times, Sunday Business*, September 1.
Trow, M. 1974. "Problems in the Transition from Elite to Mass Higher Education." In *OECD Policies for Higher Education*, 55–101. Paris: OECD.
Western Association of Schools and Colleges (WASC). 2013. "WASC Concept Papers: 2nd Series. The Changing Ecology of Higher Education and Its Impact on Higher Education." WASC. Available online at: http://www.wascsenior.org/redesign/conceptpapers; accessed on September 5, 2013.

Chapter 8

Questing for Entrepreneurship and Innovation for Enhancing Global Competitiveness in Hong Kong
Academic Reflections
Ka Ho Mok

Introduction

In view of uncertain times, Hong Kong, aspiring to continue as an international world city in Asia, has confronted increasing economic, social, and political challenges since it became the special administrative region of China in 1997. In the 2014–2015 budget, the financial secretary of the government of the Hong Kong Special Administrative Region (the Hong Kong government, hereafter) made a remark that Hong Kong has reached a critical juncture and thus people in the city-state should work together to prepare for the future, to strengthen further the solid foundation relied upon, "four traditional economic pillars"—financial services, trade and logistics, tourism, and professional and other service industries. Yet these industries are facing ever-mounting challenges from regional competitors such as Shenzhen, Shanghai, and Singapore in recent years. Its strive for becoming a knowledge economy has become even more acute after the 1997 handover and the Asian financial crisis in 1997–1998, when sustainability of Hong Kong's finance-centered economy was questioned. Being too heavily dependent on finance and trade, the role of the government in promoting research and development (R&D) has been criticized for being insufficient to compete with other nearby countries. The Hong Kong government used to assume technological development to be a linear process and that innovation will spread from upstream scientific research by universities to downstream commercialization process by enterprises. Hence, it simply acted as an infrastructure builder and funding provider without playing any important role during the process (Baark and Sharif 2006). However, since the past decade, there has been more government investment in R&D activities, especially in promoting increased regional innovation cooperation with mainland China. Most recently, the Hong Kong government has reiterated its ambition to restructure its economy in response to the growing challenges after the global financial crisis. One major strategy being adopted by the Hong Kong government is to encourage more university-industry cooperation by turning research findings into commercial products. Against the brief context outlined above, this chapter sets out to examine how the Hong Kong government has tried to encourage its public universities to engage with industry and business to promote innovation and R&D, knowledge-transfer, and research capacity of universities in the city-state. The present chapter also discusses how academics assess the growing trend of university-industry-business cooperation.[1]

Promotion of Innovation

In the colonial period, the government put less emphasis on industrial development than on service/financial industry because of the fiscal conservatism adopted by the British rulers (Tsui-Auch 1998). The major economic drives came from banking and service sectors instead of industries. Thus before the 1990s, Hong Kong government's role regarding the industrial development was mainly as a provider of infrastructure (e.g., support of industrial land, trained manpower, transport and communications, water, electricity, fuels and raw materials, financial and business services) and a facilitator (e.g., supply of technical information and advice, laboratory and bureau services that help entrepreneurs to enhance their productivity, quality, and innovation) (Yeh and Ng 1994, 460). At that time, R&D linkages among manufacturers, governmental supportive organizations, and higher education institutions (HEIs) were underdeveloped (Leung and Wu 1994). It wasn't until recent years that the government became more serious in developing strategies to support innovation and technological development.

During the past decade, Hong Kong's innovation system has expanded. Trade statistics show that the exports of high-tech products have risen in the last decade. The increase in research capacity of Hong Kong can be also seen by the increase of R&D personnel and R&D expenditure. As discussed above, the higher education (HE) sector and the private sector were the biggest spenders and employers, indicating that the government barely conducted its own research. Yet the government is important in its role as funder; in the last decade, it contributed over 40 percent of the total R&D expenditures.[2]

More importantly, since the 2000s, the government has become more active in formulating public policies and launching public projects to promote innovation and technology. Inspired by the successes of South Korea and Taiwan, the government completed the construction of the Hong Kong Science Park in 2000. Like any other science park across the world, the Hong Kong Science Park, located next to the Chinese University of Hong Kong (CUHK), also emphasizes "industry-university collaboration," establishing networks to facilitate partnership among enterprises, strengthening the talent pool, bringing expertise together into university and industry, and organizing training seminars, as well as promoting successful research outputs and developing products.

One of the key functions of the Hong Kong Science Park is to incubate business start-ups. Since 1992, the incubation programs have nurtured 277 start-ups, nearly 80 percent of which (216 out of 277) were still in operation as of 2011. Since April 2003, angel/venture capital investment has amounted to HK$699 million, 444 IP registration applications filed, 204 technical/design and management awards, and 16 IPO / merger and acquisition / joint venture / spin-off transactions (Hong Kong Science and Technology Parks Corporation 2011, 30–31). As of March 2011, the Hong Kong Science Park housed 258 companies, with 31 percent of them specializing in electronics, 29 percent in IT and telecommunications, 14 percent in biotechnology, 11 percent in green technology, 9 percent in precision engineering, and 6 percent in professional services. Most of the companies residing in the science park were local companies (60.2%), followed by those from the United States and Canada (13.6%), Europe (10.6%), Asia Pacific (8.6%), and mainland China (7%) (27).

The science park also aims to serve as a platform linking the academy and the industry. To help enterprises search for R&D personnel, it organized recruitment talks and set up an online Talent Pool Career Platform to help job seekers and students to better locate their desirable jobs in partner companies as well as at the science park. In 2010, the recruitment day attracted 2,000 candidates to apply for 400 jobs offered by 60 partner companies in the science park; the Talent Pool Career Platform registered over 1,000 job opportunities. In addition, the science park also aims at building talent pool networks through the partner universities—such as the CUHK's MBA program, Hong Kong University of Science and Technology's (HKUST) Business School, and the final-year program of the University of Ontario Institute of Technology—to get access to experienced pools of working executives (Hong Kong Science and Technology Parks Corporation 2011, 39). In terms of liaising the potential entrepreneurs and capital investors, in 2010, the science park co-established the Hong Kong Business Angel Network (HKBAN) with four local universities (i.e., University of Hong Kong [HKU], HKUST, CUHK, and Hong Kong Polytechnic University [HKPU]) and the Hong Kong Venture Capital and Private Equity Association, which aims to conduct funding matching between entrepreneurs and investors for potential R&D projects.[3]

After establishing the science park in 2000, the government continued to put more efforts in R&D promotion over the following decade. In 2000, it established the Hong Kong Applied Science and Technology Research Institute (ASTRI) as the public research institute of Hong Kong. By 2010, the tenth anniversary of establishment, ASTRI had completed over 360 technology transfers and had 130 patents granted. More than HK$160 million in income was received from the industry sector. The Industry Collaborative Project scheme, which at that time involved 10 projects, was expected to receive a committed income of about HK$47 million (ASTRI 2011, 2). Also in 2000, the government established the Innovation and Technology Commission (ITC) to devise and implement the government policies to promote innovation and technology as well as to run the Innovation and Technology Fund (ITF), which comprises a number of financial supporting programs and training schemes. Since the majority of companies in Hong Kong are small- and medium-sized enterprises (SMEs), their needs should be core to the government's innovative policies. Hence, the Hong Kong government has set up various research funds for the SMEs to apply. Since the beginning of the fund till January 31, 2012, ITF had already approved HK$6,292.1 million for 2,708 projects, many of which are related to electrical, electronics and/or information technology.

Since the inception of these programs, the government has continued to invest in them in order to help more SMEs. Taking the Small Entrepreneur Research Assistance Program as an example, in 2007 it relaxed the eligibility of applicants from companies of less than 20 employees to less than 100, so that the program could cover up to 99 percent of the companies in Hong Kong (Legislative Council, Panel on Commerce and Industry 2007). Approved projects would be offered a grant of up to HK$6 million on a dollar-for-dollar matching basis. The government's support measures offered to SMEs include not only more funding for their own research but also training schemes to upgrade their employees and incentive measures to encourage them to cooperate with the universities. To assist companies in training their staff to acquire skills in using a new technology, ITC launched the New Technology Training Scheme administered by the Vocational Training Council (VTC). The different forms of support include overseas training courses or internship, preapproved local training courses, and tailor-made training courses for individual companies.

To help SMEs employ new employees after the global financial crisis in 2009, the ITC internship program, which previously only covered universities and research institutes, has been extended to cover the private companies engaged in R&D projects funded by ITF. Monthly allowances for first-degree graduates and those with masters or higher degrees are HK$10,000 and HK$12,000, respectively. With regard to encouraging private-public R&D partnership, the government also allocated about HK$200 million to launch the "Research and Development Cash Rebate Scheme" in 2010. Under the scheme, businesses are offered a cash rebate equivalent to 30 percent of their R&D expenditures in projects under the ITF or projects funded by the companies and conducted by designated local research institutions, including six public universities,[4] the R&D centers under ITF,[5] the Hong Kong Productivity Council, and the VTC.

Besides the organizational infrastructures such as the science park and the ITC, the government also considered establishing public research institutes. Apart from the ASTRI, in June 2004 the ITC issued a consultation paper titled "New Strategy of Innovation and Technology Development," which put forward a new direction for Hong Kong's innovation system that emphasized a focus on selected strong industries, market relevance, industry participation, leverage on the mainland China, as well as a better coordination among stakeholders. Two proposals in the consultation paper are worth highlighting. First, the Paper proposed 13 technology focus areas[6] that Hong Kong should direct enough resources to develop. Second, the paper proposed to set up five research centers under the Hong Kong R&D Centers Program,[7] some of which are hosted by leading universities in Hong Kong. Together with the Hong Kong Jockey Club Institute of Chinese Medicine, these six government-university-industry cooperated centers are among the leading research centers in Hong Kong. Finally, the government has allocated HK$358.7 million from the ITF to pursue the plan.

The setting up of these research centers in 2006 was a breakthrough for R&D in Hong Kong, especially demonstrating the fact that the Hong Kong government was willing to set aside its conventional "noninterventionist" industrial policy and take up a more proactive role. The government explains that the government-led initiative has "the aim to harness

Hong Kong's advantages in applied research, intellectual property protection, business-friendly environment, and proximity to the manufacturing based in the Pearl River Delta (PRD), to thrive as a regional technology service hub."[8] The establishment of the following five R&D centers was a significant step forward for closer R&D cooperation among the government, industry, and university: (1) Automotive Parts and Accessory Systems R&D Center (APAS), (2) Hong Kong R&D Center for Information and Communications Technologies under the Hong Kong ASTRI, (3) Hong Kong Research Institute of Textiles and Apparel (HKRITA), (4) Hong Kong R&D Center for Logistics and Supply Chain Management Enabling Technologies (LSCM), and (5) Nano and Advanced Materials Institute (NAMI).

After a few years of operation, the government further allocated HK$369 million from the ITF in 2009 for the continued operation of five R&D centers up to 2013–2014. However, the government was not satisfied with the performance of these centers and hinted that its longer-term commitment would be contingent upon several factors such as cost-effectiveness, the performance in technology transfer and commercialization, and whether the centers could meet the targeted level of industry contributions. Originally, the government set the target at 40 percent of ITF in 2005; however, it lowered the expectation to 15 percent in 2009 because of the unsatisfactory performance of the centers (Legislative Council, Panel on Commerce and Industry 2011a). The government proposed that unless the centers achieved the industry contribution target it would consider ceasing the funding (2011b). Therefore, it is clear that the Hong Kong government has taken a more active role while investing in R&D activities in the past decade and has acted as an initiator to promote R&D activities through creating a more conducive environment for the private sector to engage in R&D endeavors. In addition to promotion of innovation, the Hong Kong government has attempted to enhance HE development to raise the research profile and level of innovation of universities in the city-state.

Promotion of Knowledge Transfer

In face of the improvements in R&D activities, in recent years the government has recognized the need of knowledge transfer, which aims to extend the benefits of the research outputs to the community. In November 2007, the University Grants Committee (UGC) co-organized the "Knowledge Transfer in a Knowledge-Based Economy Symposium" with the City

University of Hong Kong and the HKUST. Representatives from prestigious overseas universities, such as Stanford University, Oxford University, University of Leeds, and venture capital firms were invited to share their technology and knowledge-transfer experiences with Hong Kong stakeholders. In 2009, UGC set up HK$50 million annual funding to support public universities to promote knowledge-transfer activities. UGC has incorporated "knowledge transfer"—the UGC definition of which includes capacity building, frontline knowledge-transfer activities, and knowledge generation—into its mission statement and the institutions' role statements of its funded public universities.[9] According to UGC, knowledge transfer is "the systems and processes by which knowledge, including technology, know-how, expertise, and skills are transferred between higher education institutions and society, leading to innovative, profitable, or economic, or social improvements."[10] That means, knowledge transfer includes but is not limited to the commercialization of R&D products in the science and technology (S&T) fields. In order to carry out knowledge transfer, public HEIs in Hong Kong, under the auspices of UGC, have to submit annual reports to UGC to report the achievements of the previous year.

The government's commitment to knowledge-transfer activities has huge impact on the universities' organizational structure, finances, rules and regulations (particularly those regarding R&D activities), and the promotion of entrepreneurship education. However, compared to the counterparts in South Korea and Taiwan, universities in Hong Kong were relatively late in engaging in entrepreneurial activities. It wasn't until the 1990s that some of them started to seek ways to explore the potential of university-industry partnership, mainly through setting up spin-off companies and technology transfer office (Sharif and Baark 2008). For example, HKU set up the Technology Transfer Office and a company called Versitech. In 1998, HKU revisited its vision and mission, which now pledges to place more emphasis on applied research. In the 2000s, HKU incorporated knowledge transfer as a key pillar in its Strategic Development Plan 2009–2014. In the academic year 2010–2011, all ten faculties of HKU set up their own knowledge-exchange units as a formal structure led by the faculty dean or associate dean. In the face of more knowledge-exchange activities, the university council approved the intellectual property rights policy to set a framework for knowledge-exchange activities, especially for those conducted with external entities. For inducing knowledge transfer, in 2010–2011, a competitive funding scheme was launched to encourage faculty members to undertake innovative projects that have social, economic, environmental, or cultural impacts for industry, business, or the community. The Faculty Knowledge Exchange (KE) Award Scheme was also launched to recognize the faculty members' achievements in knowledge transfer. In terms of entrepreneurship education, the Technology Transfer Office established the Entrepreneurship Academy to organize workshop series in entrepreneurship for research staff, research postgraduate students, and alumni of related postgraduate programs (HKU 2011).

As for CUHK, with the UGC funding for knowledge transfer, it set up a Knowledge Transfer Project Fund for staff to apply for carrying out technology- or nontechnology-based knowledge-transfer activities. In 2009–2010 there were 45 applications, while in 2010–2011 the number jumped to 62. Additionally, the Technology Transfer Office launched the Patent Application Fund to encourage investors to apply for intellectual property rights protection, and also the Technology and Business Development Fund to explore the commercial potential of their research outputs. The number of patents filed increased from 109 in 2009–2010 to 148 in 2010–2011, and the number of patents granted also increased from 36 to 68 in the same period. The increases of the number of licenses and intellectual property rights income were most notable in the fields of biomedical, healthcare, and life sciences. In 2010–2011, CUHK's overall income was more than HK$248 million and the income generated from intellectual property rights accounted for HK$18.67 million (CUHK 2011). In 2010, the Center for Innovation and Technology (CINTEC) of the Faculty of Engineering launched the CUHK Open Innovation Network (COIN) to offer industrial companies with free consultancy on technical subjects, organization of regular seminars to disseminate CUHK innovations, newsletters updating CUHK innovations, and freely provided assistance to employers to conduct recruitment activities on campus. The CINTEC director explained,

> In the past, connections between the Faculty of Engineering and the industry mainly took the form of industry seeking advice from the Faculty or research collaborations. It's neither comprehensive nor proactive. COIN enables CUHK to systematically and proactively build a network with the industry.

Within a year since inception, COIN recruited about a hundred industry members. COIN anticipates that as the number accumulates, the collected information can be used for the construction of a database for industrial contacts shared with university members (CUHK 2011, 12–13).

Like HKU and CUHK, HKUST is a comprehensive university but with a stronger emphasis on S&T research and entrepreneurial activities. Since the 1990s, HKUST has established three key units to promote innovation and entrepreneurship within the campus, namely the Technology Transfer Center, the Entrepreneurship Center, and the HKUST R and D

Corporation Ltd. Through the Technology Transfer Center, from 1991–1992 to June 2011, HKUST has been granted 279 patents and has 1,222 pending patent applications. About 30 percent of the patents/patent applications are used by private companies in new products development or technology integration.[11] In recent years, with the auspices of the government's Knowledge Transfer Fund, the Technology Transfer Center introduced the Proof-of-Concept Fund to enable university staff to develop technology projects with commercial potential.[12] In 2000, the Entrepreneurship Center was established to promote entrepreneurial knowledge and activities among university staff and students and encourage them to participate in the commercialization of new technologies.[13] The HKUST R and D Corporation Ltd. is the business arm of HKUST, which seeks partnership with the industrial sector through R&D, consultancy, licensing and technology transfer, analytical and testing services, joint ventures, and model agreements.[14]

In the past decade, HKUST has had some remarkable achievements in industry-academia collaboration. From 1999 to 2010, HKUST has received HK$573.9 million from the ITF. In the same period, it received HK$577.3 million in funding from industry partners for contact research and collaborative R&D (HKUST 2010). Taking the 2008–2009 period as an example, collaborative projects were conducted with different local and foreign industry partners, such as the Mass Transit Railway (MTR) and the Hong Kong International Terminals in Hong Kong, and the Boeing Company and Motorola Inc. in America. Apart from some one-off projects, there were some partnerships for building research infrastructures. For example, HKUST received funding from the telecommunications company Huawei to set up the Huawei-HKUST Innovation Laboratory to conduct R&D projects on wireless communications (HKUST 2009).

Taking knowledge transfer more seriously, HKUST has created a new senior management position, associate vice president for research and innovation (AVP-RI), to assist the vice president for research and graduate studies in the planning and execution of knowledge-transfer activities. With regard to funding support for staff, under the support of knowledge-transfer funding by government, the Technology Transfer Center launched the Proof-of-Concept Fund to steer mid- to downstream research toward commercialization. Further, to better promote knowledge transfer and technology marketing, HKUST conducted a number of exhibitions, sharing sessions, seminars, conference, delegations, and visits (HKUST 2011).

More recently, the financial secretary of the HKSAR government made a remark suggesting, "Our competitive edge cannot be taken for granted, nor is it self-sustaining. It is up to us to keep honing it by seizing every opportunity to improve ourselves" (Government of the HKSAR 2014,

2). In order to maintain and enhance the global competitiveness of Hong Kong, the financial secretary has announced an increase in investment in R&D in the 2014–2015 budget by pursuing innovation and making good use of technology through accelerating technology transfer of upstream R&D results to translate more innovations into commercialized mid- and downstream R&D products or services. In order to further promote innovation and knowledge transfer, the financial secretary has announced two new measures to enhance the application and commercialization of R&D results, including the following (18):

1. Setting up an Enterprise Support Scheme (ESS) to replace the Small Entrepreneur Research Assistance Program. The ESS will provide funding support for R&D activities of private sector companies, irrespective of size, with the funding ceiling for each project raised from HK$6 million to HK$10 million. While the recipient company must bear at least half of the cost, it may retain all the intellectual property rights of the project.
2. Extending the scope of funding to development work and system integration, industrial design, compliance testing, and clinical trials. This will render stronger support to downstream R&D and commercialization activities, allowing full exploitation of the technological edge of local industries.

Obviously, these new measures have been adopted to further enhance R&D in Hong Kong and the government is keenly exploring the establishment of an innovation and technology bureau as a centralized body to coordinate and promote innovation and technology policy in the city-state. Meanwhile, the government has decided to allocate HK$24 million to the 6 designated universities to provide seed money for the R&D projects they recommend, encouraging their students and faculty to start downstream R&D businesses and commercialize their R&D results (19).

Networking with Mainland China

Apart from the knowledge-transfer initiatives, the R&D of Hong Kong universities has also undergone profound changes under the closer relationship of Hong Kong with mainland China. In the 1990s, it was commonly envisaged that after handover, Hong Kong's innovation system would be increasingly integrated with that of mainland China. In fact, Hong Kong's proximity to mainland China has always been an attraction for overseas companies based in Hong Kong. According to a consultancy report on a study Hong Kong Science Park conducted in the early 1990s, out of the 560 technology-based firms interviewed in 17 countries, 63 of them (mainly from mainland China, west-coast US, and the strongest European economies) expressed interest in establishing firms in the park, citing the possibility of exploring the market, manpower, and technological potential of China as the main reasons (Yeh and Ng 1994).

Since the 2000s, aiming to develop Hong Kong's innovation capacity, the government has tried to position Hong Kong as a regional service hub for the Pearl River Delta (Baark and Sharif 2006). This vision became a reality when Shenzhen and Hong Kong signed the "Shenzhen–Hong Kong Innovation Circle Cooperation Agreement" in May 2007. The newly developed innovation circle aims to establish innovation bases, service platforms, and initiate major R&D projects. One of the goals is to set up a Shenzhen–Hong Kong industry-university-research base for Hong Kong's universities. The circle has three key pillars—innovation foundation (provision of laboratories or facilities), service platform (sharing of technological resources and provision of technological services platform) and major R&D projects (cooperation in particular technological areas, such as solar battery) (Hong Kong Information Services Department 2009). In 2008, the government successfully made a deal on the first megaproject under the concept of the innovation circle. The US firm DuPont has agreed to establish the Global Thin Film Photovoltaic Business/R&D Center in Hong Kong Science Park, while setting up its production line in Shenzhen.

At the same time, the Hong Kong HE sector has been strengthening its ties with mainland China after the handover but more so in recent years. The increasing cooperation between Hong Kong and mainland China in HE is propelled by Hong Kong universities' own demands to expand the operation scale and harness more resources, as well as by mainland China's policy needs. For instance, in December 2008, the National Development and Reform Commission of the Chinese government promulgated *The Outline of the Plan for the Reform and Development of the Pearl River Delta (2008–2020)*, proposing the cross-border HE collaboration with the region. It stated, "The prestigious universities of Hong Kong and Macao will be encouraged to establish cooperative institutions of higher education in the Pearl River Delta, the authority for undertaking cooperative education with overseas organizations will be expanded, and the all-sided, multidisciplinary, and multiform cooperation on intellect introduction and talent cultivation will be encouraged, so as to optimize the structure of talent development" (Civic Exchange 2009, 65). Therefore, it expects that by 2020, the cities of Guangzhou, Shenzhen, and Zhuhai in the Guangdong Province will establish joint HEIs with three to five famous foreign universities. In 2011, China launched its twelfth Five-Year Plan, which stresses the need of developing technology-based strategic industries. All these policy plans are viewed by Hong Kong policy makers as opportunities for Hong Kong R&D to grow. An ASTRI chairman commented that, the launch of China's twelfth Five-Year Plan would provide a golden opportunity for Hong Kong to increase R&D investments (ASTRI 2011, 6). In fact, back in 2008, ASTRI had already set up the ASTRI Science and Technology Research (Shenzhen) Co. Ltd, a wholly owned subsidiary, on the mainland.

And for the HE sector, HKUST is among the first HEI in Hong Kong to establish strong ties with mainland China. The cooperation between HKUST, government agencies, and HEIs in mainland China, especially in South China (i.e., Nansha), date back to the late 1990s. In 1999, the Nansha Information Technology Park was approved by the Ministry of Science and Technology to be a key component of Guangzhou high-tech industries. In 2007, Fok Ying Tung Graduate School was established, which was named after Fok Ying Tung, a close friend of the Chinese government and a prominent "red capitalist" in Hong Kong. In 2010, the HKUST Light Emitting Diode and the Flat-Panel Display (LED-FPD) Technology R&D Center was established at Foshan with the financial support from the Foshan government. HKUST hopes that the center "will strengthen HKUST's research infrastructure and activities in the Pearl River Delta region and provide HKUST with a platform to reach out for collaboration opportunities and funding sources in the Mainland" (2010). Other prominent projects of HKUST in the mainland include the HKUST Shenzhen Research Institute and the HKUST R and D Corporation (Shenzhen) Ltd.

Joining the bandwagon, HKU and CUHK have also started to deepen their ties with mainland China, especially in R&D. For HKU, some landmark initiatives include the Hong Kong–Shenzhen Institute of Research and Innovation, the Hong Kong–Guangdong Stem Cell and Regenerative Medicine Research Center co-established with the Chinese Academy of Sciences Guangzhou Institute of Biomedicine and Health, and the HKU Shenzhen campus, which is in operation since 2013. As for CUHK, it is also establishing a new campus in Shenzhen.

Despite the trend of increasing HE cooperation between Hong Kong and mainland China, many difficulties abound that remain to be solved. A Hong Kong government-commissioned report found that the major difficulties include a lack of research talent due to the government restraints on Hong Kong HEIs independent ownership and independent student recruitment, the lack of Chinese government policy and financial support to commercialize the research, the need to pay tax for equipment acquisition, and the lack of technology transfer platform due to the immaturity of the alliance between government, industry, and

HEIs in China (Central Policy Unit 2011). Moreover, the difficulties in transferring research talents and research money between Hong Kong and mainland China also hinder the cooperation (Bauhinia Foundation Research Centre 2009, 52). Our above discussions have highlighted the recent developments of university-enterprise-industry cooperation; the following will examine how academics assess the growing trend of university-enterprise cooperation.

Academic Reflections

In order to understand how academics perceive and evaluate the growing trend of driving universities to become more entrepreneurial to reach out to the industry and business, the author conducted a comparative study of how academics working in Hong Kong, Taiwan, South Korea, and Singapore comment on the university-industry-business cooperation. The surveys are part of the research project funded by the Research Grant Council (RGC) of the HKSAR government. All nine universities/institutes in Hong Kong were selected for questionnaire distribution, namely, HKU, CUHK, HKUST, HKPU, Hong Kong Baptist University, City University of Hong Kong, Lingnan University, Hong Kong Shue Yan University, and the Hong Kong Institute of Education.

The targeted academic staffs (professors, associate professors, assistant professor, and lecturers) of all academic departments of these nine universities/institutes were asked to respond to an online survey. A total of 5,933 people were interviewed and we ultimately received 386 questionnaires. Findings of the survey are reported below.

- When asked if they "agree that university-enterprise cooperation should be strengthened," around 85 percent of the respondents supported the statement, with only 15 percent showing disagreement.
- When asked if they "agree that university-enterprise cooperations in South Korea, Singapore, and Taiwan are more successful than Hong Kong," about 58 percent believed Hong Kong had lagged behind the other Asian Tiger economies in terms of university-enterprise cooperation, while 14 percent and 28 percent of them disagreed or were not sure of the validity of the statement, respectively.
- When asked if they "agree that university-enterprise cooperation will cause a conflict of interest," about 52 percent of the respondents agreed with the statement, while 48 percent disagreed.

- When asked about "whether the government should monitor fund operation in university-enterprise cooperation," 60 percent supported the proposed management method, while 40 percent disapproved it.
- When asked to comment on "the government's role in providing more funding support to university-enterprise cooperation," the majority of the respondents showed their support (67%), while only 33 percent did not support the proposal.

When evaluating the deepening cooperation between university and industry, one major concern was related to the potential threat to academic freedom and the pressure that the academics may feel while engaging in commercialized research.

- When asked about their "views on academic freedom in the context of the growing trend of university-enterprise cooperation," the majority of the respondents did not think that more university-enterprise cooperation would affect academic freedom in a negative way (64%), while 36 percent of the interviewees gave indication of worries.
- The majority of the respondents (88%) thought university-enterprise cooperation would enhance student learning and the academic learning time of students would not be sacrificed when they do their internships in enterprises.
- When asked about "university-enterprise cooperation helping to increase the employment rate," 82 percent of the respondents showed their agreement to the statement, while only 17 percent and 2 percent showed disagreement or were not sure, respectively.
- Similarly, the majority of interviewees think university-enterprise cooperation will enhance the quality of graduates with around 80 percent of them supporting the statement.

In short, the survey shows positive support of the respondents in strengthening the university-enterprise cooperation since both parties would benefit from each other. Since R&D would not only help enhance innovation in producing new commercialized products based upon research outputs, the majority of the respondents think the university-enterprise cooperation would raise the reputation and image of the enterprises involved.

- Regarding the relationship between university-enterprise cooperation and university ranking, most of the respondents (51%) did not see a causal relationship between the two.
- When asked if they "agree that if university and enterprise do research and development together, not only can the scale and scope

of the research project be enlarged, they can jointly bear the risk of the research project," about 82 percent agreed, while 17 percent disagreed.
- When asked if they "agree that university-enterprise cooperation can reduce their operational risks," 56 percent of them showed disagreement, while 44 percent supported the statement.
- When asked if they "agree that goal difference is the main obstacle to university-enterprise cooperation," over 70 percent of the respondents supported the statement, while 29 percent did not consider it right.
- When asked if "the publication of research papers of university will release the commercial secrets of its partner enterprise," the majority (71%) disagreed with the statement, while 29 percent of them supported the claim.
- Meanwhile, around 58 percent of the respondents did not agree with the following statement, "universities inclined to conduct low-risk research and development projects would weaken enterprises' desire to cooperate with universities."
- Only 55 percent responded affirmatively to the question, "Do you agree that the benefit of university-enterprise cooperation cannot be estimated is a main obstacle in university-enterprise cooperation?"
- When asked if "universities should follow up graduates' employment status and adopt appropriate strategy to nurture students," most of the respondents (78%) showed their agreement.
- At the end of the survey, we asked them to comment on the following question: "Do you agree that 'strengthening and improving university-enterprise cooperation can lead to a win-win situation?'" Again, the majority of the interviewees (84%) showed their support for university-enterprise cooperation.

Discussion and Conclusion

This chapter has reviewed major initiatives that the Hong Kong government has adopted to support the HE sector's working with industry to promote research, transfer knowledge, and advancement of innovation. In order to further enhance the HE sector in Hong Kong to lead regionally and become globally competitive, the Hong Kong government has continued its support of R&D via its executive arm, UGC, to allocate funding support to HEIs in the city-state. In recent years, UGC has supported HEIs' academic research activities through different kinds of grants and funding, such as Theme-Based Research Scheme, Areas of Excellence

Scheme, General Research Fund (GRF), Collaborative Research Fund (CRF), and Joint Research Schemes with mainland China and overseas countries. UGC also encourages institutions to strengthen and broaden their endeavors in transferring knowledge, technology, and other forms of research outputs into real socioeconomic benefits and impacts for the community and society. Moreover, UGC established a research group to advise on the strategy to promote excellence in research and to review the research assessment and funding methodology.

Additional Government Fund in R&D

In response to the calls from UGC for excellence in research, the aggregate expenditure on research in 2010–2011 amounted to HK$6,948.3 million, representing 41 percent of the total expenditure in academic research of the institutions, and 0.38 percent of Hong Kong's GDP. UGC and RGC funding, in the form of block grants and competitive research grants respectively, constituted the bulk of research funding for the institutions. The various funding schemes administered by RGC represent the largest single source of funding for supporting academic research in Hong Kong's HE. These funding schemes are managed by RGC based on competition and peer review. Annual research funding to be distributed by the RGC amounts to about HK$1.1 billion starting from 2012–2013.[15]

RGC distributed HK$795 million through the Earmarked Research Grant for 2011–2012; there are four main funding schemes under the RGC Earmarked Research Grant: GRF, CRF, the Direct Allocation, and the Joint Research Schemes. The HK$18 billion Research Endowment Fund (REF) was established in February 2009 after approval was granted by the legislative council. The fund has been set up as a trust under the Permanent Secretary for Education Incorporated. Its investment income replaces a large portion of recurrent subvention originally allocated to RGC as an Earmarked Research Grant, thus providing greater funding stability and certainty. A portion of its investment income will also support theme-based research, thus allowing the institutions to work on research proposals on themes of a more long-term nature that are strategically beneficial to the development of Hong Kong. An injection of HK$5 billion into the REF was approved by the legislative council in January 2012. Of that the funds, a portion will provide research funding to the self-financing tertiary institutions on a competitive basis.[16] Our above discussion has also indicated the most recent measures proposed by the government to further boost R&D in Hong Kong through the provision of more funding support to promote innovation and knowledge transfer.

Rethinking Knowledge Transfer and New Governance

Nonetheless, depending upon the government alone would not be sufficient to promote innovation and R&D. Therefore, HEIs and industry have partnered closely in advancing innovation and R&D. The Hong Kong case clearly shows how universities/HEIs are becoming more entrepreneurial and the strengthened university-industry relationship will eventually affect the way universities are managed and the life styles of the academics in Hong Kong. When comparing Hong Kong with other Asian economies in terms of the role of government in promoting innovation, R&D, and knowledge transfer, the city-state is actually really lagging behind. If we further compare Hong Kong with the Organisation for Economic Co-operation and Development (OECD) countries, we can infer that Hong Kong should put more effort in the promotion of R&D in order to increase its global competitiveness.

One major aspect, in addition to funding support from the government, is the narrowly defined knowledge-transfer concept adopted by the Hong Kong government. It has placed emphasis on technology transfer rather than a broader sense of knowledge transfer that should not be confined to economic returns but also include social investment with social enterprises. This could promote social cohesion and social/community care if the government could well coordinate and articulate such productive forces between the university sector, business/industry, and the civil society. This chapter has clearly suggested that the Hong Kong government needs to rethink and reinterpret the concept of knowledge transfer since the existing notion of knowledge transfer is very much related to technology transfer. Although emphasis is being placed upon the Triple Helix Network through which the state, the industry, and the university can work closely together to promote innovation and knowledge transfer, what is missing in this framework is to bring back the "civil society" to partner with the different sectors in the Triple Helix Network to further boost entrepreneurship. Though the Hong Kong government has put much emphasis on commercialization of research outputs for economic entrepreneurship, what we can unleash from the society is effective use of societal forces in promoting social care and management to help people live in social harmony.

In conclusion, the discussions in the present chapter indicate the importance of the role of the government and the civil society in further enhancement of innovation and knowledge transfer. The Hong Kong government and the society at large should search for new governance in redefining and reshaping government-business-industry-civil society and university relationships.

Notes

1. Parts of the materials adopted (especially the policy background) in this chapter are based upon Mok's previous publication in 2013, revised and further developed for the current chapter. Part of the findings reported in the present chapter are generated from the funded project HKIEd GRF 750210 "Fostering Entrepreneurship and Innovation: A Comparative Study of Changing Roles of Universities in East Asia." The author wants to thank the Research Grant Council (RGC) of the HKSAR government for providing funding support to conduct the fieldwork and survey in Hong Kong.
2. Census and Statistics Department (2011; 2012).
3. Hong Kong Business Angel Network. Available online at: http://www.hkban.org/.
4. The six public universities being CUHK, City University of Hong Kong, Hong Kong Baptist University, HKPU, HKUST, and HKU.
5. The R&D centers under ITF being Hong Kong Automotive Parts and Accessory Systems R&D Center, Hong Kong R&D Center for Logistics and Supply Chain Management Enabling Technologies, Hong Kong Research Institute of Textiles and Apparel, Nano and Advanced Materials Institute, and Hong Kong ASTRI.
6. The 13 technology focus areas include the following:
    a. Advanced manufacturing technologies
    b. Automotive parts and accessory systems
    c. Chinese medicine
    d. Communications technologies
    e. Consumer electronics
    f. Digital entertainment
    g. Display technologies
    h. Integrated circuit design
    i. Logistics/supply chain management enabling technologies
    j. Medical diagnostics and devices
    k. Nanotechnology and advanced materials
    l. Optoelectronics
    m. Textile and clothing
7. Innovation and Technology Commission, the Government of the Hong Kong Special Administrative Region. "Research & Development Centres." Available online at: http://www.itc.gov.hk/en/rdcentre/rdcentre.htm.
8. Ibid.
9. University Grants Committee, Hong Kong. "Knowledge Transfer." Available online at: http://www.ugc.edu.hk/eng/ugc/activity/kt/kt.htm.
10. Ibid.
11. Technology Transfer Center, the Hong Kong University of Science and Technology. Available online at: http://www.ttc.ust.hk/en/home.asp.
12. Ibid.

13. Entrepreneurship Center, HKUST. Available online at: http://www.ec.ust.hk/index.html.
14. HKUST R and D Corporation Ltd. Available online at: http://www.rdc.ust.hk/eng/index.html.
15. Hong Kong UGC (2012, 77).
16. Ibid., 78.

References

Applied Science and Technology Research Institute (ASTRI). 2011. *ASTRI Annual Report 2010/2011*. Hong Kong: ASTRI.
Baark, E., and N. Sharif. 2006. "Hong Kong's Innovation System in Transition: Challenges of Regional Integration and Promotion of High Technology." In *Asia's Innovation Systems in Transition*, edited by Bengt-Ake Lundvall, Patarapong Intarakumnerd, and Jan Vang, 123–147. Northampton, MA: Edward Elgar.
Bauhinia Foundation Research Centre. 2009. *Hong Kong–Shenzhen Education Cooperation* (In Chinese). Hong Kong: Bauhinia Foundation Research Centre.
Census and Statistics Department. 2011. *Hong Kong Monthly Digest of Statistics: Hong Kong's External Trade in High Technology Products and Technology Balance of Payments, 2000, 2005, and 2010*. Hong Kong: Census and Statistics Department. Available online at: http://www.censtatd.gov.hk/hkstat/sub/sp120.jsp?productCode=FA100045.
———. 2012. *Hong Kong Innovation Activities Statistics 2011*. Hong Kong: Census and Statistics Department. Available online at: http://www.statistics.gov.hk/pub/B11100102011AN11B0100.pdf.
Central Policy Unit. 2011. *Case Study of Hong Kong-Guangdong Cooperation in Education and Science and Technology in Nansha*. Hong Kong: Central Policy Unit, HKSAR Government.
Chinese University of Hong Kong (CUHK). 2011. *Annual Report on Recurrent Funding for Knowledge Transfer in the 2009/10 to 2011/12 Triennium for the Period 1 July 2010–30 June 2011*. Hong Kong: CUHK.
Civic Exchange. 2009. *The Outline of the Plan for the Reform and Development of the Pearl River Delta (2008–2020)*. Hong Kong: Civic Exchange.
The Government of the Hong Kong Special Administrative Region (HKSAR). 2014. *The 2014–15 Budget*. Hong Kong: Government Printer.
Hong Kong Information Services Department. 2009. "Three-Year Action Plan on Shenzhen/Hong Kong Co-operation in Innovation and Technology." Hong Kong: Hong Kong Information Services Department. Available online at: http://www.info.gov.hk/gia/general/200903/31/P200903300269.htm.
Hong Kong Science and Technology Parks Corporation. 2011. *Annual Report 2010/2011*. Hong Kong: Hong Kong Science and Technology Parks Corporation.

Hong Kong University of Science and Technology (HKUST). 2009 *Annual Report 2008–2009*. Hong Kong: HKUST.
———. 2010. *Annual Report on Research Activities 2009–10*. Hong Kong: HKUST. Available online at: http://research.ust.hk/report1.pdf.
———. 2011. *Knowledge Transfer Annual Report 2010/11*. Hong Kong: HKUST.
Legislative Council, Panel on Commerce and Industry, HKSAR. 2007. "Improvements to the Small Entrepreneur Research Assistance Program and the University-Industry Collaboration Program under the Innovation and Technology Fund." LC Paper No. CB(1)2088/06–07(05), Legislative Council, Panel on Commerce and Industry, HKSAR. Available online at: http://www.legco.gov.hk/yr07-08/english/panels/ci/papers/ci0115cb1-549-4-e.pdf.
———. 2011a. "Comprehensive Review of R&D Centers Set up under the Innovation and Technology Fund." LC Paper No. CB(1)624/11–12(05), Legislative Council, Panel on Commerce and Industry, HKSAR. Available online at: http://www.legco.gov.hk/yr11-12/english/panels/ci/papers/ci1220cb1-624-5-e.pdf.
———. 2011b. "Updated Background Brief on Research and Development Centres Set up under the Innovation and Technology Fund." LC Paper No. CB(1)624/11–12(06), Legislative Council, Panel on Commerce and Industry, HKSAR. Available online at: http://www.legco.gov.hk/yr11-12/english/panels/ci/papers/ci1220cb1-624-6-e.pdf.
Leung, C. K., and C. T. Wu. 1994. "Innovation Environment, R&D Linkages and Technology Development in Hong Kong." *Regional Studies* 29 (6): 533–546.
Sharif, N., and E. Baark. 2008. "Mobilizing Technology Transfer from University to Industry." *Journal of Technology Management in China* 3 (1): 47–65.
University Grants Committee (UGC). 2012. *"3+3+4"—A New Era of Holistic Education: Annual Report 2011–2012*. Hong Kong: UGC. Available online at: http://www.ugc.edu.hk/eng/ugc/publication/report/figure2011/pdf/UGCAnnualReport.pdf.
The University of Hong Kong (HKU). 2011. *Recurrent Funding for Knowledge Transfer in the 2009/10 to 2011/12 Triennium, Annual Report 2010/11*. Hong Kong: HKU.
Tsui-Auch, L. S. 1998. "Has the Hong Kong Model Worked? Industrial Policy in Retrospect and Prospect." *Development and Change* 29 (1): 55–79.
Yeh, A. G. O., and M. K. Ng. 1994. "The Changing Role of the State in High-Tech Industrial Development: The Experience of Hong Kong." *Environment and Planning C: Government and Policy* 12 (4): 449–472.

Chapter 9

The Quest for Entrepreneurial University in Taiwan
Policies and Practices in Industry-Academy Cooperation

Sheng-Ju Chan and Ka Ho Mok

Introduction

In responding to the changing needs of social and economic development, universities have been encouraged to be more responsive and innovative for the past two decades. Burton Clark (1998; 2004) began to examine university behavior and analyze why some are more successful than others in adapting to changing environments. The key factor in raising university performance lies at the core spirit of "entrepreneurship." If universities are more entrepreneurial, it means institutions are more likely to meet new social and economic demands through innovative measures (Sporn 1999). It is not just the institution that needs entrepreneurship but individuals also require such capacity. According to UNESCO (n.d.), "Fostering entrepreneurship attitudes and skills in secondary schools raises awareness of career opportunities, as well as of ways young people can contribute to the development and prosperity of their communities." In other words, having such skills or capacity can create more employment opportunities and even help in driving the advancement of local communities. Due to such wide concerns a wide range of governments in Asia are also keen to promote the concept of "entrepreneurial university" to bring greater advantages to the whole society (Wong 2011).

As one of the most recently developed countries, Taiwan has been keen to transform into a knowledge-based economy. Building upon its previous success, universities in Taiwan are required to broaden "third mission" services in order to enhance the application of cutting-edge technology to company production, maintaining its competitiveness at the global level (Liu et al. 2011). It is based on this assumption that a wide range of government department initiatives has been put forward to deepen the collaboration between industry and the academy. This chapter uses industry-academy cooperation (IAC) as an example to illustrate the policies and practices of entrepreneurial universities in Taiwan. Our research findings indicate that a state-led approach characterizes the IAC. With narrowly defined focuses and practices, Taiwanese IAC should go beyond the scope of hard sciences or tangible products. Humanities and social sciences are becoming important in knowledge-based societies in order to enhance innovation and entrepreneurship such as popular arts, music, and tourism. Universities, therefore, should not only be concerned with financial advantages and monetary benefits. Instead, they have to fulfill their "public" duty through "social entrepreneurship." This chapter is composed of seven major sections. After a brief introduction, the authors give a broader view of the dynamic relationship among economy, technology, and entrepreneurship in Taiwan. This is followed by some conventional practices of the entrepreneurial university in Taiwan. In this section, some relevant theories and concepts in relation to IAC are discussed and used empirically. The fourth section deals with the interdepartmental efforts in promoting IAC including ministries from education, economy, and research. The focus of the fifth section is on the institutional mechanisms and practices in the Taiwanese context. Based on previous sections, in the sixth section we argue that Taiwanese universities have undergone dramatic organizational transformations due to the quest for entrepreneurship. These discussions lead to conclusions and implications in the final section.[1]

Economy, Technology, and Entrepreneurship in Taiwan

As an emerging economy, Taiwan has been very keen in transforming its industrial structure from a labor-intensive, agricultural, and low-skills oriented economy to an innovative, high-tech, and knowledge-based entity for the past several decades. In seriously pursuing this mega transformation, economic growth in Taiwan has been very significant. In 1992–2002, the gross domestic product (GDP) of the four little dragons (Taiwan, South Korea, Hong Kong, and Singapore) has grown from 3.6 to 5.6 percent. In this decade, Taiwan saw a 5.0 percent average annual growth in GDP (Zanran n.d.). However, in 2013 this figure dropped to 2.43 percent after decades of rapid growth while the GDP per capita rose to NT$20,328. In other words, Taiwan is one of the leading countries in the Asian region in terms of economic performance. As a matter of fact, this achievement is based on its strong technology advancement. Known as the "Silicon Valley of the East," Taiwan has developed very competitive information and communication technology industries since the late 1970s and 1980s. Some leading companies produce cutting-edge products in computers, information technology, semiconductor, or manufacturing sectors. Compared to other Asian countries, Taiwan's technology development level is among the top (Japan and other four tigers are rated at the same level). This technological advantage boosts the further growth of Taiwan's economy.

In examining such continuous development of this island state, another main factor emerges—entrepreneurship. Taiwan has been improving its wider environment for ease of doing business in recent years. Moreover, entrepreneurial attitudes, intentions, and behaviors in Taiwan are rated relatively high among the high-income economies in East Asia. Table 9.1, showing the relative ranking on the ease of doing business, indicates that Taiwan's ranking is getting better since 2006, improving to sixteenth place in 2013. This persistent improvement provides a positive and stable sign for doing business to domestic and international companies and industries. With such supportive policies, mechanisms, and institutions, Taiwan has been keen to facilitate the expansion of economic activities in turn promoting the advancement of technology. As far as entrepreneurial attitude and perceptions are concerned, Taiwan, compared to other neighboring countries, performs pretty well. Particularly, Taiwanese people rate entrepreneurial opportunities quite high. As can be seen in Table 9.2, 70 percent of those surveyed regard entrepreneurship as a good career choice and 63 percent believe that successful entrepreneurs enjoy high social status and respect. These comparative figures demonstrate that there is a favorable atmosphere for entrepreneurial activities and innovations. It is against the context discussed above that may contribute to the deeper involvement of universities in relevant undertakings.

Table 9.1 Ranking on the ease of doing business

Country	Rank				
	2013	2012	2010	2008	2006
Singapore	1	1	1	1	2
Hong Kong	2	2	2	4	6
New Zealand	3	3	3	2	1
United States	4	4	5	3	3
Denmark	5	5	6	5	7
Norway	6	6	7	11	8
United Kingdom	7	7	4	6	5
South Korea	8	8	15	30	23
Iceland	14	9	14	10	11
Ireland	15	10	8	8	10
Taiwan	16	25	34	50	47

Source: Data from World Bank (2013). Table created by author.

Table 9.2 Entrepreneurial attitudes and perceptions in selected countries, 2012 (% of survey respondents)

Country	Perceived opportunities	Perceived capabilities	Entrepreneurial intentions	Entrepreneurship as a good career choice	High status to successful entrepreneur
Japan	6	9	2	30	55
South Korea	13	27	13	59	70
Singapore	23	27	16	50	63
Taiwan	39	26	25	70	63

Source: Data from Xavier et al. (2012). Table created by author.

Entrepreneurial University: Traditional Practices in Taiwan and Emerging Concepts

Traditional Practices of the Entrepreneurial University in Taiwan

While examining the prototype of the entrepreneurial university in Taiwan, it would be better to look at some traditional practices in relation to the current situation. Technological and vocational institutions can be one of the cornerstones of a modern type of entrepreneurial university. Based on the Stanford report released in 1962, a large number of junior colleges (later became colleges and now universities) were set up in order to provide mid-level workforce for emerging manufacture and industrial sectors from the 1970s to 1990s (Wu et al. 1989). These institutions have been under the supervision of the Department of Technological and Vocational Education (DTVE), Ministry of Education (MOE), to nurture and provide practical and applied knowledge and skills to industry. In view of a greater alignment with industry, they often run sandwich courses, internship programs, and cooperative education with employers. Such joint initiatives can be seen as amateur entrepreneurial activities, which were particularly important for the Taiwanese economy before 1990s since small- and medium-sized enterprises (SMEs) were the main beneficiaries of these activities. Such bridging arrangements help to facilitate transition between college/university to work/job. Therefore, these traditional vocational colleges retained a "service-oriented" function, to some extent, in an attempt to cater to the needs of the society.

In addition to the technological and vocational track having a direct link to entrepreneurial origin, general universities were strongly encouraged to engage with the local industries and companies in areas other than the pursuit of abstract or theoretical knowledge. The dynamic relationship between the science park and university can highlight such entrepreneurial innovation. In order to further strengthen the roots of the economic development, Hsinchu Science Park in Taiwan was established in 1980 with some high-tech companies and enterprises (Mok et al. 2013). Two neighboring universities, namely, National Tsing Hua University (清華大學) and National Chiao Tung University (交通大學), emphasize natural science, engineering, and computer sciences providing high-end labor force to this newly established science park. If we examine these two sectors closely, there is an alignment/tango between the constituent discipline of the two universities and industries at Hsinchu Science Park. The major industries concentrate on semiconductor, computer, telecommunication, optoelectronics, and advanced precision mechanics while these two universities also pay special attention to these disciplinary areas. Many successful leaders and managers at the Hsinchu Science Park have received their higher education (HE) at these two universities. In a sense, the science park is a conduit or platform for promoting better and synergetic collaboration between the academy and industry. The two universities contribute to the science park by mainly target the needs of industrial development in general. These unique interactions pave the way for the engagement of Taiwan's universities in entrepreneurial activities. However, it remains unclear what entrepreneurialism actually means in a more commercialized environment. We will discuss this in more depth later.

Emerging/Broadening Concepts

There has been a general belief that the entrepreneurial university concentrates on pursuing a business goal and commercial benefits, or even generating income from the outside world. The origin of the attachment of such goals to the entrepreneurial university stems from the greater needs of diversifying or earning resources from wider capital markets. There are those who think that the entrepreneurial university is equivalent to privatization, the market principle, and corporate management. Such negative or neoliberal impressions reflect a mainstream stereotype that the university should not be under the command of the private market or be purely driven by a need to generate external funding in order to maintain its feature of "public goods." In exploring such developments, some scholars even use "academic capitalism" to describe certain behaviors of the entrepreneurial university, particularly in relation to privatization and commercialization (Slaughter and Leslie 1999; Deem 2001). However, if we look at the term "entrepreneurialism" closely, it appears more complex. According to Shattock (2009, 4), an eminent scholar in promoting entrepreneurship at Warwick University in the United Kingdom, the broad sense of entrepreneurialism is "a reflection both of institutional adaptiveness to a changing environment and of the capacity of universities to produce innovation through research and new ideas." The main driver for such institutional transformation encompasses the needs of adaption to changing of wider societies by providing new services or functions in forms of research, teaching, or consultancy. Judging from this broad definition, entrepreneurialism is not only concerned with commercial or business-oriented activities with respect to resources generation or corporate behaviors but also with wider application of HE outputs (i.e., research, teaching, and service) to social and economic development at local, national, regional, and international levels (Clark 1998). If this loose meaning is accepted, there are different types of theories and concepts that are highly relevant to the discussion here.

First, apart from research and teaching, the "third stream" of HE focuses on the application and promotion of university's all services and products to the outside world (Wedgwood 2006). It stresses the important role of the university to connect to the development of local economy and regional communities. This concept supports the idea that HE should be devoted to adopting innovative measures in assisting regional social and economic development. Some examples from the field have shown that even humanities or social sciences subjects such as literature, counseling, or history can be vital factors in successfully restructuring the local community. Such deep linkages between academic knowledge and practical application indicate that university's innovative and adaptive measures (also entrepreneurial) are key to new socioeconomic environments. This breaks away from the traditional curiosity-driven and theory-focused practices of knowledge production. The new way of creating knowledge outlined previously, named as "Mode 2," asserts that knowledge production is context-driven, problem-focused, and interdisciplinary (Gibbons et al. 1994). Therefore, application does matter and is critical for driving knowledge advancement. No doubt, such wider orientation covers the basic nature of entrepreneurialism, broadly defined by institutional innovation and adaption as suggested by Shattock (2009) and Clark (2004).

There has been growth in terms of universities' greater engagement into social and economic development. In response to the increased pressure of globalization and international competition, HE sectors across the globe are expected to raise national or societal competitiveness by providing a wide range of services (Mok et al. 2013). One of the main forms of such services, considerably related to entrepreneurialism, is IAC. IAC refers to a situation where two sectors help each other to achieve a common goal in a broad sense. Aiming at providing workforce, technology, and consultancy, HE can engage industry widely. Based on previous successful experiences such as the dynamic cooperation between the science park and universities or sandwich/internship courses provided by technological universities, more recent initiatives have been launched to encourage greater cooperation between academy and industry, as universities have an important role to play in creating new knowledge and innovations for wider industries and societies. IAC is considered as one of major activities of entrepreneurialism. In this chapter, IAC in Taiwan will be the main area to be explored and used as the bases for discussion on entrepreneurship in general.

Major Initiatives in Pursuit of Entrepreneurial University

In examining the policies proposed by Taiwan's government in the quest for the entrepreneurial university through IAC, there are interdepartmental engines that intersect among education, economy, and research. Three major ministries stand out, namely, MOE, Ministry of Economic Affairs (MOEA), and National Science Council (NSC). However, they also collaborate with each other to maximize their joint potential. We will explore relevant policies according to the previous sequence.

MOE: General Platforms and Regulations

Acting as a promoter and regulator, the MOE was active in promoting IAC in the past and established rules such as the "Regulation for Industry and Academy Cooperation for Tertiary Education" that govern and encourage IAC. According to the MOE, "We would like to encourage the universities to put equal emphasis on education and internship, and enhance the cooperation between enterprises and schools. Besides the tasks of research and teaching, the universities should also be engaged in social service" (2007). This statement regards IAC activities as an essential channel for universities to engage enterprises and companies, echoing the idea of the third stream outlined earlier. In deepening the cooperation with industries, not only the institutional structures need to be designed for such objectives but more importantly the core value or culture of the university is also expected to shift to adapt to these needs. Therefore, "universities should be managed with a spirit of entrepreneurship; the programs of the institutes and colleges should be designed based on the principle of pragmatism" (ibid.). From the official perspective, entrepreneurship is the fundamental element in achieving better IAC; this advantage should be realized through the pragmatic design of courses in order to meet the demands of the wider society. Thus, it is clear that IAC in Taiwan becomes a critical measure to turn traditional academic institutions into "entrepreneurial" organizations.

With an eye to promoting IAC, the DTVE, in the MOE, has commissioned National Kaohsiung First University of Science and Technology to establish an integrative website ("教育部產學合作資訊網" ["Industry-Academy Cooperation Information"], http://www.iaci.nkfust.edu.tw/Industry/index.aspx) as a common platform. This website contains relevant policies, practices, and outcomes of IAC and provides implementation manuals, cases, and results. These major initiatives are carried out by technological and vocational institutions supported by a wide range of centers sponsored by DETV such as the Centre for Regional IAC (區域產學合作中心) (six centers nationwide), Centre for United Technical Development (聯合技術發展中心), and Centre for Technical Research (技研中心). One of the major policies launched in 2010 is "Restructuring Technological and Vocational Education Sector" (技職再造), which attempts to realign the resources of industry, government, university, and research institutes to meet the needs of enterprises and companies. Three strategies adopted under this policy are "adjusting institutions," "revitalizing curriculum," and "promoting employment." Through such a reform at technological and vocational institutions, Taiwan's industries aim to build a knowledge-based economy with cutting-edge products and technology.

Six vital industries specifically selected to deepen IAC include precision machinery and opto-mechatronics, leisure and service innovation, cultural innovation and digital service, biotech medicine and precision agriculture, electronics and communication, and green energy and environmental ecology.

Such ambitious moves toward the high-tech society and economy through entrepreneurial activities are also supported by another initiative called Model University of Technology Program (典範科技大學計畫). In 2013, the MOE initiated this program by selecting 12 technological universities for establishing closer connection with industries. The main aim is to "diversify the development of talent cultivation and technology innovation so as to enhance the value of intellectual property" (MOE 2013). Selected universities have to collaborate with industry and government in devoting resources to certain innovative fields and linking the institutional mission to the national and regional needs of economic growth. In other words, the MOE tries to reshape the image and function of technological universities by requiring greater integration with certain industries through talent cultivation and technology advancement. These innovative reforms target the upgrading of local enterprises and raising their technological capacity by transfer of technology from university to industry. As a matter of fact, as far as enhancing technological ability is concerned, the MOE even began to pioneer an alternative route under the name "Professional Expert" ("專技教師") for university faculty since 2006. This new type of faculty helps the university to recruit teachers specializing in certain technical/vocational skills in order to enhance the linkage between industry and HE. Professional experts stress professional skills and practical innovation and avoid overemphasis on academic publication, journal articles, and written papers. This new faculty track encourages promotion through technical reports, innovative products, and intellectual property (patent) developments instead of traditional academic papers/publication. We can say that this innovative way to hire faculty with entrepreneurial spirit is concerned with bridging latest technology or skills between industries and higher education institutions (HEIs). On the one hand, these faculty can help to educate students with practical and skillful abilities; on the other hand, universities with such professional experts have the first hand knowledge of real industry and become more entrepreneurial due to their engagement with both academy and industry.

With an eye on assessing and encouraging IAC activities, the MOE in Taiwan carried out a project to evaluate each university's performance in IAC against a wide range of indicators and stated that "teachers and students who have performed well in the collaboration should be rewarded" (MOE 2007). This annual IAC Accountability Assessment (大專校院產學合作績效評量) is applicable to all colleges and universities in Taiwan

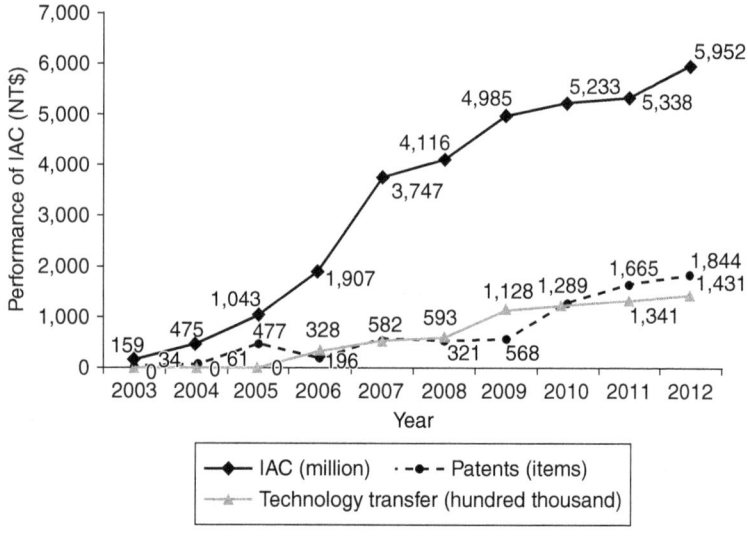

Figure 9.1 Increasing performance of IAC, 2003–2012 (NT$).

since 2007. The objective of this IAC assessment is to understand, monitor, and compare the relative performance of IAC at Taiwanese universities. The dimensions to be evaluated include fund and efficiency, coverage (teacher participation and partners), and outcome of intellectual property and application benefits. Quantitative approaches and institutional ranking are employed to reward the universities with performance of high standards. Figure 9.1 shows that after the introduction of the annual IAC Accountability Assessment in 2007 the overall performance of Taiwanese universities is improving dramatically. The number of patents and the level of technology transfer doubled or even tripled within five years. This excellent outcome indicates the effectiveness of such assessment in raising university's motivation for IAC in general.

The exceptional performance in IAC actually is also driven by the world-class university project in Taiwan. In the twentieth century, the era of the knowledge economy, innovation and research and development (R&D) has become the key to national competitiveness. Whether knowledge can make further progress depends primarily on universities' R&D results. Therefore, "Plan to Develop First-class Universities" and "Top-level Research Centers" supported by MOE requires better IAC to strengthen the advantages in cutting-edge technology. Such synergy raises the universities' R&D capacity and creates more opportunities for intellectual property rights including patents, technology transfers, and professional works. These knowledge-intensive products in turn can be translated into companies' competitive advantage. In this sense, through application, R&D becomes a crucial dimension of the third stream for the university in pursuit of entrepreneurship. These IAC projects can "provide R&D support and consultation services to high-tech industries," having a direct impact on industry upgrades and related innovations as well as R&D (MOE 2012). These high-tech industries include electronics, communication, optoelectronics, biochemistry, medical care, nanotechnologies, environmental protection, and conventional manufacturing.

MOEA: Assisting SMEs

Since IAC proved to be beneficial to economic development, MOEA began to assist SMEs at the start-up stage by encouraging the establishment of (innovation) incubation centers within the universities or research institutes in 1996. Incubation centers are regarded as supportive units for disseminating the knowledge and skills of operation, consultation, R&D, business management, market extension, and enterprise development. Since more than 70 percent of companies in Taiwan are SMEs, these incubation centers play a major role in nurturing such enterprises and providing relevant industrial knowledge, skills, and even advice to corporate management. As we have discussed previously, Taiwanese colleges and universities are seen to be responsible for regional economic development as per the idea of the third stream/mission. Incubation centers, on the one hand, pave a platform for greater IAC, and on the other hand, can be a trigger for universities' "entrepreneurial behavior" for faculty, staff, and students. According to the statistics of MOEA, there are 132 incubation centers in 2013. Among them, 73 percent (97 centers) come from the HE sector. That means that about 60 percent of universities (now totaling 162 in Taiwan) set up incubation center. This coverage and distribution is quite widespread. Moreover, in the last decade more than 2,651 start-up companies were created and investment rose to NT$84.6 billion (equivalent to US$2.8 billion) (SME Administration, MOEA 2014). Coinciding with the current strengths of Taiwanese industries, 49 percent of the incubation centers, as indicated at Table 9.3, focus on IT and electronics, biotechnology, and machinery. They are followed by tourism and recreation (8.91%), education and culture art (6.80%), environmental protection industry (4.90%), and medical industry (4.77%), respectively. It is clear that the main function of incubation centers is to assist in the continuous growth of emerging SMEs. MOEA does this job quite well in strengthening IAC

Table 9.3 Top ten categories of incubation centers in Taiwan, 2013

Rank	Category	Distribution (%)
1	IT and electronics	22.08
2	Biotechnology	16.67
3	Machinery and electric machinery	10.09
4	Others	9.46
5	Tourism and recreation	8.91
6	Education and culture art	6.80
7	Environmental protection industry	4.90
8	Medical industry	4.77
9	Multimedia and broadcasting	4.47
10	Livelihood industry	3.93

Source: Data from SME Administration, MOEA (2014). Table created by author.

for the past two decades. However, in recent years it has shifted its focus to cutting-edge technology and leading knowledge production.

MOEA acknowledges that knowledge-based economy entities require major innovation or breakthroughs in technology in order to have a comparative advantage globally. In view of such a national ambition, MOEA is aiming for cutting-edge technology in collaboration with the NSC since 2013. MOEA and NSC have initiated the project of Major League IAC (產學大聯盟) to engage in R&D of the most critical and advanced technology by involving domestic companies, HE sector, and research institutes in the form of a consortium. The size of a typical research grant is no less than NT$80 million (equivalent to US$2.7 million). The awarded projects include National Taiwan University (semiconductor and intelligence device) and National Cheng Kung University (steel materials). Both universities collaborate with leading companies in Taiwan and aspire to have groundbreaking discovery or innovation in these two fields. This project indicates an obvious development that modern IAC has gone beyond the traditional forms of teaching and learning and technical services. Greater cooperation in R&D between leading universities and large companies has become the key element in upgrading industry and enhancing national competitiveness. This is the reason why MOEA and NSC have to collaborate with each other and increase this interdepartmental synergy.

NSC: Combining University Research and Industry

As the most important official funding arm for research, NSC has a long history of promoting IAC in Taiwan. Hsinchu Science Park was established in 1980 under its full support; subsequently, more such parks have been set up such as Southern Taiwan Science Park, in 1997, and Central Taiwan Science Park, in 2002. As indicated previously, there are multilayered relationships between universities and industries in the science park. Another major role played by NSC is to finance research projects for universities and research institutes. Among these research projects, some initiatives are related to IAC. Three different types of research projects in relation to IAC are designed for various developmental stages of an emerging company in 2013. The first one is Major League IAC (產學大聯盟) in collaboration with MOEA for cutting-edge technology as described above. Another type is Minor League IAC (產學小聯盟) for SMEs consistent with the mission of incubation centers supported by MOEA. The final type of IAC research project is the Applied Research Program for Start-ups (應用型研究育苗專案計畫), which targets early stage novel research with capacity for product development and application. The comprehensive coverage of different types of IAC research can have systematic impacts on university behaviors toward entrepreneurship in general. As a matter of fact, in order to provide systematic assistance to IAC, NSC passed the Regulation for Funding Advanced Technology Programs (補助產業前瞻技術計畫作業要點) in 2013. With this rule, NSC is able to support new business models for key technologies in emerging or existing industries.

Institutional Mechanisms and Practices in Taiwanese Universities

Having examined the diverse policies proposed and implemented by three major ministries including education, economics, and research, we pay attention to relevant institutional mechanisms and practices regarding IAC. In fact, Taiwanese universities tend to have a mission statement to assist IAC or regional/local (economic) development, particularly technological institutions. For instance, National Tsing Hua University, a top institution, publicly states in their Institutional Development Plan that "promoting IAC" has been the cornerstone of attaining academic excellence status (2009, 4). Due to such motivation and policy guidance/enforcement, there have been a variety of institutionalized agencies in relation to IAC within the university. Using National Chung Cheng University as an example, there are at least four agencies dealing with some aspects of IAC. First, the Office of Research and Development (研發處) is in charge of R&D issues including management of academic and industrial research services. Under this wider umbrella, there is the

IAC Division and Center of Technology Promotion. The latter specializes in management and promotion of technology and intellectual property rights. As indicated previously, National Chung Cheng University also operates an incubation center under the support of MOEA focusing on high-tech manufacturing. In addition, extra mechanisms might be found at technological-oriented universities such as the center for regional IAC or the center for technology development or research. In other words, such institutionalized mechanisms point to one fact that the very essence of IAC has been deeply rooted in the daily operation of many universities in Taiwan (Mok 2013). IAC development is about not only government policies, strategies, and research programs at national level but also there are corresponding administration divisions and centers at the university level for facilitating the implementation and planning of IAC.

Apart from the organizational institutionalization within the campus, human capital and capacity provide the fundamental basis for advancing IAC. In bettering student's IAC literacy, entrepreneurship education can serve a variety of purposes. With this, students can have better knowledge or skills for employment or even starting enterprises (Chen et al. 2013). This might be able to ease the problem of unemployment and poverty. It is particularly relevant in Taiwan because of the rising unemployment rate for college graduates. SMEs occupy a very important position in the whole of Taiwan industry also making entrepreneurship education more critical and necessary. Usually, entrepreneurship education programs are provided in parallel with the existing resources of the university and are one of the most valued areas of the university. National Donghua University, National Taiwan University, National Sun Yat-Sen University, and Southern Taiwan University are planning more professional courses related to these important areas. Yuan Ze University stresses entrepreneurship courses while National United University courses emphasize business management and financial planning. Most universities believe that legal courses should also be included in the program planning, for example, commercial law, patents, property rights, and other law-related courses. National Donghua University adds many economics-related subjects into the program planning, such as the basis of economics, the economic life of the commercial economy, and Taiwan's economic development. The Global Institute of Technology adds team management skills, interpersonal skills, communication skills, and other practical application courses into the program planning. This shows different universities have different entrepreneurship education programs and focus on different subjects. The diverse elements of programs and courses reflect the multifaceted nature of entrepreneurship education while adapting to the changing societal needs.

Entrepreneurial University: A Grand Transformation in Taiwan

In this chapter, we use IAC as a term to depict and examine the behavior of the entrepreneurial university in Taiwan. According to the reviewed policies and practices at national and institutional level, we argue that there is a unique approach for the Taiwanese university to be entrepreneurial. The classical theory asserts that healthy dynamics of IAC is composed of three major forces, namely, state, university, and industry (see Figure 9.2). This "triple helix" indicates a balanced synergy if cooperation remains sustainable. Empirical experiences in Taiwan have shown that this system mainly relies on the nation-state as the driving force to make IAC possible and effective. We have seen a strong state steering through a top-down approach with diverse and detailed cross-departmental support (education, economy, and research). In an attempt to make the entrepreneurial university feasible, the Taiwanese government seeks to align the HE sector with the development of industry. All possible means such as regulations, funding, and outcome monitoring have been mobilized to assure such alignment. This centralized governance for IAC reflects the spirit of new public management or new managerialism in the wake of accountability (Deem and Brehony 2005). Critically speaking, entrepreneurship should have autonomy in institutional decision making (Clark 2004). People need to be cautious of the external imposition from the central government on the realization of core values. The top-down approach might cause some challenges to "real" entrepreneurship since it narrows the space for innovative and adaptive options.

In order to effectively respond to global competition and pressure, Taiwanese universities are required to address the cutting-edge technology with a strong vision to revive or stimulate the local and regional economy. However, it is interesting to note that international entrepreneurial adventures are not equally encouraged in easing such pressures. On the contrary, interdepartmental policies and initiatives entirely focus on the assistance of local and domestic industries in the form of incubation centers or other research projects. These emphases are a mirror of nationalism (or local concern) by stressing domestic-oriented development rather than cross-border collaboration or internationalization as has been the experience of Hong Kong and Singapore (Chan 2012). This may need further evidence to examine how successful this domestic-focused approach is in responding to global competition. The formation of such an approach to some extent is related to the larger share

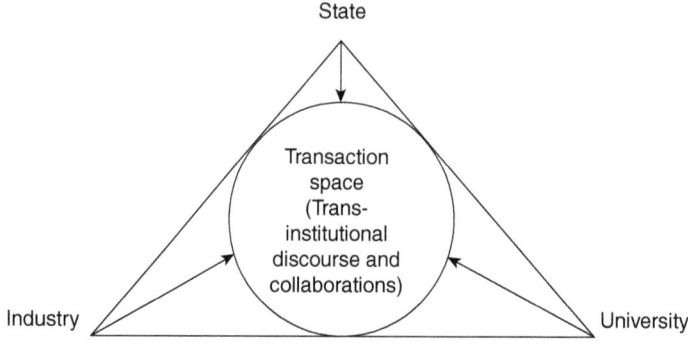

Figure 9.2 The dynamics of IAC.

of SMEs in the Taiwanese industrial structure (about 70%). Therefore, the focus of IAC is dependent on SMEs. Now it has begun to shift to major or larger enterprises by stressing on cutting-edge technology, intellectual property rights, and patents. In transforming its industrial structure into a knowledge-based economy, Taiwan begins to pay more attention to leading companies since they can produce more value-added products and services. Therefore, the world-class university project in Taiwan stresses upon the importance of IAC. The greater collaboration of leading organizations, both in the HE sector and industrial sector, can be very effective in technology advancement and raising national competitiveness in an increasingly globalized world. This redirection of IAC highlights the emerging role of R&D in a changing scenario of technological revolution and provides new opportunities for Taiwanese universities to pursue greater entrepreneurship.

As a matter of fact, in further realizing entrepreneurship, some major transformations have been underway to further promote entrepreneurship as discussed above. For instance, IAC has been regarded an important and necessary mission of every university. In a border sense, entrepreneurialism, to some extent, has become the "gene" of Taiwanese universities. Most people understand that IAC has such a long history in Taiwan with a wide range of supporting policies and strategies. Universities even have specialized internal administrative units and provide relevant courses or programs in entrepreneurial education. Thus, we would argue that each university seems to have an imperative to carry out IAC as well as be innovative while adapting to the wider socioeconomic development. However, overemphasis on the dominant role of government in driving IAC might pose serious challenges to the balance of the triple helix (i.e., state, university, and industry). From our field observation and dialogue in Taiwan, there are two major criticisms for current IAC (fieldwork interview, August 2013). On the one hand, some faculty are not very motivated to implement IAC largely because of a lack of systematic rewards, such as financial benefits, or punishments. On the other hand, the private sector, particularly SMEs, are reluctant to invest in joint activities and tend to rely on governmental sponsorship (or public research funds as discussed above). This inert corporate culture with respect to IAC prevents universities from further entrepreneurial activities.

In addition, another feature of Taiwanese IAC systematically privileges "hard science" or "tangible product" over "soft science" and intangible immersion subjects such as art, design, psychology, community studies, and so on (Wedgwood 2006). The very concept of IAC for many officials, university leaders, and faculty in Taiwan is that it is only applicable to the fields of sciences, engineering, medicines, and certain forms of business-related research. Such notions considerably distort and narrow the broader application of entrepreneurialism proposed by Shattock (2009) and Clark (1998; 2004). Certainly, it restrains the potentials of social sciences, arts, and humanities from realizing the function of the third stream. Utilized suitably, IAC or engaging community development can be very similar and complementary concepts that involve a wide range of academic subjects, knowledge, and skills. For example, in addition to introducing productive industries, other issues such as mental health, environmental aesthetics, and historical heritage should be carefully reviewed while restructuring a traditional community. Therefore, it is our intention to argue that the entrepreneurial university is not just about income generation, market principle, or even academic capitalism. It can be an innovative and creative institution that mobilizes teaching, research, and social service as effective instruments to solve practical problems in the real world. IAC, as a major form of entrepreneurial activities, retains huge potential for leading to organizational transformation for greater social benefits.

As far as the quest for entrepreneurship is concerned, Taiwanese universities also experienced successful transformations within the institutions. Nearly every university/college has its own internal governance unit/structure to enhance its outreach to local industries and enterprises. However, they are fragmented or duplicated in some ways. These administrative units, often endorsed by different central departments, are responsible for various aspects of IAC or entrepreneurial activities. It is our suggestion that streamlining these internal units can provide more powerful and coherent organizational support to entrepreneurialism.

Conclusion and Implications

The active and long history of IAC points to an undeniable fact that Taiwanese universities have been exposed to entrepreneurship intensively. However, theoretical reviews also reveal that Taiwanese policies and practices are biased and imbalanced. The highly state-led approach, although inspiring universities to be entrepreneurial, may not be sufficient to guarantee a more sustainable development. A greater participation and engagement of university and industry/enterprise is urgently required. From the university side, there are some major transformations needed. First of all, effective policies and strategies should be adopted to develop an entrepreneurial faculty/culture (Lambert 2009), which offers endless power in pursuit of innovative and creative engagement with societal development. Moreover, institutional autonomy and less regulation are also desirable for better entrepreneurship (Mora and Vieira 2009). As we have argued, overt intrusive intervention, due to new managerialism, could be harmful for forming such a culture or value. Finally, internal coordination is needed at the university level to remove duplication of governing structures.

Another major lesson for Taiwanese entrepreneurial universities is their narrowly defined focuses and practices. IAC should go beyond the scope of hard sciences or tangible products. Humanities and social sciences are becoming important in the knowledge-based society for enhancing innovation and entrepreneurship such as popular arts, music, tourism, and so on. This assertion is consistent with the emerging concept of the third stream, which combines research and teaching for social services (Laredo 2007). Therefore, universities are not only concerned with financial advantages or monetary benefits but they also have to fulfill their public role through social entrepreneurship. The expanded concept of entrepreneurialism is composed of a wide range of academic subjects and knowledge and aims at enhancing public benefits. It is our conclusion that Taiwanese universities have to begin to ponder over this new development and change current outdated policies and practices to succeed in its quest for a healthy, balanced, and sustainable entrepreneurship.

Note

1. Part of the findings reported in the present chapter are generated from the funded project HKIEd GRF 750210 "Fostering Entrepreneurship and Innovation: A Comparative Study of Changing Roles of Universities in East Asia." The authors want to thank the Research Grant Council (RGC) of the HKSAR government for providing funding support to conduct the fieldwork and survey in Taiwan.

References

Chan, S. J. 2012. "The Emergence of Nationalism in an Internationalized Context: Higher Education Reforms in Japan and Taiwan." Paper presented at International Symposium on Internationalization of Higher Education: Ideas, Practices and Implications for Asia and Pacific, The Hong Kong Institute of Education, February 24.

Chen, S. C, H. C. Hsiao, J. C. Chang, C. M. Chou, C. P. Chen, and C. H. Shen. 2013. "Can the Entrepreneurship Course Improve the Entrepreneurial Intentions of Students?" *International Entrepreneurship and Management Journal.* DOI 10.1007/s11365-013-0293-0.

Clark, B. 1998. *Creating Entrepreneurial Universities: Organizational Pathways of Transformation.* Bingley, UK: Emerald Group Publishing Limited.

———. 2004. *Sustaining Change in Universities: Continuities in Case Studies and Concepts.* Maidenhead, UK: Open University Press.

Deem, R. 2001. "Globalization, New Managerialism, Academic Capitalism, and Entrepreneurialism in Universities: Is the Local Dimensions Still Important?" *Comparative Education* 37 (1): 7–20.

Deem, R., and K. Brehony. 2005. "Management as Ideology: The Case of 'New Managerialism' in Higher Education." *Oxford Review of Education* 31 (2): 217–235.

Gibbons, M., C. Limoges, H. Nowotny, S. Schwartzman, P. Scott, and M. Trow. 1994. *The New Production of Knowledge. The Dynamics of Science and Research in Contemporary Societies.* London: Sage Publications.

Lambert, B. H. 2009. "Impediments, Inhibitors, and Barriers to University Entrepreneurialism." In *Entrepreneurialism in Universities and the Knowledge Economy: Diversification and Organizational Change in European Higher Education*, edited by M. Shattock, 142–182. Maidenhead, UK: Open University Press.

Laredo, P. 2007. "Revisiting the Third Mission of Universities: Towards a Renewed Categorization of University Activities?" *Higher Education Policy* 20 (4): 441–456.

Liu, P. C. B., D. Z. Chen, and J. D. Chiou. 2011. "University Technology Commercialization in Taiwan: National Taiwan University (NTU) and National Taiwan University of Science and Technology (NTUST)." In *Academic Entrepreneurship in Asia: The Role and Impact of Universities in National Innovation Systems*, edited by P. K. Wong, 199–222. Cheltenham, UK: Edward Elgar Publishing.

MOE. 2007. *Industry-Academia Partnerships a Win-Win Strategy.* Taipei: MOE. Available online at: http://english.moe.gov.tw/ct.asp?xItem=6844&ctNode=504&mp=2.

———. 2012. *Plan to Develop First-class Universities and Top-level Research Centers.* Taipei: MOE. Available online at: http://english.moe.gov.tw/ct.asp?xItem=7131&ctNode=505&mp=1.

———. 2013. *An Introduction to Model University of Technology Program.* Taipei: MOE. Available online at: http://www.iaci.nkfust.edu.tw/Upload/UserFiles/1020308發展典範科技大學計畫說明會簡報.pdf.

Mok, K. H. 2013. "Meeting Point of the East and the West: Globalizing or Localizing Higher Education in East Asia." In *The Dynamics of Higher Education Development in East Asia: Asian Cultural Heritage, Western Dominance, Economic Development, and Globalization*, edited by D. Neubauer, J. C. Shin, and J. N. Hawkins, 81–118. New York: Palgrave Macmillan.

Mok, K. H., K. M. Yu, and Y. W. Ku. 2013. "After Massification: The Quest for Entrepreneurial Universities and Technological Advancement in Taiwan." *Journal of Higher Education Policy and Management* 35 (3): 264–279.

Mora, J. G., and M. J. Vieira. 2008. "Governance, Organizational Change, and Entrepreneurialism: Is There a Connection?" In *Entrepreneurialism in Universities and the Knowledge Economy: Diversification and Organizational Change in European Higher Education*, edited by M. Shattock, 74–99. Maidenhead, UK: Open University Press.

National Tsing Hua University. 2009. *Long and Mid-term Plan for Institutional Development*. Hsinchu, Taiwan: National Tsing Hua University.

Shattock, M., ed. 2009. *Entrepreneurialism in Universities and the Knowledge Economy: Diversification and Organizational Change in European Higher Education*. Maidenhead, UK: Open University Press.

Slaughter, S., and L. L. Leslie. 1999. *Academic Capitalism: Politics, Policies, and the Entrepreneurial University*. Baltimore, MD: John Hopkins University Press.

SME Administration, Ministry of Economic Affairs (MOEA). 2014. *The Current Status of Incubation Centers in Taiwan*. Taipei: SME Administration, MOEA. Available online at: http://www.moeasmea.gov.tw/ct.asp?xItem=5959&ctNode=469&mp=2.

Sporn, B. 1999. *Adaptive University Structures: An Analysis of Adaptation of Socioeconomic Environments of US and European Universities*. London; Philadelphia, PA: Jessica Kingsley Publishers.

UNESCO. n.d. *Entrepreneurship Education*. Paris: UNESCO. Available online at: http://www.unesco.org/new/en/education/themes/strengthening-education-systems/secondary-education/entrepreneurship-education/.

Wedgwood, M. 2006. "Mainstreaming the Third Stream." In *Beyond Mass Higher Education: Building on Expansion*, edited by I. McNay, 134–157. Maidenhead, UK: Open University Press.

Wong, P. K., ed. 2011. *Academic Entrepreneurship in Asia: The Role and Impact of Universities in National Innovation Systems*. Cheltenham, UK: Edward Elgar Publishing.

World Bank. 2013. *Doing Business 2013: Smarter Regulations for Small and Medium-Size Enterprises*. Washington, DC: World Bank. Available online at: http://www.doingbusiness.org/~/media/GIAWB/Doing%20Business/Documents/Annual-Reports/English/DB13-full-report.pdf.

Wu, W. H, S. F. Chen, and C. T. Wu. 1989. "The Development of Higher Education in Taiwan." *Higher Education* 18 (1): 117–136.

Xavier, S. R., D. Kelley, J. Kew, M. Herrington, and A. Vorderwülbecke. 2012. "Global Entrepreneurship Monitor 2012 Global Report." Available online at: http://www.leo.itesm.mx/GEM/Reporte%20Global%202012.pdf.

Zanran. n.d.. "GDP Growth Rate Forecasts for Asian Economies." Available online at: http://www.zanran.com/q/GDP_growth_rate_forecasts_for_Asian_Economies.

Chapter 10

The University-Community Compact
Innovation in Community Engagement
Robert W. Franco

Introduction

American higher education (HE) has a rich history of university-community engagement. Today, however, most colleges and universities find themselves still cloistered in "town versus gown" issues with their publics and legislatures. These issues are having a significant negative impact on community and legislative willingness to fund HE at local, state, and national levels. Some institutional types are at greater risk of confronting their demise.

This chapter will focus on one institutional type: the American community college. The chapter will briefly discuss the evolution of the American community colleges movement and then discuss major advances in university-community engagement since 1985. These advances include the work of Campus Compact, Ernest Boyer and the Carnegie Foundation for the Advancement of Teaching, the American Association of Community Colleges (AACC), Association of American Colleges and Universities (AAC&U), and the Science Education for New Civic Engagements and Responsibilities (SENCER) initiative at the National Science Foundation (NSF).

The author has been leading community and civic engagement initiatives at Campus Compact and AACC for nearly 20 years. Using insights and innovations from these organizations, Kapi'olani Community College

(KCC) has developed nationally recognized innovations in community and civic engagement. These innovations have resulted in significant community benefit while improving student engagement, learning, and achievement within an evolving ecology of learning. The chapter concludes with the suggestion that greater civic and community engagement may make a difference in the survival of our colleges and universities.

The Evolution of the American Community College

In 1862, American HE experienced its first wave of increased community engagement when President Abraham Lincoln signed the Morrill Act. This act led to the establishment of "Land Grant" colleges and universities in states across the nation. According to McDowell (2001), Kerr (1963), and Ward (2003), the Morrill Act represented a teleological shift in the history of HE in America as HE opportunities became available to a much wider portion of the nation's population, applied sciences became appropriate for university study, and expertise of the university was linked with the needs of the community. After America's Civil War, the German model of HE influenced the development of land grant universities into research universities that could address both national and societal needs.

Early in the twentieth century, a second wave of HE community engagement began when Dean Alexis Lange of the University of California School of Education and other national leaders "urged the junior colleges to give high priority for programs that would prepare their students for effective participation in community life" (Gleazer 1994, ix). Lange called for a junior college department of civic education with a curriculum that would "quicken students' communal sympathies," "deepen their sense of indissoluble oneness with their fellows," and encourage them to "participate vigorously, militantly, if need be, in advancing community welfare" (Bogue 1950, 336–337).

In the United States, the early decades of the twentieth century were a period of heightened attention to the urban migration of African Americans and international migration of Southern and Eastern Europeans and East Asians, and an emerging social Darwinism. Lange and other elite university presidents also promulgated another, largely hidden mission for the community college:

> Fearing they would be "overrun" by hordes of unqualified students and yet recognizing the powerful political pressures for more open access to

universities in a society emphasizing upward mobility through education, the elite universities saw the junior college as an essential safety valve that would satisfy the demands for access while protecting their own institutions...they saw the two-year institution as existing less to offer new opportunities to obtain a bachelor's degree to excluded segments of the population than to divert them away from four-year colleges and universities. (Brint and Karabel 1989, 208)

In 1922, the American Association of Junior Colleges, in their first revision to their statement of purpose asserted,

The junior college may, and is likely to, develop a different type of curriculum, suited to the larger and ever changing civic, social, and vocational needs of the entire community in which the college is located. (Gleazer 1994)

In 1936, Hollinshead reasserted,

The junior college should be a community college, meeting community needs; that it should serve to promote a greater social and civic intelligence in the community...that the work of the community college should be closely integrated with the work of the high school and of other community institutions. (Witt et al. 1994, 24)

From the 1930s, junior colleges realigned to offer more vocational/career two-year terminal degrees to support local and state workforce and economic development. This vocational/career realignment, combined with the continuing emphasis on local students gaining access to and succeeding at the university, resulted in what is now called the American "community college."

In 1947, the Truman Commission called on community colleges to become "centers of learning for the entire community." The commission also boldly asserted the need for public education to be "made available, tuition-free, to all Americans able and willing to receive it, regardless of race, creed, color, sex, or economic and social status (Gleazer 1994, xi).

The return of millions of service personnel from both the European and Pacific theaters and pressure to extend educational opportunities to them resulted in the passage of the GI Bill in 1944. This bill provided HE support to military veterans and resulted in soaring enrollments in community colleges through 1946, when nearly 43 percent of junior college students were veterans (Witt et al. 1994, 126).

From 1950 to 1970, the number of American community colleges increased from 412 to 1,058. Through the 1960s, America built "nearly one community college per week" and enrollments soared to 2.5 million students (Witt et al. 1994, 185). Throughout this decade, these two-year colleges found themselves "in communities caught in the throes of change" and substantial ethnic, racial, and political unrest.

From 1960 to the present, the community college has educated an unprecedented diversity of students. In many American cities, these campuses have often been the setting for the first genuine and sustained interactions among racial and cultural groups.

Today, America's 1,132 community colleges educate 13 million students. About half (52%) of these students are White and half (48%) are Hispanic, Black, Asian/Pacific Islander, Native American, or Other. Almost half of all American undergraduates (45%) are in community colleges.

Major Advances in Campus-Community Engagement

Campus Compact was founded in 1985 by the presidents of Brown, Georgetown, and Stanford Universities and the president of the Education Commission of the States. Concerned about media representations of college students as materialistic and self-absorbed and more "interested in making money than in helping their neighbors," these presidents founded Campus Compact to help colleges and universities create support structures, including offices and staff, to coordinate community engagement efforts, train faculty members to integrate community work into their teaching and research, create scholarships and other student incentives, and develop the institutional will to make civic and community engagement a priority.

Campus Compact is a national coalition of more than 1,100 college and university presidents—representing some 6 million students—who are committed to fulfilling the civic purposes of HE. As the only national HE association dedicated solely to campus-based civic engagement, Campus Compact promotes public and community service that develops students' citizenship skills, helps campuses forge effective community partnerships, and provides resources and training for faculty seeking to integrate civic and community-based learning into the curriculum. Campus Compact's membership includes both public and private two- and four-year institutions across the spectrum of HE.[1]

Campus Compact has affiliated offices in 34 US states; these offices are usually housed on the campuses of leading universities in these states. For example, Hawaii-Pacific Islands Campus Compact is housed at the University of Hawaii at Manoa.

In 1999, Elizabeth Hollander, Campus Compact executive director, and Harry Boyte, senior fellow, Humphrey School of Public Affairs, University of Minnesota, convened a Wingspread Conference. The conference was coordinated by the University of Michigan Center for Community Service and Learning, with sponsorship by the Association of American Universities, American Association for Higher Education, American Council on Education, AAC&U, Campus Compact, New England Resource Center for Higher Education, University of Pennsylvania Center for University Partnerships, and the Johnson Foundation and support from the W. K. Kellogg Foundation.

The conference produced the Wingspread Declaration on the Civic Responsibilities of Research Universities. The document identifies ways in which a new vision for "public engagement" by research universities will impact students and faculty, including teaching staff, staff, administrators, and institutions.[2]

In the first years of the new millennia, Campus Compact focused their research agenda on civic engagement as an institutional priority. With funding from the Carnegie Corporation of New York, from 2002 to 2006, Campus Compact staff, Senior Faculty Fellows, and leaders in the field conducted and published national studies of institutional civic engagement in two-year colleges and minority-serving institutions. The two reports by Zlotkowski et al. (2004; 2005) provided specific strategies for deepening civic and community engagement in American higher education.

Ernest Boyer and the Carnegie Foundation for the Advancement of Teaching

Ernest Boyer was the president of the Carnegie Foundation from 1979 to 1995. In 1987, he and his colleagues published *College: The Undergraduate Experience in America*. This research made the powerful and lasting case that HE should not only prepare students for productive careers "but also enable them to live lives of dignity and purpose, generate new knowledge, and channel that knowledge to humane ends, and study government, and help shape a citizenry that can promote the public good."

In 1990, in his publication, *Scholarship Reconsidered*, he advocated for an expanded definition of scholarship and research. For Boyer, traditional research, or the scholarship of discovery, had been the center of academic life and crucial to an institution's advancement. Boyer argued that scholarship needed to be broadened, more interdisciplinary, and applied, so that colleges and universities could address new social and environmental challenges beyond the campus. His vision was to change the research mission of universities by introducing the idea that scholarship needed to be redefined. He proposed four different categories of scholarship as follows:

1. The scholarship of discovery that includes original research that advances knowledge
2. The scholarship of integration that involves synthesis of information across disciplines, across topics within a discipline, or across time
3. The scholarship of application (also later called the scholarship of engagement) that goes beyond the service duties of a faculty member to those within or outside the university and involves the rigor and application of disciplinary expertise with results that can be shared with and/or evaluated by peers
4. The scholarship of teaching and learning that the systematic study of teaching and learning processes—differs from scholarly teaching in that it requires a format that will allow public sharing and the opportunity for application and evaluation by others

In 1988, Boyer consulted with the AACC on a Kellogg-funded project titled "Building Communities: A Vision for a New Century." The publication set some new directions for America's community colleges with a focus on curriculum, faculty, partnership, and community development. The community colleges' presidents engaged in this work eloquently defined community as "a region to be served and a climate to be created."

KCC led efforts to develop international education as part of the "Building Communities" project. The college published a four-volume set titled "Beyond the Classroom: International Education and the Community Colleges."

Boyer's vision has influenced every corner of American HE; it was appropriate that the Carnegie Foundation would develop their Classification of Community Engagement in 2006 based on Boyer's vision.

In 2006, the Carnegie Foundation for the Advancement of Teaching developed a new benchmarking tool for documenting "Community Engagement" at American colleges and universities. According to Amy Driscoll, associate senior scholar at the Carnegie Foundation, the tool used insights from two major sources (2006):

1. Campus Compact's study and publication of the indicators of community engagement at community colleges, an assessment tool developed by Community Campus Partnerships for Health, and the Defining and Benchmarking Engagement Project of National Association of State Universities and Land Grant Colleges.
2. A pilot study sponsored by Carnegie to examine community engagement practices as indicators for a documentation framework

conducted at 14 institutions (see Carnegie website for list of pilot institutions).

In this latter pilot study, there was an active debate about whether to emphasize institutional "civic engagement" or "community engagement."

The 2006 Wingspread Conference called attention to the different ways "engagement" was being used within different constituencies within American HE. The discourse of civic engagement had soared to new "rhetorical heights...these statements are impressive. But there are some extraordinary things happening across the country. Now is the time to bring together rhetoric, leadership, and hard work" (Rice, cited in Sandaman and Weerts 2008).

Below are some of the most eloquent phrasings of civic engagement (Levine 2012).

> Civic engagement is the participation of private actors in the public sphere, conducted through direct and indirect interactions of civil society organizations and citizens-at-large with government, multilateral institutions and business establishments to influence decision making or pursue common goals.[3]
>
> In American history, the citizen has been not only a voter or a rights-bearing member of the nation or a consumer of services. The citizen has also been a producer, a public-spirited agent in problem solving and common work...Addressing the tough challenges we face today will require people to reconceive of themselves as citizens...It will require widespread civic involvement that taps the common sense, energy, insight, and effort that comes from citizens with different talents and points of view working together, often across lines of sharp cultural, partisan, racial, and economic differences. Without active citizenship, we will continue to struggle with narrow, unfulfilling roles and ineffective institutions. With restored citizenship, we act as co-creators of history, reclaiming our birthright as democratic citizens to be full participants in shaping our common life.[4]
>
> [Civic engagement is] being sensitive to and understanding the world's problems as well as addressing them through collaboration and commitment.[5]
>
> Civic Participation: Individual and collective actions designed to address public issues through the institutions of civil society. Political Awareness: Cognitive, attitudinal, and affective involvement in the polity. Civic Engagement: The combination of Civic Awareness and Civic Participation.[6]
>
> A morally and civically responsible individual recognizes himself or herself as a member of a larger social fabric and therefore considers social problems to be at least partly his or her own; such an individual is willing to see the moral and civic dimensions of issues, to make and justify informed moral and civic judgments, and to take action when appropriate.[7]

Our mission is to educate and empower people to engage in hands-on democracy in order to individually and collectively take strategic actions to identify and address the root causes of local, state, federal, and global issues of social and economic injustice and concerns.[8]

[Civic engagement is] active involvement in the discourse dealing with the need to develop and utilize knowledge for the improvement of society, to use talents and offer wisdom for the greater good, and to provide opportunities for education in the spirit of a democratic society. A civically educated and engaged citizen is one who is skilled in coalition-building, collaboration, negotiation, and synthesis of multiple perspectives.[9]

Active citizens seek to build, sustain, reform, and improve the communities to which they belong, which range from small voluntary associations to the world. Active citizens deliberate with peers to define public problems and then collaborate with peers to address those problems. In doing so, they honor certain virtues; such as equal respect for others and a degree of loyalty to their communities that does not preclude critical thinking and dissent. Collaboration—actual work—is just as important as deliberation. People who merely talk about public issues are ineffectual and often naïve or misinformed; we learn from acting together. By collaborating, citizens construct or build public goods: tangible goods like schools and markets, and intangible ones like traditions and norms. In doing so, they create civic relationships, which are scarce but renewable assets for civil society.[10]

Many of the 14 institutions engaged in the Carnegie Foundation's pilot study aspired and continue to aspire to civic engagement as a central role for their colleges and universities. These colleges and universities are fundamentally committed to specific student learning and development outcomes, that is, preparing students, now and into the future, for active citizenship, democratic participation, and societal improvement.

However, many of the institutions saw their primary engagement roles and responsibility as improving the quality of life in their communities, and secondarily about student learning and development outcomes.

In the pilot study, the term "community engagement" was deemed more useful as it was more inclusive. The concept could include services (e.g., extension services) and programs at universities rooted in their Land Grant history and mission, the workforce and economic development programs of community colleges, the applied research work of universities, and civic engagement as a student learning and development outcome.

Rather than the soaring rhetoric of civic engagement, the Carnegie definition of community engagement is eloquently simple and clear: community engagement is the collaboration between institutions of HE and their larger communities (local, regional/state, national, and global) for the mutually beneficial exchange of knowledge and resources in a context of partnership and reciprocity.

The current Carnegie Community Engagement Classification recognizes HE's commitment to community engagement. Drawing its criteria heavily from Campus Compact's Indicators of Engagement Project, the new classification reaffirms institutional commitment to deepen the practice of service and to further strengthen bonds between campus and community.

In January 2015, the Carnegie Foundation for the Advancement of Teaching selected 240 US colleges and universities to receive its 2015 Community Engagement Classification. Of this number, 83 institutions are receiving the classification for the first time, while 157 are now reclassified, after being classified originally in 2006 or 2008. These 240 institutions join the 121 institutions that earned the classification during the 2010 selection process. The foundation congratulates all 361 campuses on gaining this important designation.

The documentation framework for the classification includes the following:

A. Foundational indicators
  1. Institutional commitment
     - Mission/vision
     - Recognition
     - Assessment/data
     - Marketing materials
     - Leadership priority
  2. Institutional identity and culture
     - Infrastructure
     - Budget and fund-raising
     - Tracking and documentation
     - Assessment/data
     - Strategic plan
     - Professional development
     - Community voice
     - Recruitment and promotion
     - Student leadership

B. Curricular engagement describes teaching, learning, and scholarship, which engage faculty, students, and community in mutually beneficial and respectful collaboration. Their interactions address community-identified needs, deepen students' civic and academic

learning, enhance the well-being of the community, and enrich the scholarship of the institution (Saltmarsh 2013).
C. Outreach and partnership describe two different but related approaches to community engagement. The first focuses on the application and provision of institutional resources for community use. The latter focuses on collaborative interactions with community and related scholarship for the mutually beneficial exchange, exploration, discovery, and application of knowledge, information, and resources (e.g., research, economic development, and capacity building) and related scholarship (Saltmarsh 2013; Saltmarsh and Hartley 2011).

Colleges intending to submit applications for the 2015 Carnegie Classification have already been identified.

AACC and AAC&U: Service Learning (SL) and Civic Responsibility

While this work was underway at Campus Compact, Carnegie, and the Wingspread Conferences, the AACC's "Horizons" project and AAC&U were sharpening their focus on SL as a high-impact pedagogy and civic responsibility as a student learning and development outcome.

Gail Robinson directed the AACC Horizons SL project from 1995 to 2012. Gottlieb and Robinson (2006) defined civic responsibility as, "Civic responsibility means *active participation in the public life of a community in an informed, committed, and constructive manner, with a focus on the common good*" (emphasis added). This definition is widely used across two- and four-year campuses since it points to specific knowledge (informed), attitudes (committed), and skills (constructive manner) that the civically responsible student would need to develop. It also emphasizes that these outcomes contribute to and result from active participation in the public life of a community and that this participation must contribute to the common good. Many two-year campuses have incorporated this definition into their SL programs.

In 2011, AAC&U identified SL and community-based research as high-impact teaching practices.[11] These high-impact practices are identified using research from the National Survey of Student Engagement (NSSE). The community version of this survey is called the Community College Survey of Student Engagement (CCSSE).

In 2012, AAC&U and the National Task Force on Civic Learning and Democratic Engagement published *A Crucible Moment: College Learning and Democracy's Future* (Musil 2012). This publication called for five essential actions:

1. Reclaim and reinvest in the fundamental civic and democratic mission of schools and all sectors within HE.
2. Enlarge the current national narrative that erases civic aims and civic literacy as educational priorities contributing to social, intellectual, and economic capital.
3. Advance a contemporary, comprehensive framework for civic learning, embracing US and global interdependence.
4. Capitalize upon interdependent responsibilities of K-12 and HE.
5. Expand the number of robust, generative civic partnerships and alliances, locally, nationally, and globally.

AAC&U's Diversity and Democracy initiative actively supports campus-based publications focused on strengthening diversity, civic engagement, and democratic practice in American HE.

NSF: SENCER Initiative

NSF's SENCER initiative is a major driver of undergraduate science reform.[12] SENCER is housed at the National Center for Science and Civic Engagement (NCSE). SENCER uses brain-based "science of learning for the learning of science." SENCER faculty develop undergraduate science courses that teach canonical science concepts through compelling, capacious, and contested public policy issues.[13] NCSE also houses the "Great Lakes Innovative Stewardship through Education Network," which has developed a unique and promising model employing students as "Undergraduate Stewardship Liaisons" to support faculty and community partners in service and research while also improving the quality of Great Lakes ecosystems (Odenbrett 2012). SENCER's Chesapeake Bay Regional Center is focused on the complex issues confronting the Chesapeake Bay ecosystem, their region's most important natural resource. The SENCER Center for Innovation for the Western Region, housed at Santa Clara University, is focusing on water issues in the west. In October 2010, KCC, Hawaii-Pacific Islands Campus Compact, and Hawaii's NSF Experimental Program to Stimulate Competitive Research (EPSCoR) hosted a two-day symposium titled "Resources, Energy, and Island Sustainability." This symposium served as a catalyst to sustainability teaching and learning at KCC.

KCC has been engaged in most of the national initiatives discussed above and we have adapted these insights into our SL, civic, and community engagement work.

KCC's SL

With AACC Horizons funding in 1995, the college developed a strong SL program that continues to grow today. At KCC, SL is a teaching and learning method that integrates critical reflection and meaningful service in the community with academic learning, personal growth, and civic responsibility. More than ten thousand students have completed course-based community service experiences since 1995. More than five thousand evaluations of students have been completed by their community and project supervisors. These evaluations focus on students' reliability and responsibility, communication skills, willingness to learn, and sensitivity to clients.[14] We have conducted various assessments of student learning, engagement, and achievement over the last 15 years.

Organizationally, the SL program has ten key features (Hill et al. 2014):

1. It is focused on student engagement, learning, and achievement.
2. It is faculty driven, interdisciplinary, and innovative.
3. It celebrates the diverse multicultural traditions of service and social responsibility in Hawaii, the Pacific region, and the American experience.
4. Students serve in issue-based pathways across multiple semesters for university transfer and degree completion: education, environment, health, long-term care, intercultural perspectives, art, history, and culture. These pathways enable students to understand and to ameliorate pressing social problems in Honolulu. Community partnerships are managed and organized under each pathway.
5. One SL outreach coordinator supervises six to ten paid-student pathway leaders, and facilitates quality student experiences that are beneficial to our community partners. This coordinator also works with an institutional researcher to facilitate SL student tracking and assessment.
6. One SL faculty coordinator (0.20–0.40 FTE) oversees faculty development, discipline coaches, and ongoing pedagogical improvement.
7. Ninety SL course sections are offered each semester and faculty teaching these courses identify specific pathways for students' SL.

8. More than 320 students complete the SL assignment each semester. Each is required to submit an end-of-semester capstone essay addressing reflection prompts aligned with KCC's General Education Student Learning Outcomes (SLOs).
9. These outcomes are derived from the Essential Learning Outcome developed by AAC&U and from the general education requirements of the Accrediting Commission for Community and Junior Colleges, Western Association of Schools and Colleges. Rubrics to assess the student capstone essays are derived from AACU Value Rubrics.
10. One SL faculty member coordinates and facilitates the learning outcomes assessment process (refining reflection prompts, assessment protocol, rubrics, scoring, and reporting). The SL Leadership Team (SLLT) formed by staff, faculty, and student leaders assesses student capstone essays from both the fall and spring semesters. Based on these assessments, new "treatments" are developed to improve student learning.

The major community impacts of this sustained Service-Learning and Civic and Community Engagement program are as follows:

1. Science, technology, engineering, and mathematics (STEM) education support for children and college preparation for adults at Palolo public housing
2. Supporting STEM and sustainability programs at public and charter schools
3. Improvements in the quality of Native Hawaiian watersheds on Oahu
4. Assisting elderly immigrants to become US citizens
5. Development of a Sensory Stimulus Garden model for elders in long-term care
6. Development of web resources for descendants of the Kalaupapa Hansen's Disease Settlement
7. Healthy Campus—Healthy Community initiatives (HIV/AIDS prevention, smoke free campus, blood bank drives.)
8. Active generation of community support for Japan relief after the tsunami on March 11, 2011, by international SL students in KCC's International Cafe

SL faculty and staff have recently completed a three-year program review and are advocating the integration of sustainability teaching and learning into all six SL pathways. These faculty and staff argue that to truly understand the importance of sustainability for Hawaii, students and faculty need to be actively engaged in civic and community work. The fit between SL and sustainability is so strong that we renamed the program to "Service and Sustainability Learning."

Kapi'olani Engagement, Learning, and Achievement (KELA) Model

In 2010, KCC's Office for Institutional Effectiveness (OFIE) developed the KELA model to focus administration, faculty, and staff on 12 quantitative Institutional Effectiveness Measures (IEMs), as well as quantitative and qualitative assessments and improvements of SLOs in both courses and programs.

Five of these IEMs are tracked through CCSSE administered in even-numbered years:

1. Active and collaborative learning
2. Faculty-student interaction
3. Academic challenge
4. Student effort
5. Support for learners

Another seven IEMs focus on clearly defined student achievement data that can be gathered and evaluated each semester and year with consistent definitions of student populations and time periods:

1. Course success rates
2. Fall to spring reenrollment
3. Fall to fall reenrollment
4. Annual certificate and degree completions
5. Three-year certificate and degree completion rates of entering fall cohorts
6. Annual transfers to University of Hawai'i 4-year campuses
7. Three-year transfer rates of entering fall cohorts

The KELA model has also shaped a new campus brand: "Kapi'olani Community College: Engage, Learn, Achieve." Further, the Hawaiian word "kela" means excellence in English and aligns with Queen Julia Kapi'olani's and the college's motto: to strive for the highest.

In 2012, OFIE staff and SL faculty conducted numerous studies to examine the relationship between SL participation and student learning, engagement, and achievement.

Relationship between SL and Student Achievement

1. Compared with the non-SL participating students in the classes that offered SL opportunities, the SL participants (in fall 10, spring 11, and fall 11 cohorts) improved their three-semester average successful course completion rates in all courses, while non-SL students' success rates were lower than the previous semester in all courses.
2. Examining the same three cohorts (fall 10, spring 11, and fall 11) of SL students in comparison with their non-SL counterparts in the SL-offering classes, the average next-semester reenrollment rate was higher for the SL students at 76.1 percent compared to 61.0 percent for non-SL students. The SL students in these cohorts also had higher rates in getting certificates, graduation, and transfer (13.1%) in comparison with non-SL students (10.5%). The same pattern is true for each annual cohort.
3. In the fall 10, spring 11, and fall 11 SL cohorts, the students who repeatedly participated in SL had a higher successful course completion rate (93.2%) than the first-time SL participants (87.8%) averaged across three semesters. However, the first-time SL participants enjoyed a higher level of improvement in successful course completion rates in their SL participating term (87.8%) than the previous term (84.1%), a 3.7 percent increase, in comparison to the repeated SL participants who had only minimal improvement of 0.7 percent.
4. In terms of persistence, the average three cohorts (fall 10, spring 11, and fall 11) performance showed that the repeated SL participants reenrolled at a slightly higher rate (79.9%) than their first-time counterparts (75.7%) and had a slightly higher rate of attaining certificates, graduation, or transfer (14.4%) than first-time SL students (12.3%). Although the relative proportion of reenrollment and graduation/transfer varies across three cohorts, the repeated SL students always had lower dropout rates than their first-time counterparts.

Relationship between SL and Student Indirect Learning

In the spring 2012 semester, a survey evaluating the effect of SL on a student's diversity attitudes, sense of social justice, self-esteem, and learning experience was given to all the classes that offered SL opportunities—once in the beginning and once at the end of the semester. The data from 101 respondents with matching IDs on the pre- and post-survey showed that the SL participants' gains on two social justice items were statistically significant from those of the non-SL participants. The SL participants agreed more to the statement that "in order for problems to be solved, we need to change public policy" and "we need to institute reforms within the current system to change our communities" at the end of the semester.

Relationship between SL and Student Engagement

Using participation in a community-based project as part of a regular class as an indicator for SL participation and CCSSE benchmark scores as the indicator for student engagement, the 2010 and 2012 CCSSE results showed that participants with higher-level SL participation had higher level of student engagement in all CCSSE benchmark areas:

- Active and collaborative learning
- Student effort
- Academic challenge
- Student-faculty interaction
- Student support

The results suggest that SL participation has a positive relationship with student engagement.

Qualitative Learning Assessment

In summers 2011 through 2014, a SL assessment team comprised faculty, staff, and student leaders assessed required, end-of-semester reflection essays composed by SL students. Of these essays, 60 are randomly selected from more than 600 SL essays submitted to a web-based archive annually. The reflection prompts are aligned with the KCC's general education outcomes and the essays are scored using a qualitative rubric. These assessments have resulted in new service and sustainability journals in fall 2013 and 2014 to guide student service and learning and a new online "Service Learning Research Organizer" to guide community-based research.[15]

In fall 2013 the quality and comprehensiveness of our SL program and the KELA-model assessment was recognized by the Teagle Foundation of New York, which awarded US$360,000 to the Community College National Center for Community Colleges and KCC to lead a national project titled "Student Learning for Civic Capacity: Stimulating Moral, Ethical, and Civic Engagement for Learning That Lasts."

With six other community colleges, De Anza in California, Delgado in Louisiana, Kingsborough in New York, Mesa in Arizona, Queensborough in New York, and Raritan Valley in New Jersey, the project will (1) develop 70 courses in the humanities and other fields that build students' current and future commitment to civic and moral responsibility; (2) develop strategies for students' continual building of this commitment across curricular and cocurricular programs to degrees and transfer; (3) develop, review, and refine a qualitative rubric-based assessment methodology for campus use and national dissemination; (4) develop, review, implement, and refine a quantitative pre- and posttest methodology for campus use and national dissemination; (5) create communities of faculty, staff, students, and administrators on each of the seven campuses to build program and institutional commitment to civic and moral responsibility; (6) engage in campus, statewide, and national dialogues on curricular and pedagogical reform promoting civic and moral responsibility; and (7) leverage additional resources from campus, state, federal, and foundation sources.

Each semester six KCC faculty will integrate the following big question into SL and sustainability designated courses in developmental education, arts and humanities, language arts, and social and natural sciences: "How do we build our commitment to civic and moral responsibility for diverse, equitable, healthy, and sustainable communities?" The college will provide state, regional, and national leadership in preparing students to be engaged citizens and scholars building a healthier and more sustainable Hawaii.

These seven community colleges have agreed to have students in selected courses write end-of-semester essays with the same reflection prompts and to score the essays using the same assessment rubrics. The reflection prompts are as follows:

Statement of the Issue/Activities: Identify the issue you focused on and explain how it relates to diversity, equity, health, or sustainability. Describe the activities you engaged in that addressed this issue. Discuss the impact your activities had on the issue.

Academic/Applied Learning: Describe 3–5 central course concepts or theories that engaged you and deepened your understanding of the issue you focused on. [Instructor should specify possible concepts/theories and specific course competencies/objectives/goals/learning outcomes that they address.] Describe how you applied them in your activities. Explain how your activities deepened your understanding of these course concepts or theories.

Change: Explain how your coursework and activities have shaped your personal, academic, and/or career goals. Explain how you have come to see yourself as an agent of change as a result of your coursework and activities.

Moral and Civic Engagement: As an informed individual and citizen, discuss the issue you focused on as a problem. What elements of unfairness or injustice does the problem have? Do you believe more people should care about the problem? Why or why not? As an informed individual and citizen, discuss possible solutions to the problem.

Commitment/Action: From the list below, select three actions and discuss in detail the actions you will take to reduce the impact of the problem.

1. Support people in my family and my friends who are affected by the problem
2. Take another course to gain a new perspective on the problem
3. Join, start, or lead a campus student group working on the problem
4. Serve at a community-based organization working on the problem
5. Convene a dialog with policy-makers working on the problem
6. Advocate with public officials and legislators who work on the problem
7. Fund-raise to support non-profit organizations working on the problem
8. Complete a degree that will provide me with the knowledge, skills, and attitudes to work on the problem in my career
9. Other (specify)

The seven campuses are also piloting a common pre- and post-survey instrument to quantitatively assess the impact of new project implementations on student learning, engagement, and achievement.

KCC's Ecology of Learning

With the completion of the KCC's strategic plan for 2008–2015, the college has been contextualizing our learning-centered work within a new ecology of learning. This new ecology places central importance on active-collaborative teaching and learning in the classroom environment and integrates student learning experiences in college centers and labs, cocurricular campus programs, community- and place-based learning through service, undergraduate research, internships, study abroad in Asia and the Pacific, and cyber-enabled and distance education.

As we construct and adapt this new ecology, we are positioning community in the middle of our learning environment, not on the margins. With this new ecology we can continually assert our institution's civic purposes, and our central place in genuine, sustained, and creative interactions among racial, socioeconomic, gender, and age groups (Franco 2010).

Conclusion

The contributions of research universities to economic development and societal improvement are every day manifest in our communities, states, regions, nation, and planet. Still our publics and legislatures continue to provide inadequate financial support.

These institutions are also situated in communities that suffer from illiteracy, poverty, pollution, and health disparities. The current trajectory of these problems indicates an increase, especially in the context of climate change, which may act as a natural selective force, resulting in the relocation of large populations in coastal regions, drought-prone areas, and low lying islands. The weak and the hungry will be at more, not less, risk.

At this time of great urgency, if our institutions increase their community and civic engagement and we commit to our public-serving roles and responsibilities, this can only result in greater public and legislative support. Further, if our civic and community work helps to reduce the severity of environmental and societal problems, through the social capital and service of students as well as the intellectual capital and service of faculty, then these costs will be less burdensome on public and legislative funding sources.

Across the United States, many models exist for greater institutional engagement in real world problem solving. These models will need to deepen and multiply in the years ahead. Community engagement may make the difference in the survival of colleges and universities across the American HE landscape.

Notes

1. Available online at: http://www.compact.org.
2. See Boyte and Hollander (1999, 9–14).
3. The World Bank (n.d.).
4. The staff and partners of the *Center for Democracy and Citizenship*. Available online at: http://www.cpn.org/partners/center4democracy.html.
5. Duke University. Available online at: http://civic.duke.edu/.
6. Michael Delli Carpini (n.d.), dean of the Annenberg School for Communication.
7. Colby and Ehrlich (2000).
8. OccupyLA Civic Engagement (n.d.).
9. Portland State University, Center for Academic Excellence, statement developed through a Delphi process on campus.

10. From Peter Levine (2012; drawing from recent testimony to the National Academy of Sciences' Committee on Science, Technology, and Law and a forthcoming book on civic renewal).
11. AAC&U (2008).
12. Available online at: sencer.net.
13. See "SENCER Model Courses," available online at: sencer.net.
14. More detail available online at: kapiolaniserve.weebly.com.
15. Kapi'olani Community College. "Service Learning Research Organizer." Available online at: http://guides.library.kapiolani.hawaii.edu/servicelearning.

References

AAC&U. 2008. *High-Impact Educational Practices: A Brief Overview.* AAC&U. Available online at: http://www.aacu.org/leap/hip.cfm.

Bogue, J. 1950. *The Community College.* New York: McGraw-Hill.

Boyer, E. 1987. *College: The Undergraduate Experience in America.* New York: Harper and Row.

———. 1990. *Scholarship Reconsidered: Priorities for the Professoriate.* Princeton, NJ: Carnegie Foundation for the Advancement of Teaching.

Boyte, Harry, and Elizabeth Hollander. 1999. "Wingspread Declaration on Renewing the Civic Mission of the American Research University." Available online at: http://www.compact.org/wp-content/uploads/2009/04/wingspread_declaration.pdf.

Brint, S., and J. Karabel. 1989. *The Diverted Dream: Community Colleges and the Promise of Educational Opportunity in America, 1900–1985.* New York: Oxford University Press.

Carpini, Michael Delli. n.d. "Michael X. Delli Carpini's Definitions of Key Terms." Available online at: http://spotlight.macfound.org/blog/entry/michael-delli-carpinis-definitions-key-terms.

Colby, A., and T. Ehrlich. 2000. "Introduction." In *Civic Responsibility and Higher Education*, edited by T. Ehrlich, xxi–xliii. Westport, CT: Oryx Press.

Driscoll, A. 2006. "The Benchmarking Potential of the New Carnegie Classification: Community Engagement." Available online at: http://www.compact.org/resources/future-of-campus-engagement/the-benchmarking-potential-of-the-new-carnegie-classification-community-engagement/4257/.

Franco, R. 2010. "Faculty Engagement in the Community Colleges: Constructing a New Ecology of Learning." In *Handbook of Engaged Scholarship: Contemporary Landscapes, Future Directions*, edited by H. Fitzgerald, C. Burack, and S. Seifer, 149–163. East Lansing, MI: Michigan State University Press.

Gleazer, E. J. 1994. "Foreword." In *America's Community College: The First Century*, edited by A. Witt J. Wattenberger, J. Gollattschek, and J. Suppinger, viii–ix. Washington, DC: Community College Press.

Gottlieb, K., and G. Robinson. 2006. *A Practical Guide to Integrating Civic Responsibility into the Curriculum*. 2nd ed. Washington, DC: Community College Press.

Hill, Y. Z., T. Renner, F. Acoba, K. Hiser, and R. Franco. 2014. "Service-Learning's Role in Achieving Institutional Outcomes: Communities, Capabilities, and Competencies." In *Service-Learning at the American Community College: Theoretical and Empirical Perspectives*, edited by A. Traver and Z. Perel, 170–181. New York: Palgrave Macmillan Publishing.

Kerr, C. 1963. *Uses of the University*. Cambridge, MA: Harvard University Press.

Levine, P. 2012. "What Is the Definition of Civic Engagement?" *Huffington Post*, December 11.

McDowell, G. R. 2001. *Land Grant Universities and Extension into the 21st Century: Renegotiating or Abandoning a Social Contract*. Ames, IA: Iowa State University Press.

Musil, C. 2012. *A Crucible Moment: College Learning and Democracy's Future*. Washington, DC: Association of American Colleges and Universities.

OccupyLA Civic Engagement. n.d. Available online at: http://www.ustream.tv/channel/occupylacivicengagement.

Odenbrett, G. 2012. "The Unique Leadership Role of GLISTEN Undergraduate Stewardship Liaisons: Recruiting, Orienting, and Training the Next Generation of Great Lakes Ecosystem Stewards." In *Environmental Leadership: A Reference Handbook*, edited by D. R. Gallagher, ch. 94. San Francisco: Sage Publications.

Saltmarsh, J. 2013. "Carnegie Classification of Community Engagement." PowerPoint presentation. The Massachusetts Community College Conference on Teaching, Learning, and Student Development, April 5.

Saltmarsh, J., and M. Hartley. 2011. *To Serve a Larger Purpose: Engagement for Democracy and the Transformation of Higher Education*. Philadelphia, PA: Temple University Press.

Sandaman, L. R., and D. J. Weerts. 2008. "Reshaping Institutional Boundaries to Accommodate an Engagement Agenda." *Innovative Higher Education* 33 (3): 181–196.

Ward, K. A. 2003. *Faculty Service Roles and the Scholarship of Engagement*. ASHE-ERIC Higher Education Report 29 (5). San Francisco: Jossey-Bass.

Witt, A., J. Wattenberger, J. Gollattschek, and J. Suppinger. 1994. *America's Community Colleges: The First Century*. Washington, DC: Community College Press.

World Bank. n.d. *What Is Civic Engagement?* World Bank. Available online at: http://web.worldbank.org/WBSITE/EXTERNAL/TOPICS/EXTSOCIALDEVELOPMENT/EXTPCENG/0,,contentMDK:20507541~menuPK:1278313~pagePK:148956~piPK:216618~theSitePK:410306,00.html.

Zlotkowski, E., D. Duffy, R. Franco, S. B. Gelman, K. H. Norwell, and J. Meeropol. 2004. *The Community's College: Indicators of Engagement at Two-Year Institutions*. Providence, RI: Campus Compact.

Zlotkowski, E., R. J. Jones, M. M. Lenk, J. Meeropol, S. B. Gelman, and K. H. Norwell. 2005. *One with the Community: Indicators of Engagement at Minority-Serving Institutions*. Providence, RI: Campus Compact.

Chapter 11

Management of Research, Development, and Innovation
A Case Study of Universiti Sains Malaysia
Chang Da Wan and Molly N. N. Lee

Malaysia is a middle-income country with a multiethnic population of 28 million. In 2011, Malaysia was ranked thirtieth in the economies of the world with a gross domestic product (GDP) of RM853[1] billion, a growth rate of 5.1 percent, and GDP per capita of RM29,404 (Department of Statistics Malaysia 2012). The vision of Malaysia is to become a high-income country with an economy that is inclusive and sustainable and to establish a progressive society that is scientific and innovative (Malaysia 2009). The government recognizes the importance of science and technology in national development. A number of national policies have been outlined since the 1980s to formulate and implement various initiatives and programs to enhance the national capabilities of research, development, and innovation (RDI) (Ministry of Science, Technology, and Innovation 2012).

RDI is a key activity in enhancing the generation of new products, processes, services, and solutions. The Gross Expenditure on Research and Development (GERD) as a proportion of GDP in Malaysia has increased constantly over the last two decades. Although the ratio has increased from 0.22 percent in 1996 to 0.82 percent in 2008 (Ministry of Science, Technology, and Innovation 2012), it remains relatively low in comparison to regional and international averages. For instance, the Asian average in 2007 was 1.6 percent (UNESCO Institute of Statistics 2010). By 2020, Malaysia aims to increase the ratio to 2.0 percent.

Higher education institutions (HEIs) play an important role in the development of RDI in Malaysia. GERD of HEIs has increased steadily, from RM40.4 million in 1996 to RM1,188.3 million in 2008 (Ministry of Science, Technology, and Innovation 2012). Although the proportion of GERD of HEIs in 2008 remained at only 20 percent of the total GERD in Malaysia and government research institutes (GRIs) took up another 10 percent, these public institutions have two important roles in the development of RDI. First, government funds for basic research in Malaysia were almost exclusively directed to these public institutions. Second, as in 2008, there were 28.5 researchers, scientists, and engineers per 10,000 workforce in Malaysia; interestingly, 85 percent of researchers are located in the public HEIs and GRIs.

Recognizing the important role of HEIs, the government has outlined in the National Higher Education Strategic Plan (NHESP) the need to develop a critical mass of 100 researchers, scientists, and engineers per 10,000 workforce and to produce 100,000 PhD holders by the year 2020 (Ministry of Higher Education [MOHE] 2007). The implementation of NHESP was entrusted to the MOHE[2] and HEIs, and operationalized through programs such as *MyBrain15* and the Academic Staff Training Scheme (ASTS) to fund postgraduate education.

More importantly, realizing the importance of HEIs in the development of RDI, the government grants a number of public universities with the status of Research University (RU). The designated status of RU comes together with an annual block grant of RM400 million to support the institution to develop and enhance its RDI agenda. In addition, the number of undergraduate students in public HEIs with the RU status is expected to decrease, while that of the postgraduate students is expected to increase. To date, five public HEIs[3] in Malaysia are granted the RU status.

Universiti Sains Malaysia (USM) is one of the five RUs in Malaysia. On top of that, USM is the only university in Malaysia to be awarded the Accelerated Program for Education Excellence (APEX) status. The APEX status is one of the initiatives within the NHESP where a university is selected based on its capabilities and preparedness to attain world-class status (MOHE 2007; USM 2011). USM was awarded the APEX status in 2008 based on a submission titled "Transforming Higher Education for a Sustainable Tomorrow," which encapsulates the university's commitment to the idea of sustainability within a globalized context and to the use of blue ocean strategy to help the "bottom billion" to transform their socioeconomic well-being. The APEX strategy involves significant changes on a wide range of aspects in the university in terms of autonomy, governance, accountability, talent management, sustainability as well as global relevance and RDI. The RDI priority areas include environmental protection, social justice, and cultural diversity (Dzulkifli 2010).

This chapter focuses on the ways in which RDI is managed in a public university in Malaysia and USM has been selected as a case study. USM has been selected because it is one of the research universities and as an APEX university it has received additional government funding to develop its RDI. The chapter is structured as follows. The first section examines the conceptual framework on the knowledge and skills required to manage RDI at different levels. The second section provides a detailed analysis of how RDI is managed in USM. The third section summarizes and concludes the chapter.

The Conceptual Framework

Research is a personal activity and highly dependable on the ideas and imagination of individuals or group of individuals. As Taylor (2006, 2) described,

> Academic staffs feel a fierce personal ownership of their research; it shapes and dictates their career development and their status with their peers. Research is ultimately linked with fundamental beliefs about academic freedom and the opportunity to challenge longstanding orthodoxies. Moreover, research, by its very nature, is unpredictable, moving in unforeseen directions with unexpected consequences; further, it is this unpredictability that often gives rise to some of the most important outcomes and is therefore to be applauded, not curbed.

This description clearly points to the fact that research is inherently an individualistic, important yet unpredictable activity. Importantly, the description has also suggested that it is difficult to control and manage these activities due to the nature of research. Yet, as the culture of "new public management" began to exert stronger influence in the university, the management of RDI became important and the focus has shifted onto the institutional level (Deem and Brehony 2005; Olssen and Peters 2005; Taylor 2006). Issues related to RDI such as funding and optimization of resources, controlling quality and performance, increasing efficiency and effectiveness, handling legal and ethical issues as well as risk management have to be incorporated into the new management structure of universities. University central management began to take a greater interest in RDI by taking administrative measures such as undertaking centralized planning to set research priorities for development and channeling resources into these research areas. It is clear that research is an important activity for both individuals and universities but as rightly pointed out by Fox (1992, 105), "Institutions do not do research, individuals do; but institutional conditions affect productivity." This proposition suggests the influence of both institutions and individuals on RDI activities, and therefore, the understanding of RDI management in a HEI should be explored at both the institutional and individual levels.

For the understanding of RDI management, Pettigrew and colleagues (2013) outlined a typology of the knowledge and skills required for effective leadership and management of RDI (see Table 11.1). The typology consists of six themes across three levels: government, institutional, and group. Within each theme, there are subthemes that outline the specific areas to explore the knowledge and skills required for effective leadership and management of RDI. However, as this chapter focuses on the case study of a university, the analysis of RDI management will focus on Theme 2 to Theme 6.

RDI in USM

USM was founded in 1969 in the state of Penang and is the second public university in Malaysia. The university comprises the main campus on the island of Penang and two branch campuses—Engineering Campus in Nibong Tebal, a town on the mainland at the border between the states of Penang and Perak; and Health Campus in Kubang Kerian in the state of Kelantan. The mandate of the university is to promote and develop higher education (HE) and to provide for research, advancement, and dissemination of knowledge in the fields of natural sciences, applied sciences, medical and health sciences, pharmaceutical sciences, building sciences and technology, social sciences, humanities, and education. From the very beginning, USM has adopted the school system, instead of the traditional faculty system, with the intention to provide an interdisciplinary approach to produce multiskilled graduates (USM 2011). In 2011, USM had a total enrollment of 28,277 students, of which 18,659 were undergraduates (MOHE 2012). As a comprehensive university, USM offers undergraduate and postgraduate programs across 26 schools and 24 research institutes, centers, and units.

To allow a more insightful yet systematic description of RDI management in USM, this section is divided into four subsections: (1) The overall RDI management structure of USM; (2) RDI management structure in research institutes, centers, and units; (3) RDI management structure in

Table 11.1 Typology for knowledge and skills required for effective leadership and management of RDI

Theme	Theme description	Subthemes
Theme 1: Leadership in RDI by government	This theme refers to governments and policy makers in providing the context for development of RDI in a country.	National priorities (and funding) for: o Research o Innovation o Infrastructure o Capacity building o Funding mechanism; incentives o Supporting collaboration o Research ethics and integrity o Compliance and regulation o Communication
Theme 2: Leadership of RDI in institutions	This theme focuses on the leadership within an institution such as university, GRI, or private corporation.	o Awareness o External settings and environment o Internal condition and capacity o Institutional governance o Planning o Implementing institutional change o Cultivating a sound research ethos o Risk—be prepared o Communication
Theme 3: Management to support leadership of RDI in institutions	This theme outlines the managerial aspects that support the leadership at the level illustrated in Theme 2.	o Organizational structure o Executive and management operations o Committees o Research management and administration o "Research Office"
Theme 4: Leadership of researchers in institutions	This theme focuses on leadership of a group of researchers within institutions, e.g., research groups, schools, and faculties in university.	o Research students o Early career researchers o Established researchers o For all researchers o Dealing with difficult situations
Theme 5: Management to support leadership of researchers	This theme illustrates the managerial aspects that support the leadership at the group level of Theme 4.	o Research management and administration o Offices – Postgraduate Research Office – Personnel Office – Human Resources Office

continued

Table 11.1 Continued

Theme	Theme description	Subthemes
Theme 6: Personal behaviors and qualities of RDI leaders and managers	This theme focuses on the traits and characteristics of individuals across the institutional and group levels.	o Behaviors that have a positive influence

Source: Data from Pettigrew et al. (2013). Table created by author.

schools; and (4) the interaction between institution and group (research institutes, centers, units, and school) levels.

Overall RDI Management of USM

Prior to receiving the official status of RU, USM had been a "research-intensive" institution of higher learning. In 2001, the then vice chancellor of USM in his maiden speech to the campus community proposed that USM become a world-class institution; this was followed by the setting up of an Advisory Committee on World Class Programs. One of the major tasks of the advisory committee was to conduct an internal exercise to assess the impact and sustainability of the university's research activities and to identify potential areas of research to be nurtured (Lee 2004). This kind of internal quality assessment was the first of its kind to be carried out in a Malaysian university.

It is fair to suggest that prior to the internal assessment of 2001, RDI activities in USM were carried out without much involvement from the university central administration. RDI activities were left to the initiative and ability of individuals or groups of researchers. From the report of the advisory committee (Lee 2004), the top 16 research programs in USM were assessed using impact and sustainability as the main criteria. The research findings show that there was a lack of focus and strategic direction, an overreliance on existing cohort of researchers, a lack of second generation researchers, a strong dependence on local sources of funding, a lack of exposure to compete for external funding, as well as usual problems such as limited facilities and infrastructure and technological constraints. The advisory committee then recommended that the vice chancellor and his management team play an active role in managing and enhancing RDI activities in USM.

One of the major recommendations was to transfer the management of RDI to the offices of the vice chancellor and the deputy vice chancellor of research and innovation (DVC R&I). The rationale to centralize the management of RDI to the top offices of USM was to intensify its focus on the importance of RDI to the institution (Lee 2004). As a result, a research management office was established to plan, manage, and execute all research management matters, including strategic planning, monitoring and evaluation, product development, marketing and promotion, and technology and intellectual property (IP) management. This office is currently known as the Research, Creativity, and Management Office (RCMO) and is under the leadership of the DVC R&I. The centralization of managing RDI in USM was further institutionalized through a number of initiatives recommended by the advisory committee, which include (1) the activation of the University Research Council as a high-level strategic panel to strategize and plan the RDI direction; (2) the revision of the role and function of the University Research Committee; (3) the creation of an advisory panel of eminent academics and scholars that function like a think tank to plan, monitor, and assess RDI activities and to advise the leadership of USM on the strategies, direction, and management of RDI; and (4) the establishment of research clusters to promote greater integration and sharing of knowledge, resources, and facilities. By 2012, many of these recommendations had been implemented and incorporated into the organizational structure of RDI management in USM.

However, as recent as the beginning of 2013, there was a major reorganization of RDI management. The restructuring also happened concurrently with a change of leadership in the position of the DVC R&I. Hence, over a relatively short period, from 2012 to 2013, there were some major changes to the organization structure of RDI management in USM and the major changes are summarized in Table 11.2.

The major changes include a change in the role of RCMO and a change from the seven research platforms to five Centers for Research Initiatives (CRIs). The role and responsibilities of the RCMO are to administer and monitor research projects and grants. In contrast, the role of the CRIs is to focus on policies and strategies pertaining to the direction of RDI in the five selected broad research areas, namely, life sciences, natural sciences, liberal arts and social sciences, clinical sciences and health, and engineering and technology. Matters that required knowledge and insights on research are now reassigned to the academic staffs in the CRIs while administrative matters remain with the university administrators in the RCMO.

Besides, the RCMO and the CRIs, there are two other entities at the institutional level that have major roles to play in managing RDI activities in USM: Innovation and Commercialization Office (ICO) and USAINS.

Table 11.2 Major changes to the organizational structure of RDI management in USM between 2012 and 2013

	2012	2013
RCMO	RCMO is the one-stop center in the university, which is tasked to create a research environment. This includes o formulating policies and creating processes for RDI management; o promoting research culture; o generating research opportunities; and o deploying and managing research projects. Administratively, the DVC R&I concurrently leads the RCMO as its de facto director and is assisted by university administrators.	The role of RCMO focuses mainly on the administrative aspect of RDI management, particularly to monitor and administer research grants. RCMO is now led by a director, who is an academic staff and is assisted by a relatively similar team of university administrators.
Research clusters	There are seven research platforms: o Biomedical and health sciences o Clinical sciences o Engineering and technology o Fundamental sciences o Information and communication technology o Life sciences o Social transformation Their primary role is to coordinate research activities within its area of specialization, which primarily focuses on the administrative functions of monitoring and managing research projects. Each platform is led by a research dean and is assisted by university administrators.	There are now five CRIs: o Life sciences o Natural sciences o Liberal arts and social sciences o Clinical sciences and health (based in the health campus) o Engineering and technology (based in the engineering campus) One important task undertaken previously by RCMO concerning policy and strategic matters has now been put under the portfolio CRIs. Each CRI is led by a director, who is an academic staff with the major responsibilities to (1) provide strategic direction for RDI in the particular area, (2) develop the culture of research in their respective area, (3) oversee the development of centers of excellence, (4) encourage interdisciplinary research, and (5) strengthen external collaboration with industry and other universities.

The ICO, which reports directly to the DVC R&I, has been setup to evaluate the viability and potential of research to be patented or commercialized. It handles all the logistical arrangements for researchers in USM to promote their research at international and national exhibitions. In addition, the ICO provides "seed funds" to assist researchers in commercializing their research and development (R&D) products. The ICO is led by a director, who is part of the academic staff and is assisted by a university administrator and other staff members recruited based on their expertise, such as the patent evaluation officer, commercialization officer, research officer, and designer. On the other hand, USIANS is the corporate arm of the university, which was established in 1998 when the Malaysian government began to corporatize the public HEIs. The main function of this company is to generate revenue for the university and this includes undertaking an active role in commercializing R&D products from the work of researchers in USM, as well as coordinating the consultancy services and contract research carried out by the academics as solution providers to the external businesses and industries. Despite the changes in the management structure of the DVC R&I office, the roles and functions of the ICO and USAINS have remained relatively unchanged.

However, apart from the structural change, there was a change of leadership in the office of the DVC R&I toward the end of 2012. This change of leadership has led to a notably different managerial style and focus in the management of RDI as the two DVCs R&I came from remarkably different backgrounds.

The former DVC R&I is a prominent scientist of international standings. During her tenure, the focus was to cultivate the research ethos and to put in place a managerial structure to manage RDI. Her policies have led to an institutionalized incentive scheme that provides different types of research grants as well as recognition for research and monetary rewards to those who publish in high-impact journals. The idea was to get all the academics in the USM to be active in RDI activities. Due to the fact that the DVC R&I oversaw the strategic, managerial, and administrative aspects of RDI, her efforts have resulted in tremendous progress in developing the research ethos in USM. While in the past only 20 percent of academics held research grants, by the end of 2012, the percentage increased to 85 percent.

The current DVC R&I is a renowned academic and management consultant with vast experience in conducting contract research and providing consultation to industries and the corporate world. Under his leadership, while continuing to recognize the importance of RDI, there has also been some realization that there should be a change in the ways in which RDI activities should be managed in USM. The idea is to empower the researchers and to gradually reduce the bureaucratic role of the institution in managing RDI. To operationalize this idea of reducing the institutional role is to allow researchers with more flexibility to manage their own research projects, especially in terms of human resources management and usage of funds. The role of the institution is to provide some form of check-and-balance for accountability purpose. In addition, it is believed that by reducing the administrative and managerial role of the institution on RDI, it will allow leaders to focus on policy and strategic matters concerning the overall direction of RDI for USM. This includes developing a more coherent research policy for USM and strengthening of institutional collaboration and networking with the industry, other universities, and society.

Apart from the major changes in the organizational structure of RDI management, it is important to recognize that RDI activities in USM are not confined to the offices directly under the purview of the DVC R&I. In part, RDI activities at the institutional level also involve the office of the DVC of academic and internationalization (DVC A&I), the office of the DVC of industry and community network (DVC ICN), and the International Office and Institutional Development Division. For example, academic programs, in particular the postgraduate research programs such as the PhD and master's by research are under the purview of the office of DVC A&I. Therefore, this office also plays a role in managing RDI activities in USM, particularly those activities involving research students. Similarly, as the office of DVC ICN is tasked to enhance the linkages with industry and community, many of the collaboration between university and the industry do involve RDI.

Hence, a University Management Committee (UMC) was set up to coordinate the various RDI activities carried out by different offices within the institution. The UMC meets fortnightly, is chaired by the vice chancellor, and involves the top management of the university, namely, the four deputy vice chancellors, the registrar, bursar, chief librarian, and chief legal advisor. In short, the UMC functions like the cabinet in a government setup. Through these regular meetings, the various offices report on the work they undertake; if there is an overlap between offices, for example, on external collaboration of RDI activities with industry or foreign universities, the overlapped involvement is sorted out to avoid duplication of resources within the institution. Subsequent to the decisions made at UMC, the DVC R&I meets with the directors of CRIs, deputy deans of research and innovation in schools, and deputy directors in various research institutes, centers, and units to communicate these decisions for further implementation. The DVC R&I also communicates directly through regular meetings and forums with young researchers to share with them the research direction of USM as well as with inactive academics regarding the university's expectations and to encourage them to carry out more RDI.

RDI Management in Research Institutes, Centers, and Units

USM has 24 research institutes, centers, and units[4] that focus on a wide range of topics. Each of these institutes was established uniquely to cater to a particular need in its area of specialization and is managed and administered with notable differences. Three research institutes—Center of Drug Research (CDR), Institute for Research in Molecular Medicine (INFORMM), and National Higher Education Research Institute (NaHERI)—were chosen to provide a more in-depth understanding of the management at the group level. It is interesting to note that CDR and INFORMM are recognized by the MOHE as Higher Institution Centers of Excellence (HICOEs). This kind of recognition comes together with an annual block grant from the ministry.

The history underlying these three research institutes is different and is needed to be made clear in order to understand the ways in which these institutes are organized and RDI is managed. CDR was established in 1978 under the senate of USM with the aim to undertake research on drugs during a period where drug abuse was a matter of critical concern to the country. The establishment of CDR was a top-down initiative by the government and the university. Similarly, NaHERI was also established as a top-down initiative by the National Council on Higher Education (NCHE) in 1997 and is hosted in USM (NaHERI 2007). NaHERI is accountable to the NCHE and the vice chancellor of USM (USM 2011). NaHERI was established to serve as a platform to conduct research on HE; it acts as a think tank to the NCHE and the Ministry of Education. On the contrary, INFORMM was established as a bottom-up initiative. The internal quality assessment carried out by the Advisory Committee on World Class Programs in USM in 2001 clearly indicated that medical biotechnology was the only area in USM at that point in time that could be recognized immediately as "world class." Thus, the researchers in the field of medical biotechnology in USM were gathered to set up INFORMM in the Health Campus in 2003 to further enhance RDI activities in this field.

Besides having relatively different backgrounds, the three research institutes are organized in contrasting manner. On the one hand, as both CDR and INFORMM were established as research institutes under the senate of

USM, these institutes are considered as academic entities in the university, which means that these institutes function exactly like a school where academic staffs are based permanently in these institutes and the institute can confer academic degrees. Both CDR and INFORMM offer postgraduate degrees. By the end of 2012, CDR had 19 PhD and 28 master's students and INFORMM has approximately 100 PhD and master's students. On the other hand, NaHERI for a long time (from 1997 to 2002) was a one-man institute that relied entirely on the director. However, even the position of the director is a joint appointment where the director maintains his primary role and responsibility as an academic staff in a school. It was only in 2002 when NaHERI successfully bid a commissioned research project that a team of researchers across various Malaysian universities and disciplines came on board the project. Having completed the project, several researchers stayed on with NaHERI as associate research fellows on a voluntary basis (NaHERI 2007). Hence, unlike CDR and INFORMM, NaHERI continues to operate based on voluntary participation of researchers. As this institute was not established under the senate, NaHERI is not able to recruit permanent researchers and offers postgraduate degrees.

The status of an academic entity in the university has implications not only to the provision of postgraduate degrees and the hiring of researchers but also to the development of human capital within these institutes. As academic entities, CDR and INFORMM are able to utilize the funding from USM under the ASTS to send young researchers abroad to pursue postgraduate degree. The ability to utilize this fund has been essential to the development and sustainability of RDI in these institutes. For example, as CDR began to venture into neuro-related blood brain barrier research, the institute sent two researchers to pursue a doctorate in the United Kingdom at a world-renowned institution in this particular area of research. Although NaHERI has managed to send a researcher abroad for a doctorate, it was an exception made by the top management of USM. However, to date NaHERI is still exploring the possibility of having permanent researchers, instead of relying solely on associate research fellows across various universities, to carry out its research work. The current voluntary arrangement has become increasingly challenging, particularly with the institutionalizing of RDI management and the use of Key Performance Indicators (KPIs). The voluntary participations of associate research fellows of NaHERI, at times, have been perceived as problematic to the leaders and administrators in their respective departments and universities due to the difficulties in measuring the KPIs of these fellows and the research work carried out and published under the banner of NaHERI. Interestingly, this illustrates some forms of tension in the management of RDI across institutes, schools, as well as across HEIs. More importantly, as the associate research fellows of NaHERI are academic staffs from a wide range of disciplines, such as management, law, languages, economics, humanities, and education, the tension may also imply the difficulties of departments and institutions in measuring and managing inter- and multidisciplinary RDI activities.

Internally, each of the three research institutes has introduced its own ways of managing RDI activities. The management of RDI activities includes ways in which a research project is proposed, administered, and monitored. First, as the research area of CDR is relatively broad, which includes drug discovery, biomedical analysis, epidemiology, behavioral science, and more recently, blood brain barrier, the effort to propose a research project and to source funding is very much left to the individual effort of the researchers themselves. Individual researchers in CDR setup a team to propose or bid for research projects from a wide range of grants from Ministry of Science, Technology, and Innovation (MOSTI), MOHE, and companies such as BioTech Corporation, as well as international bodies such as UNICEF and WHO. Second, as the research focus of INFORMM is much more focused on molecular medicine and the institute is comparatively bigger in terms of the number of researchers, INFORMM has established an internal committee to oversee processes such as the application of grants, monitoring of the status of applications, and the implementation of projects. The establishment of this internal committee is to ensure that the proposals submitted are of quality, research projects are progressing, and research funds are spent accountably. Importantly, the arrangement of a committee is also a form of informal mentoring for the established and experienced researchers to guide the younger ones in preparing and applying for research grants, as well as managing research projects. In short, INFORMM has developed a systematic approach to manage RDI and has been awarded the ISO 9100 for the standard operating procedure on its work instruction. Third, as NaHERI has developed expertise in various areas of HE research, namely, curriculum development, governance of universities, development of academic work and career, transnational HE services, regional engagement, HE systems, and comparative international HE, a large number of research projects undertaken by NaHERI were commissioned by MOHE, as well as international bodies such as UNESCO and Organization for Economic Co-operation and Development (OECD). Furthermore, as researchers of NaHERI come from different universities across the country, the management of research projects is typically coordinated by a research officer designated to the project. The research officer can be based either in NaHERI or at the office of the project leader. As such, NaHERI has a relatively fluid mechanism to manage and monitor RDI activities as compared to the much more structured CDR and INFORMM.

RDI Management in Schools

Schools in USM are not only involved in teaching undergraduates and postgraduates but are also actively involved in RDI activities. Four Schools—School of Biological Sciences, School of Chemical Sciences, School of Educational Studies, and School of Materials and Mineral Resource Engineering—were chosen to help us understand the management of RDI activities at the school level, as well as the Institute of Postgraduate Studies (IPS) was chosen to understand the development and training offered to future researchers through postgraduate degrees.

Across the four schools, RDI is a major part of the KPIs. The academics and the schools are assessed in terms of the number of publications, number of research grants, and their amount. A large majority of research grants at the school level are from MOHE as well as a significant proportion is from MOSTI. Administratively, RDI at the schools are led by the dean and assisted by the deputy dean of research and innovation. The structure and ways of how research is conducted in the school is similar to INFORMM and CDR with the only exception differing between schools and the research institutes being that the former have undergraduate programs. The schools, despite an increased emphasis on RDI, are obliged to continue offering the undergraduate programs and the master's programs via coursework. In other words, the academics in schools have to teach and do research at the same time.

Although the structure of the schools across USM is similar, the ways in which and the extent to which RDI is managed differs considerably; these differences reflect the different leadership styles of the deans, deputy deans, and administrators. While there are schools that tend to be more laissez-faire, there are also schools that tend to be more authoritative in managing RDI. A laissez-faire management style in the schools may entail the leaders encouraging academics and researchers to participate in RDI activities. For example, young researchers are encouraged to seek advice and guidance from more experienced researchers, and experienced researchers are expected to know their responsibilities to conduct research and publish. Contrastingly, the authoritative style tends to focus on the number of publications, number of grants, and amount of grants and the leaders use these statistics as yardstick to measure the performance of academics and researchers. In addition, these indicators are being used for comparison across academics and researchers within a school and to create some form of "peer pressure" to carry out more RDI. Driven by the culture of auditing and KPIs in USM, particularly after attaining the status of RU, the authoritative style is increasingly being adopted at the school level to urge academics and researchers to apply for grants, conduct research, and publish.

While a research institute is expected to emphasize RDI, increasingly, RDI has also become an important aspect among the schools in USM. Yet, while the research institutes do not seem to have a problem in getting the researchers to be involved in RDI activities such as applying for grants, conducting research, and publishing papers, and researchers in the institutes seem to understand what is expected of them, conversely, there seem to be some difficulties in getting academics in the school to be active in RDI. The schools have introduced different strategies to encourage academics in schools to apply for grants, conduct research, and publish. For example, one of the schools organized a committee internally to help academics and researchers with grant applications. And particularly in the sciences where research is laboratory based, academics are discouraged from taking on postgraduate students if they do not have research grant that can support the research of the students. Very often, schools also assume the role of "matchmaking" by putting together experienced and young researchers in some form of mentoring scheme with the intention of the experienced researchers guiding the younger ones to develop the know-how of grants application and managing a research project. At times, schools also organize writing workshops and get researchers who have experienced publishing in journals with high-impact factor to share and teach the skills of writing to the less experienced researchers. Through these different strategies, schools play an important role in developing the knowledge and skills for researchers and academics to participate more actively in research activities and to create a research ethos within the schools.

IPS is also a school but it has a different task and responsibility in relation to the management of RDI. Unlike the other schools, IPS plays an active role in the human resource development of researchers, as this school is tasked with not only administering the postgraduate programs but more importantly with overseeing the skills training of future researchers in the form of postgraduate students. While postgraduate students carry out their research projects in schools or research institutes under the tutelage of senior researchers, the role of IPS is to provide additional training to equip these students with more generic skills and capabilities.

The Postgraduate Academic Support Services (PASS) is the major training program organized by IPS. This program includes providing a statistician and an editor at the school on a full-time basis to support postgraduate students across USM in terms of the statistical and editorial work related to their research. Furthermore, PASS also includes the Personal and Professional Development (PPD) program that focuses on the personal skills, such as presentation and communication skills, as well as professional skills, such as writing research proposal and curriculum development. All postgraduate students in USM are encouraged to participate in the PASS program in addition to the knowledge and skills provided to them through supervision by their supervisors at the school level.

Therefore, on top of its responsibility as an administrative unit to manage postgraduate students, IPS in USM has widened its scope to train and support these students in preparing them with the skills and capabilities required for the research work and for becoming a researcher. The widening of its scope and responsibilities, to some extent, has also given significance to IPS not only as an administrative unit but also as an actively involved participant in managing RDI and young researchers.

The Inter-level Interactions

However, apart from the variation in the ways in which RDI is managed, one common feature in USM is the strong influence of the culture of audit using KPIs. The management of RDI has focused strongly on the measurable aspects, such as the number of research projects and publications, the amount of research grants, the ability to meet deadlines, and the "efficiency" of spending the research grant. There seems to be a lack of focus on aspects such as quality and the impact of RDI to the economy and society. In addition, although USM is a comprehensive university, the management of RDI has adopted a "one size fits all" model and inadequate consideration for the different natures of RDI activities across disciplines. For instance, publication practices of science-based disciplines, social sciences, and humanities can be quite different from one another as well as the differences in priorities of publication and commercialization of products across disciplines.

More importantly, the emphasis on audit and use of KPIs to manage RDI may have serious implications on the overall mission of a university. With the increasing emphasis on RDI, particularly in schools, academics may become more active and productive in RDI activities, but this may be done at the expense of the quality of teaching and learning. It is often reported that academics do not incorporate their research findings into their courses. In the absence of such practices, the increased emphasis in research and publications will be at the expense of teaching and learning.

In order to strike a balance between RDI and teaching and learning, USM is trying to diversify the career pathways of the academics. So far, there are at least four different paths proposed for consideration, namely, teaching and learning, research, service and engagement, and clinical. After considering these proposals, USM has instead introduced a flexible personalized weightage system to evaluate the performance of academics. In this system, an academic can decide for himself or herself the weightage in which his or her performance is to be assessed. For example, academic "A" may allocate 50, 30, and 20 percent while academic "B" may allocate 20, 40, and 40 percent for research, teaching and learning, and services, respectively.

Furthermore, USM has also taken two other measures to encourage the development of researchers. First, as a public university USM has to adhere to the civil service where all academics are classified under the education stream. However, USM has designated some positions in the university under the R&D stream of the civil service to diversify the career paths for the academics. Previously, there was a quota restriction in the R&D stream in terms of the number of staff, the promotions available, and the level the staff could attain. However, university staffs under the R&D stream will now have their career path set on RDI and similar to the education stream, there will be no quota for promotions and the number of vacancies and those in this stream will also be able attain the title of professor. Second, USM has introduced a dual-appointment scheme for academics, whereby an academic can be jointly appointed to a school and a research institute. The dual-appointment scheme is intended to provide the flexibility for academics to chart their own career paths and at the same time allow research institutes such as NaHERI that do not have permanent academics to bring in researchers on permanent basis. Recognizing the constraints in managing the human resources needed for RDI, USM has introduced these measures to provide flexibility for academics and researchers to chart their own direction for career development and at the same time, have a more transparent and accommodating model to manage a diverse set of human resources for RDI.

Discussion and Conclusion

RDI is an important agenda for USM and the management of RDI has become a significant part in the organizational structure of the institution. Interestingly, the evolution in the management of RDI at the institutional level can be summarized and divided into three phases, which we labeled as organized anarchy, institution-centered, and individual-led. The three phases can be further demarcated more clearly using the eight aspects outlined by Taylor (2006) in managing RDI in RUs (see Table 11.3).

It is important to note an individual-led phase is the ultimate destination for USM in RDI management, but at this point in time, the institution is gradually transiting from an institution-centered phase and moving toward the individual-led phase. The strategy to enable USM to move in

Table 11.3 Three evolutionary phases of RDI management at the institutional level in USM

Phase	Organized anarchy	Institution-centered	Individual-led
Management philosophy	Does not exist at the institutional level; more collegial	Active management; bureaucratic and somewhat top-down in terms of the need to conduct research and in identifying research focus	Passive management; a more bottom-up approach by individuals and groups of individuals to identify and exploit new gaps in research market
Organizational structure	No institutional involvement in RDI	Proper institutional structure focusing on RDI is established	The institutional structure is streamlined to ensure efficiency, such as redistributing the various responsibilities accordingly
Research support offices	Do not exist	These offices institutionalized in the university organizational structure; administrators play the role of regulator and enforcer	More decentralized with clearer distribution of responsibilities between offices, such as strategic planning, and administration
Resource allocation procedures	Individually managed by researchers	Centrally managed and administered	Individually managed but with proper check-and-balance mechanism at institutional level
Research plans	No institutional plan	Centralized at the top management of the university; supported and assisted by the research platforms	Partially decentralized to the various CRIs

continued

Table 11.3 Continued

Phase	Organized anarchy	Institution-centered	Individual-led
Performance management	No KPI for RDI	Clear and somewhat rigid KPIs using a one size fits all model; incentive system also present	Flexible KPIs such as personalized weightage for assessment; an avenue for specialization of tasks also present
Human resource management	Individually managed by researchers	Centralized at the institutional level	Partial autonomy given to the researchers and research groups to select and manage the research personnel
Teaching and Research	Teaching mandatory; RDI is not evaluated—up to the academics to incorporate research into teaching	Academics required to give emphasis as stipulated by the KPIs; no incentive to encourage incorporation of research into teaching	Realization about the importance of integrating research into teaching present, but still no incentive or requirement for academics to do so

this direction is twofold: it includes empowering individual researchers as well as formulating a clear institutional strategy for greater external and international collaboration among researchers and universities.

Apart from the evolution of RDI management at the institutional level, RDI management at the group level such as in the research institutes, centers, units, and schools also vary considerably. This variation across these groups in a RU can be illustrated via a continuum of aspects outlined by Taylor (2006) (see Table 11.4).

Conceptually, Type 1 and Type 2 are typologies of the extreme opposite in a continuum. The research institutions, centers, units, and schools in USM are situated in between these two extreme states across the many different aspects of RDI management. It is clear that even within a university, RDI management at the group level differs considerably. These variations and diversity have important implications on the management of RDI and development of RDI activities at the institutional level. One implication is the need for the institution to recognize and understand this diversity,

Table 11.4 Continuum of RDI management at the group level in USM

Type 1	Aspects	Type 2
Authoritarian	Management philosophy	Organized anarchy, collegial
Structured rather permanently	Organizational structure	Team setup on an ad hoc and voluntary basis according to projects
Incorporated into the structure of the institute and school	Research support offices	Fluidly coordinated
Centrally controlled	Resource allocation procedures	Project basis
Top down	Research plans	Bottom up
Strict measure using KPIs	Performance management	Less emphasis on KPIs; more concern about the impact and usefulness of the outcomes
Permanent researchers	Human resource management	Contractual and project basis; possibly voluntary
Strong emphasis on both teaching and research but not much integration	Teaching and research	Only focused on research without teaching

resulting in initiatives and programs that are more focused yet flexible enough to be introduced in managing and encouraging RDI activities.

Institution has a major role to play in managing RDI activities, which are fundamentally individualistic in nature, important yet unpredictable. However, this case study of USM highlights an ongoing evolution of RDI management at the institutional level as well as the diversity and variation of management style at the group level within the institution. Clearly, institution has a role, not in conducting research, but as Fox (1992) suggested, in providing conditions that may determine the productivity of RDI activities. Therefore, there is a need for the institution to strive for a balance between providing a structure to manage RDI activities effectively and accountably, and at the same time, offering a space to inspire the creativity, interest, and passion of individual researchers and academics to carry out RDI activities.

Notes

1. On August 1, 2013, the currency exchange rate was US$1 = RM3.20.
2. In May 2013, the MOHE was merged into the Ministry of Education.

3. The five research universities are Universiti Malaya (UM), Universiti Sains Malaysia (USM), Universiti Kebangsaan Malaysia (UKM), Universiti Putera Malaysia (UPM), and Universiti Teknologi Malaysia (UTM).
4. The term "research institute" will be used in the remaining chapter.

References

Deem, R., and K. J. Brehony. 2005. "Management as Ideology: The Case of 'New Managerialism' in Higher Education." *Oxford Review of Education* 31 (2): 217–235.
Department of Statistics Malaysia (DOSM). 2012. *Malaysia @ a Glance*. Putrajaya: DOSM. Available online at: http://www.statistics.gov.my/portal/index.php?option=com_content&view=article&id=472&Itemid=96&lang=en; accessed on December 14, 2012.
Dzulkifli, A. R. 2010. "Foreword." In *Understanding Reform and the Universiti Sains Malaysia Agenda*, edited by J. Campbell, vii–viii. Available online at: http://www.usm.my/images/pdf/h.pdf; accessed on February 14, 2015.
Fox, M. F. 1992. "Research Productivity and the Environmental Context." In *Research and Higher Education: The United Kingdom and the United States*, edited by T. G. Whiston and R. L. Geiger, 103–111. Buckingham: SRHE and Open University Press.
Lee, M. 2004. *Research Assessment in Institutions of Higher Learning*. Penang: Universiti Sains Malaysia Press.
Malaysia. 2009. *New Economic Model*. Putrajaya: Prime Minister's Office.
Ministry of Higher Education (MOHE). 2007. *The National Higher Education Strategic Plan beyond 2020*. Putrajaya: MOHE.
———. 2012. *Malaysia Higher Education Statistics 2011*. Putrajaya: MOHE.
Ministry of Science, Technology, and Innovation (MOSTI). 2012. *National Science, Technology, and Policy (2013–2020)*. Putrajaya: MOSTI.
National Higher Education Research Institute (NaHERI). 2007. *Celebrating 10 Years of Excellence and Achievements*. Penang: NaHERI.
Olssen, M., and M. A. Peters. 2005. "Neoliberalism, Higher Education, and the Knowledge Economy: From the Free Market to Knowledge Capitalism." *Journal of Education Policy* 20 (3): 313–345.
Pettigrew, A., M. N. N. Lee, L. Meek, and F. B. de Barros. 2013. "A Typology of Knowledge and Skills Requirements for Effective Research and Innovation Management." In *Effectiveness of Research and Innovation Management at Policy and Institutional Levels: Cambodia, Malaysia, Thailand and Vietnam*, edited by A. Olsson and L. Meek. Paris: Organization for Economic Cooperation (OECD).
Taylor, J. 2006. "Managing the Unmanageable: The Management of Research in Research Intensive Universities." *Higher Education Management and Policy* 18 (2): 1–25.

UNESCO Institute of Statistics (UIS). 2011. *Global Investments in R&D*. UIS. Available online at: http://www.uis.unesco.org/FactSheets/Documents/fs15_2011-investments-en.pdf.
Universiti Sains Malaysia (USM). 2011. *Universiti Sains Malaysia Prospectus 2011*. Penang: USM.

Chapter 12

Dynamics and Challenges of Public and Private Partnership in Thai Higher Education Institutions in Promoting a Creative Society
Implications for Research[*]

Prompilai Buasuwan and Bordin Rassameethes

It does not take much vision to realize that we are living in a world of rapid change and increased uncertainty. As a recent Organization for Economic Co-operation and Development (OECD) report noted, "In the opening decades of the twenty-first century there is a good chance that four simultaneous and powerful societal transformations will give rise to more variety and interdependence: from the uniformity and obedience of the mass era to the uniqueness and creativity of a knowledge economy and society; from rigid and isolated command planning to flexible, open and rule-based markets; from predominantly agricultural structures to industrial urbanization; and lastly, from a relatively fragmented world of autonomous societies and regions to the dense and indispensable interdependencies of an integrated planet" (OECD 2000).

Our world is faced with critical challenges on a global scale in areas such as rapid population increase, environment, environmental pollution, fresh water and food resources, technology, health, energy resources, climate change, economics, lifestyles, and politics. Thailand is one of many nations that are striving to make the transition to a creative society and economy with sustainable growth, tolerance, and inclusion at its heart. Although much emphasis is placed on education, we believe that primary, secondary, and tertiary education systems will not be able to support this transition without the partnership and strong support of government and the private sector. In this chapter, we suggest some ways in which the education, government, and private sectors can assist this transition to a more creative society. In order to develop a more sustainable and fruitful world, human creativity will be required in many areas of human activity including education, politics, economics, health, science, technology, and so on (Jones and Buasuwan 2011).

During the past decade a new paradigm of economic development has emerged with the notion that creativity, knowledge, and access to information are powerful drivers of development in a globalizing world. Although productivity and efficiency will still be important, the driving force of the economy will be creativity and innovation. This new paradigm allows developing countries to become more competitive in the global economy because creativity is found in all societies and countries—rich or poor, large or small, advanced or developing (United Nations Conference on Trade and Development [UNCTAD] 2008).

The project "Design Thailand 2019" conducted by the Knowledge Network Institute of Thailand (KNIT) outlined three scenarios that Thailand might follow in the next ten years. One of these scenarios suggests that Thailand has a good chance of moving toward a creative society with its development focused on self-reliance in the framework of the creative economy concept. Also, since Thailand and its ASEAN partners are moving ahead toward a single ASEAN community in 2015, there is an urgent need for Thailand to prepare its people and institutions for the transformations that will result from this single community.

The Thai government has proclaimed its commitment to the development of a creative economy in the Eleventh National Economic and Social Development Plan (2012–2016) and called on Thai researchers to link their research work with the creative economy concept, in order to strengthen Thailand's economic and social development. The importance of public-private partnership (PPP) in developing Thailand as a creative economy hub in ASEAN was highlighted in former prime minister Abhisit Vejjajiva's keynote address on "The Role of Thailand in the ASEAN Economic Community," given at a gathering of members of the public and private sectors in Bangkok on October 13, 2010. The former Thai prime minister also stressed the importance of PPPs in higher education (HE) in Thailand and ASEAN during his keynote address at the 6th ASEAN Leadership Forum in Bangkok on June 19, 2009.

If HE learning is to be a means of sustaining economic growth, producing social transformation, and developing and supporting a creative society, some of the following questions need to be answered:

1. What are the roles of universities in supporting these developments?
2. What should be the new paradigm of practices for Thai universities?
3. What roles should PPPs play?
4. What guidelines should be adopted for forging PPPs in HE?

The answers to these questions are difficult and will require contributions from many people. In the present chapter, we present some preliminary findings from an investigation into Thai higher education institutions (HEIs) and the cooperation between public and private sectors that is helping to promote a creative society. Some challenges facing these endeavors are also discussed.

What Is a Creative Society?

Although the general idea of a creative society is reasonably clear, it is difficult to give a precise definition. Richard Florida's *The Flight of the Creative Class* says, "Wherever talent goes, innovation, creativity, and economic growth are sure to follow" (2005). He goes on to say, "Today the terms of competition revolve around a central axis: a nation's ability to mobilize, attract, and retain human creative talent." In 2007, John Hartley proposed that creative industries are developing toward a kind of "creative society." He described the evolution of creative industries from creative clusters (output) to creative service (input) and further to the creative citizen (consumer) or the creative society. Desmond Hui (2006) believes that government-level policies in areas such as wealth and employment creation are a necessary basis and premise for developing creative industries. However, he points out that the development of creative industries is not sufficient to develop and support a creative economy and society. To develop a truly creative society it is also necessary to develop every individual's potential creativity.

Haavisto (2004) also observes that in the idea of a "Creative Society," creativity and creative attitudes are embraced and championed as central driving forces of a socially responsible performance. She argues that creativity does not only belong to the "Creative Industries" or to the "Creative Class" but that it also belongs to, and should include, every active member of our society at every level of professional activity. Creativity enriches and develops actions in every area of public and private life. She goes on to say that the goal of the creative society is to ensure living standards in an era of global competition. More importantly, a balance between economic growth and the everyday welfare of people must be sought. Before that, however, she contends, the idea of the creative economy has to permeate the whole realm of economics and society. Tolerance for diversity and social inclusion must be embraced at the heart of a creative society.

Many leading Thai social critics and higher learning communities have echoed Haavisto's proposition on creative society. They contend that emerging global issues require human creativity, which must be fostered in a creative environment. A creative society is a society that harnesses individual creativity, which must be examined in a holistic dimension of socioeconomic and political aspects. A creative society should not be restricted to creative industries and be only for the pursuit of economic prosperity, but rather it should be a pathway to lead the whole society toward sustainable well-being of humanity and the planet.

An example of the importance of the creativity of the people is the megaflood that struck Thailand in 2011. This flood unleashed Thai people's innate creativity. While university, intellectual, and many richer people affected by the flood were scattering and seeking available shelter, many innovations were made by street vendors and those who we call "non–ivory tower people" in order to survive under the harsh conditions.

Roles of HEIs in Promoting a Creative Society

A creative society starts with individual creativity, which can be innate and then further developed through both formal and informal learning experiences. There is a growing recognition of the need to find practical ways of cultivating creativity at every stage of the education system. Creativity, in this sense, goes beyond artistic ability. Rather, it is more about equipping people with the skills that they need to respond creatively and confidently to new situations in all areas of their life, whether it is at home, at school or university, or at work. These skills also enable the people to make a positive contribution to their communities and society at large (Department for Culture, Media, and Sport [DCMS] 2008).

Resnick (2007) states that, "unfortunately, few of today's classrooms focus on helping students develop as creative thinkers" and that "many students learn to solve specific types of problems, but they are unable to adapt and improvise in response to the unexpected situations that inevitably arise in today's fast-changing world."

Araya (2010, 228) gives the interesting insight on the changing role of education:

> Education will require enormously disruptive transformation to move it beyond its roots in nineteenth-century mass education. Yet, the interconnected forces of technology, globalization, and cultural hybridity are together a democratizing agency, moving authority away from institutions of education and towards learners themselves. The model of education as transmitted content is unraveling. As students become meaning makers in the context of their own trajectories, questions about the formal role of systems of education become problematic.

Universities provide formal learning experiences to individuals at an advanced level, with one of the aims being to train people for professions such as medicine, law, education, engineering, and so on. Universities also play a vital role in developing and sustaining a creative society through activities such as teaching, research, research and development (R&D), assistance to government and industry, and academic services. Some of the many contributions of universities to the economy include education of people for government and industry, generation of new inventions and patents, spin-offs in the form of start-up companies, consultation and advice on company or government projects, and employee training. Florida et al. (2006) found naivety in tying research universities too closely to commercialization. They also tried to emphasize that a university had multiple roles and that it should not be regarded as just an institute for pumping out new ideas. They examined the roles of universities in a creative economy through the lens of 3Ts, namely, technology, talent, and tolerance. In technology, universities are often at the cutting edge of technological innovation and are among the major recipients of R&D funding. Universities attract talent both directly and indirectly. They directly attract talented people as faculty, researchers, and students, and they indirectly draw talented people to their area by attracting companies that employ highly educated, talented, and entrepreneurial people. Universities can increase tolerance because they can attract faculty and students from a wide range of economic, social, cultural, racial, and religious backgrounds. The interactions among people from diverse backgrounds introduce them to new ideas, which often lead to increased tolerance. This interaction can also result in increased experimentation and innovation in social and economic areas and a critical reexamination of previous beliefs.

In addition to their roles in attracting and training talented students and generating new technology, universities play a vital role in knowledge transfer from generation to generation and between university faculty and students and the general public. While knowledge transfer can be fixed and made specific and directed from universities to others, knowledge transfer in a creative society is interactive and multidirectional and should be regarded as "knowledge exchange," "knowledge interaction," and "knowledge development" between universities and others. In a creative society, knowledge is developed by all areas of society and not just by specialized researchers in universities or research institutes. Although, while it is still necessary that scientific, technological, and medical knowledge be developed mainly by highly trained scientists, engineers, and researchers based mainly in universities and government-supported and private research institutes, it is also expected that these researchers carry out research on projects that are of importance for the Thai people and economy. However, it should also be emphasized that the usefulness of research results is often completely different from the aims of the original researchers who may, in fact, just have been satisfying their own curiosity in doing the research. In other words, it will be important in a creative society to support pure research with no immediate applications as well as research aimed at particular problems of immediate importance.

The traditional roles of universities are now being challenged in this new era of creative societies. Universities are being challenged in all dimensions: teaching and learning, researching, and transferring or exchanging of knowledge. The old idea of a university as an "ivory tower" where a professor could teach and do research with no thought of what is happening in the outside world is no longer acceptable. It is now necessary for universities to help solve the important problems being faced by humanity in the twenty-first century. Therefore, universities must undertake teaching and research that can help develop the economy and the living standards of the people in the rapidly changing world. If they do so, they will be able to attract and train talented people, generate new technology, exchange knowledge with others, and harness creative assets that are responsive to market demand and lead to sustainable growth. However, this teaching and research must also include some ivory tower aspect because, in the past, the results of this ivory tower research have turned out to be vital to the solution of problems that occur at a much later date.

Dynamics and Challenges of PPP in Thai HE

While HE in Thailand is facing many challenges arising from massification and the need for Thai universities to reach and maintain world-class standards, they are also meeting challenges associated with inadequate finances, a demand for relevance, and a need to support the new hybrid knowledge-based economy that combines creativity and innovation as their central tenets. In order to meet these challenges, universities must change their educational practices in order to support this new idea of a creative society.

Thailand is one of many countries that are currently experiencing difficulties in providing sufficient funds to support growing numbers of students and costly research facilities. Also, there is increasing criticism from industries and employers that the quality of graduates is too low to meet the requirements of the industries and employers. There is also criticism that research output from many university departments is not relevant to the needs of industry or the country. In an attempt to address the future challenges to Thailand HE in areas such as competitiveness, efficiency, finance, quality, relevance, and staff development, the Office of Higher Education Commission (OHEC) of the Royal Thai government has introduced a long-term planning framework that highlights partnership and networking as one of the key mechanisms to overcome these challenges (OHEC 2008).

In addition to the demands for universities to provide academically qualified graduates, there are also demands that Thai HEIs create creative and socially responsible students and that the institutions be socially responsible. Various forums and seminars have been conducted on topics such as University Social Responsibility (USR), Creatively Sustainable University, Desirable Characteristics of Students in the Twenty-First Century, Socially Responsible Students, and so on. Most of these forums have given rise to partnerships between public and private HE sectors aimed at fostering desirable characteristics in students and at developing a sustainable creative society. Thai HEIs are currently facing a dilemma. On the one hand, HEIs have to maintain their competitiveness in a global market economy, and on the other hand, they have to be socially responsible and reach out for community development.

In order to increase the social responsibility of the Thai HEIs, the OHEC has initiated various projects such as the Research and Innovation for Technology Transfer to the Rural Communities Project. This project aims to encourage participation and promote linkages between universities and the rural community in order to improve the rural economy and rural education. Through these projects, partnership and networking between universities and other Thai educational institutions such as community colleges, and primary, secondary, and vocational schools have been strongly encouraged. The research universities are expected to develop closer ties with community colleges and vocational institutions because these institutions are closer to local communities and can have a better knowledge of the needs of the local people and local industries.

In the past the terms "public" and "private" were often perceived as dichotomous with distinctions in "power to control," "source of funding," and "ownership." While "public entities" were basically organizations or institutions that were under government control, state-funded, and state-owned, "private entities" were generally perceived as having nongovernment ownership and could be for profit or nonprofit. Nowadays, because of increasing global challenges and rapid change, the boundaries between public and private spheres have become blurred.

The term "public-private partnership" (PPP) can be defined as a partnership of the two sectors that can utilize the strengths and resources of the two sectors to overcome any limitations that the individual sectors might have. Irandoust and Kromadit (2010) point out that "public-private" arrangements can overcome financial limitations on government sector funds by utilizing the financial resources of the private section. With the increased financial resources, it is then possible to increase the funding available for education and thereby to improve the availability, quality, and efficiency of education. The introduction of the private sector into higher learning can bring improvements in educational quality and employability of graduates in areas such as marketing, finance, human resources and development (HRD), medicine, law, hospitality management, tourism, information and educational technology, and so on. In other words, through partnerships, issues of access, quality, relevance, and affordability can be overcome in a wide range of important areas. As noted by Enders and Jongbloed (2007), the dynamics of PPP in HE can be observed in public-private coordination that has occurred in funding and research and in the development of joint programs by public and private HEIs.

Creativity, diversity, and tolerance are at the heart of the creative society with creative economy as a main driving force. Creative economy institutions have been established in cooperation with seven universities as "creative academies" (Government Public Relations Department 2010). These universities include Mahidol University (MU) (performing arts, traditional medicine, and cultural and heritage tourism), Silapakorn University (design and visual arts), Chiangmai University (CU) (crafts), Thammasat University, Rangsit Campus (architecture), Kasetsart University (KU) (Thai food), Bangkok University (broadcasting), and Sripatum University (software). Four of the above universities are also public universities and classified as research universities. These are MU, CU, Thammasat University, and KU. These research universities are expected to scale up their contribution to creative industries through their research and expertise. Silapakorn University is a public university, which is not classified as a research university, whereas Sripatum University and Bangkok University are private universities.

Although these universities are expected to focus their practice on certain creative industries to scale up Thailand's creative economy, they rather adopt a whole university approach to foster a creative society. Most of them have placed their emphasis on nurturing student's creativity as part of student's character building, redesigning their practices on teaching and learning processes, conducting research, and sharing knowledge with communities. All partnerships with public and private sectors are considered to be contributing factors to the success of these endeavors as partnership can infuse new ideas and allow the universities to adapt their ways of doing things and help them overcome challenges.

Keeratikorn et al. (2010, 21) illustrated the level of partnerships and practices of PPP in Thai HEIs as given in Table 12.1. As illustrated in the table, PPPs in Thai HE include partnerships at international, regional, national, institutional, and disciplinary levels and occur in various forms such as academic, research, and resources and capacity building. HEIs have developed partnerships with the business sector, professional organizations, and nongovernmental organizations (NGOs). These partnerships play important roles in public-private contributions toward developing a creative society in the following areas.

Academic

Curriculum in a creative society must be more integrated and multidisciplinary with diverse cultural aspects. HEIs can work with private and public sectors in developing curricula and training programs that can meet the demands of the community and the Thai economy. The community organizations can provide information to the universities on demands for knowledge and innovations and on the skills needed for the workforce. Also, professional experts from the government and private sectors can be invited by the universities to be part-time lecturers, while university professors can provide academic services through consultancy or project development to the government and private industry. Job-based learning programs can also be developed that would give real-life working experiences to university students to be better prepared and more employable when they graduate. In contrast, university lecturers can provide in-house training in companies, industries, and government departments. For example, KU's Sriracha Campus is located in Chonburi province, which has a concentration of national and international industries. Nowadays, most industries are reluctant to send their workers to receive professional training at a university because it gives their workers access to connections for other job opportunities and often involves appreciable loss of work time on account

Table 12.1 PPP in Thai HEIs

Types of Partnership	U2U (Univ. to univ.)	U2I (Univ. to industry)	U2R (Univ. to research inst.)	U-P (Univ. to public agencies)	U2C+F/NGO (Univ. to communities, foundations, NGOs)
Partnership	- Universities MOU	- Thai-Nishi Institute of Technology, Technology Promotion Association (TPA Thai-Japan) and Japanese companies in Thailand - MU-Investment Fund Joint Companies - Stock Exchange of Thailand (SET) research fund to University Network	- National Center for Genetic Engineering and Biotechnology (BIOTEC) University. - External labs - CU, KU, MU, King Mongkut's University of Technology Thonburi (KMUTT) – pilot plant and eco-waste labs	- Centers of excellence sponsored by OHEC	
Strategic alliance	- Universities Memorandum of Understanding (MOU) (offshore university) - ASEAN University Network (AUN) - Southeast Asian Regional Center for Graduate Study and Research in Agriculture (SEARCA) - Southeast Asian Ministers of Education Organization-Regional Center for Higher Education and Development (SEAMEO-RIHED)	- Siam Cement Group (SCG) lab at CU - Practice schools		- Telecommunications Research and Industrial Development Institute (TRIDI) labs at ten universities - Junior Science Talent project	- Royal patronage projects
Cooperation	- Universities MOU (staff & students exchanges, research collaboration, etc.)	- Cooperative learning - Internship programs			

Source: Data from (Keeratikorn et al. 2010, 21); table created by author.

of traveling. Therefore, industries prefer to develop a customized training program with a university. Another partnership program between public and private HEIs is between KU and Panyapiwat Institute of Management. Panyapiwat is a corporate university owned by CP Corporation. Both institutions have signed an agreement to jointly develop a new program in agricultural management and entrepreneurial farming that aims to lay down a strong foundation for Thai agricultural sector. Another innovative practice that is under discussion is the development of joint degree programs between a university and corporate university. Students can learn foundation courses and general studies at the university and take professional and vocational courses at the corporate university. There are also various public university consortiums and private university consortiums such as Public Higher Education Institutions Consortium and Private Higher Education Institutions Consortium. Most disciplines also have consortiums associated with them. For example, the members of the Thailand Consortium of Business Schools (TCOBS) work together on the development of curricula for business programs. Partnerships between universities and nonprofit private agencies in developing academic and training programs can also be observed in Thailand. Students at some universities are also widely encouraged to work in local communities through project-based, work-based, and cooperative learning. Finally, Bangkok University tries to attract talented people by recruiting people with diverse backgrounds.

Research

It is commonly believed that universities are "engines of innovation," which develop knowledge that flows from university's science to commercial technology that is of benefit to the economy. However, in an analysis by Foresight National Research Council of Thailand (NRCT) research (Thanisawanyankul et al. 2010), it was found that very little of university research could be turned into patents and there was little, if any, evidence of commercialization. This indicates that university research in Thailand has probably made little direct contribution to economic growth. In addition, the produced knowledge is very specialized and limited to a single discipline. Therefore, it does not support a creative society where a multidisciplinary approach is highly valued. Some changes in research practices are, therefore, required in Thai universities if the research is to support a creative society. For this support to be achieved, the research should be more integrated and demand-driven. Although it has been argued that private industries should play larger role in providing research funding to universities, only large companies and big corporations can afford to do so. Most small- and medium-sized enterprises (SMEs) lack the resources to provide research funding, despite the fact that these enterprises are strong foundations of sustainable economy. However, there is an example where these SMEs have joined together to form an association that can share their resources to provide research funding for a university to investigate a specific shared problem. For example, the Rice Merchants Association provided a research grant to KU to invent a new breed of rice that can survive an extended flood. This indicates that private industries can work with university researchers on ideas for R&D that meet their commercial needs. Joint research projects between university and public and private sectors have also been initiated with student involvement. For example, a number of business schools have developed a partnership with the SET. This partnership gives grants to Business Schools for research on topics relevant to companies listed in the SET. Commercialization of a university's research output is commonly done on seed money and through a business incubator. Some professors' research have been commercialized by the university through university's stores such as the KU shop and utilized by the university such as for eco-design library, renewable energy, waste management, and so on. KU in collaboration with Department of International Trade Promotion has organized Thailand Innovation and Trade Expo 2013 on the theme "Creative minds that move the world," which showcases research output and innovations from all sectors.

Resources

Due to the massification of HE, many governments are having difficulty in finding resources for subsidizing HE learning. Also with the movement in Thailand toward the development of world-class universities where huge resources are required for research facilities and recruitment of high-level professionals, the universities are faced with the challenge of acquiring resources to support their endeavors. Private industry has resources. With PPP, private institutions or industries can participate in cost sharing to support student tuition, research funding, materials, facilities, and laboratories. Cost sharing of student tuition is commonly found in cooperation between Thai and international universities where joint degree and double degree programs are very attractive to students. Many joint degree programs allow a student to study in their home country to save cost prior to continuing their education abroad. Most Thai universities provide services or facilities for support of private/business activities, which brings in financial resources to universities. For example, a university may charge for the use of laboratories, studios for TV program/movie production or display of artwork, sport facilities, equipment, auditorium, and so on. As a further example, the Faculty of Business at KU is cooperating with the International Organization for Standardization (ISO) in starting a management laboratory located in the Faculty of Business. KU also subcontracts a private company to manage some university facilities such as parking space, shops, restaurants, university hotels, and so on. Various private companies also give financial support to student activities. For example, an orchestra and symphony band (KU Wind), which consists of students and alumni of the Faculty of Humanities has received over US$150,000 financial support from various private companies to participate in a world music competition in the Netherlands. In 2013, KU Wind received the first prize in the Asia group and was ranked sixth in the world. Without this financial support, these students would not have had this opportunity to participate in this competition. Also, Thammasat University aims to develop a sustainable university. One of the projects is to encourage the use of bicycle on campus. Five hundred bicycles have been supported by Coca Cola. Another project to support this endeavor is the development of electrical bus charging solar station to which Toyota will support a power grid.

Knowledge Sharing

One of the important missions of Thai HE is sharing knowledge with the community. Providing these academic services is considered a major task of Thai universities. Thai HEIs normally have a very close relationship with the community, mostly through academic services such as commercializing research output in the form of patents and providing consultancy and training programs to the community. These academic services can bring in much-needed extra income to a university. For example, KU currently earns over US$150 million from providing academic services to business and the community. Also, a program called "Farmer University" has been established at KU, Kampaengsaen Campus. This program, which has connections with farmer schools across Thailand, is a program in which university professors work with farmers in the community and share knowledge with them. Many universities are now utilizing information and communication technology (ICT) and new technology into their knowledge sharing programs with the community. ICT and social networking are being incorporated into teaching and learning processes to enhance community learning. Knowledge exchange, which is based on interaction and mutual learning, is now coming to replace knowledge transfer, which is based on the idea of one-way knowledge transfer from an expert or university professor to a nonexpert practitioner.

Conclusion

Thailand is one of many nations that are striving to make the transition to a creative society and economy with sustainable growth, tolerance, and inclusion at its heart. Although much emphasis is placed on education, we believe that primary, secondary, and tertiary education systems will not be able to support this transition without the partnership and strong support of government and the private sector. All partnerships with public and private sectors are considered to be contributing factors to the success of these endeavors as partnership can infuse new ideas, allow the universities to adapt their ways of doing things, and help them overcome challenges. This chapter illustrated the dynamics of PPPs in Thai HE, which include partnerships at international, regional, national, institutional, and disciplinary levels and occur in various forms such as academic, research, and resources and capacity building. HEIs have developed partnerships with the business sector, professional organizations, and NGOs. These partnerships play important roles in public-private contributions toward developing a creative society in various areas such as academic and learning, research, and knowledge sharing. However, the extent to which these partnerships actually foster individual's creativity and lead to the outcome of a creative society where sustainable well-being of humanity and the planet are achieved is yet to be seen.

Note

* Prompilai Buasuwan is assistant to the vice president for international relations and associate professor in the Program of Educational Administration (email: feduplb@ku.ac.th). Bordin Rassameethes is the dean of the faculty of business administration, Kasetsart University (email: fbusbdr@ku.ac.th).

References

Araya, D. 2010. "Cultural Democracy: 'Universities in the Creative Economy.'" *Policy Futures in Education* 8 (2): 217–230.
Department for Culture, Media, and Sport (DCMS). 2008. *Creative Britain: New Talents for the New Economy*. London: Department for Innovation, Universities, & Skills.
Enders, J., and B. Jongbloed. 2007. *Public-Private Dynamics in Higher Education Expectations, Developments, and Outcomes*. UK: Transaction Publishers.

Florida, R. 2005. *The Flight of the Creative Class.* New York: HarperCollins Publishers.
Florida, R., G. Gates, B. Knudsen, and K. Stolarick. 2006. "Education in the Creative Economy: Knowledge and Learning in the Age of Innovation." In *The University and the Creative Economy*, edited by D. Araya and M. A. Peters, 45–76. New York: Peter Lang International Academic Publishers.
Government Public Relations Department. 2010. *Seven Universities Selected as Creative Academies.* Bangkok: Office of Prime Minister, Government Public Relations Department. Available online at: http://thailand.prd.go.th/view_news.php?id=5435&a=2; accessed on September 28, 2011.
Haavisto, V. 2004. "Towards a Creative Society: Embracing the Diversity of Creativity." *The Finnish Economy and Society* 3:79–85.
Hartley, J. 2007. "The Evolution of the Creative Industries—Creative Clusters, Creative Citizens, and Social Network Markets." Presentation at Creative Industries Conference, Asia-Pacific Week, Berlin, September.
Hui, D. 2006. "From Cultural to Creative Industries: Strategies for Chaoyang District, Beijing." *International Journal of Cultural Studies* 9 (3): 317–331.
Irandoust, S., and V. Kromadit. 2010. "The Time Is Now for Public-Private Partnerships in Higher Learning." *The Nation.* Available online at: http://www.nationmultimedia.com/home/2010/06/04/opinion/The-time-is-now-for-public-private-partnerships-in-30130834.html; accessed on September 28, 2011.
Jones, M. E., and P. Buasuwan. 2011. "Unknown Shifts in Uncertain Times: Preparing for Tomorrow Today through Education & Partnerships." Paper presented at the ASAIHL conference at Sripatum University, November 11–12.
Keeratikorn, K. et al. 2010. "Cooperation, Strategic Alliance and Partnership in Higher Education." *ASAIHL-Thailand Journal* 14 (1): 11–25.
Office of Higher Education Commission (OHEC). 2008. *The Second* 15-Year *Long Range* Plan *on* Higher *Education (2008–2022).* Bangkok: OHEC. Available online at: www.mua.go.th/users/bpp/developplan; accessed on February 2, 2011.
Organization for Economic Co-operation and Development (OECD). 2000. *The Creative Society of the 21st Century.* Paris: OECD.
Resnick, M. 2007. "Sowing the Seeds for a More Creative Society." *Learning & Leading with Technology* 35 (4): 18–22.
Thanisawanyankul, S., B. Rassameethese, and P. Buasuwan. 2010. "Foresight Research on Results and Invention of Research Projects." Kasetsart University, Bangkok.
United Nations Conference on Trade and Development (UNCTAD). 2008. *Creative Economy Report 2008.* Geneva: UNCTAD. Available online at: http://unctad.org/en/docs/ditc20082cer_en.pdf.

Chapter 13

Subjectivity, Indigenous Perspectives, and the New Qing History
The Role and Potential of Local Dimensions in Enhancing Research and Development in a Globalized Setting

William Yat Wai Lo

Introduction

Enhancing research capacity of universities is considered as a major response to the global competition by East Asian countries. Two initiatives are widely used in the higher education (HE) sectors of the region to increase their research capacity: role differentiation and network building. The former refers to institutional arrangements that differentiate research and flagship universities from the rest of the system (Mohrman et al. 2008). The latter is to encourage the establishment and development of closer ties to the international knowledge networks through research collaboration and staff recruitment (Postiglione 2013). Both initiatives serve the goal of increasing the visibility and participation of the local academics in the global academic community.

However, the emphasis on global dimensions in academic research is controversial because, as argued in some recent studies, this may lead to the loss of traditions and the decline of local studies, especially in social sciences and humanities, in HE (e.g., Baker and Lenhardt 2008; Deem et al. 2008; Ishikawa 2009). In the light of this argument, this chapter expresses two viewpoints regarding the options for retaining local dimensions in the era of globalization. The first viewpoint outlines the relevance of institutional rearrangements in promoting local dimensions in academic research. The second examines the possibility of contributing to, rather than detracting from, their local scholarship in the process of globalization of research and development (R&D). It therefore examines the potential role and value of indigenous perspectives in academic research. The chapter uses "new Qing history," a new scholarship for assessing Qing history and its relation to Chinese modernity, as an example to demonstrate how indigenous perspective is important in achieving innovation and possibility developing academic dialogues on niche areas with global peers.

Promoting the Global Visions: Organizational Restructuring in HE Systems in East Asia

Differentiating research universities from one another in a larger system is considered as an effective policy initiative in fulfilling the goal of achieving research excellence in the globally competitive environment. As reported by Lo (2009), a common of differentiation is to form a tiered model, in which the apex usually constitutes research universities with an international outlook that serves the purpose of building a wide global network of research collaboration (labeled as "1" in Figure 13.1), in East Asia. These research-oriented universities are therefore expected to develop their own strategies for enhancing their research productivity as well as extending their international knowledge network. In return, to a certain extent financial resources concentrate on these apex research universities. Meanwhile, the majority of the HE systems are located in the lower part of the tiered system, where universities might be further divided in several tiers but are often categorized together as teaching institutions focusing on the local dimensions (labeled as "2" in Figure 13.1). In some cases, inter-tier collaborations are encouraged to promote integration of the international and local dimensions and to enhance research capacity of universities located in the lower tiers through trickle-down effect (labeled as "3" in Figure 13.1).

This framework for R&D illustrates a top-down approach in which apex universities play the role of network and innovation agents carrying global research practices and standards across tiers of the HE systems. To encourage the presence of local dimensions, Lo (2009) proposes that the

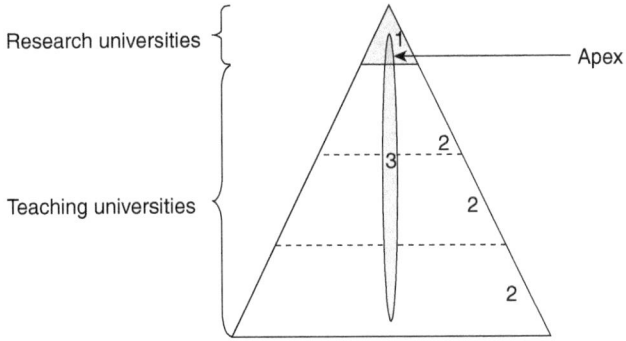

Figure 13.1 A common differentiated academic system.

notion of state building can be used to balance the globalizing trends in HE. Specifically, in the area of R&D, state building means a strong vision in local dimensions and a commitment to both basic and applied research for benefiting domestic industry and social good. According to Lo, state-building universities are primarily concerned with their presence in local community. Faculty members' participation in community services, successful cases of outreach to domestic industry and local governmental and/or nongovernment organizations, articles in local journals and newspaper columns, and graduates' role in community leadership are seen as suitable performance indicators for state-building institutions. He further argues that department-based funding is considered to be the suitable funding strategy because the activities of state building are more likely to be those of outreach and collaboration at departmental level. On the basis of this model, individual units of universities can be more autonomous to explore their ways to reach out to and serve the domestic industry and community. In terms of partnerships with industry, Lo believes that faculty members from different academic departments can be involved in outreach activities as a project team through which multi- and cross-disciplinary collaboration and partnership can be encouraged. Also importantly, state-building universities are not necessarily the comprehensive universities but strong actors in local communities. On this ground, small institutions can compete with large, comprehensive universities more equally.

These ideas illustrate a revised tiered model (Figure 13.2) in which local dimensions are preserved as universities are encouraged to develop a multidimensional profile. In this model, although the majority of universities (those located in tier 2) are still teaching oriented and locally focused, most internationalized and research-intensive universities (those located in tier 1)

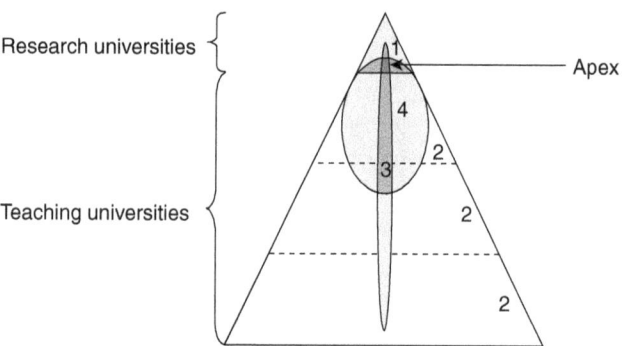

Figure 13.2 The differentiated academic system integrating the international and local dimensions.

are not necessarily located at the apex of the academic system. While, as it is in the existing system, cross-tier research collaboration cooperation (labeled as "3" in Figure 13.2) should be encouraged to strengthen the global-local integration in HE system, the apex has now shifted to universities whose research performances are outstanding in both global (labeled as "1" in Figure 13.2) and local domains (i.e., an emphasis on state-building notion and activities) (labeled as "4" in Figure 13.2).

It is argued that the goal of achieving world-class excellence and the concept of state building are not mutually exclusive. It is believed that the notion of state building is a counterbalance to the strong trends of internationalization in Asian HE. It can be used to promote institutional rearrangements that allow universities to pursue global and local visions simultaneously. Furthermore, this framework for institutional rearrangements chimes in with the machinations of managerialism well. Given the fact that managerialism has been widely accommodated by contemporary universities (Deem et al. 2007), the conceptual model proposed earlier can be easily implemented by employing "carrot-and-stick" management methodologies. A set of performance indicators relevant to the notion of state building can be listed to achieve a balance between the research-oriented global dimension and the local dimension with an emphasis on teaching. The value of this conceptual model is to reassert the importance of local dimensions in the era of globalization where scholarship within different contexts is threatened by the homogenizing effects of globalization (Deem et al. 2008; Dei 2006). In short, this chapter argues for a synergizing solution of making Asian HE globally visible and connected without losing local visions and missions.

Rethinking the Local Dimensions: The Value of Indigenous perspectives in Knowledge Production in the Transnational Context

Apart from organizational restructuring, this chapter also argues that local scholarship have the potential to play a key role in the process of globalization of R&D. The following discussion uses the new Qing history to examine how indigenous perspectives can promote innovation in academic research and conceptually offers a bottom-up approach in knowledge production.

The New Qing History

The new Qing history is a new scholarship that offers the revised narrative of the Qing period (1644–1912) in Chinese history. In traditional narrative, the Qing dynasty and its rulers did not foundationally differ from other dynasties built by the Han Chinese. In this sinicization account, the Qing court could sustain its rule over China because the Manchu leaders were willing and able to assimilate almost completely into Chinese ways. It then lapsed into a long and slow decline, in which the Qing emperors found that their ethnic special interest conflicted with their responsibility of saving China when facing threats posed by Western and Japanese imperialism. Eventually, the Qing court fell due to the 1911 revolution led by the Chinese republican nationalists.

However, the recent new accessibility of Chinese- and Manchu-language archives provided new evidence concerning the intricacy of Qing policies and practices. Some historians in the United States sought to reframe the traditional framework that is based on the sinicization thesis. The most important revelation made in the new Qing history is that the Qing conquest of China was colonial and imperial in nature. Accordingly, while the occupation of China was critical to the ambitions of the Manchu leaders, it did not constitute their sole focus of attention and did not undermine their ethnic identity. An important evidence of this revelation is that the Qing empire was divided into different linguistic or ethnic blocs in which the Manchu leaders intended to present different images to their subjects. In addition, the Manchu ways, including language and custom, were preserved and maintained and were closely tied to institutions to display the Manchu difference and distinguish the Manchu from other ethnicities in the empire. This distinction constituted a major category in the construction of the empire and became a way of maintaining the consequent status of Qing. These policies and practices are considered as Qing colonial techniques and the establishment and expansion of the Qing empire are seen as a process of colonization, according to the new Qing history (for details, see Waley-Cohen 2004).

This revelation is important, not only because it provides new criteria for assessing Qing history but also because it offers fresh insights into the boarder issues related to the development of modernity in China in particular (such as the understanding and construction of Chinese nation "*zhonghua minzu*") and in non-Western contexts in general (Waley-Cohen 2004). Obviously, the use of the Manchu-language archives is a new method. However, more importantly, the conceptual and methodological implications of new Qing history is that peripheral narrative (i.e., the Manchu perspective) is adopted to review or even challenge the existing narrative that is based on the narrative of the core (i.e., the Han Chinese). In this regard, the new Qing history demonstrates a new methodological approach for researching Chinese topics (i.e., Chinese history) in which the perspectives of the ethnic minorities are incorporated and integrated in order to provide a new understanding of the issues (Elliott 2006).

The Role and Potential of Indigenous Perspectives

The new Qing history provides a new approach in the studies of Qing history. This new approach for knowledge production reveals the potential of indigenous perspectives in promoting innovations in academic research. Methodologically, the new approach of the new Qing history is developed based on the center-periphery model in postcolonial analysis (Elliott 2006). However, it is also important to note that indigenous elements (i.e., Manchu perspectives) have played an important role in triggering the revision to existing models and paradigms by starting a debate against the sinicization thesis.

This argument provides a supplement to the call for incorporating Asian perspectives into academic research. Here we rely on Chen's "Asia as Method" to examine the relevance of Asian perspectives to innovations. On this issue, Chen (2010) borrows from Mizoguchi's "China as Method" to illustrate how the understanding of ourselves is important to intellectual work. He notes that the emphasis on Asian perspectives in academic research is a process of searching for the "self," which is seen as a way of transforming the existing knowledge structure through promoting de-Westernization, deimperialization, and decolonization in academic and scientific arena. He believes that "historical experiences and practices in

Asia can be developed as an alternative horizon, perspective, or method for posing a different set of question about work history" (xv). Similar to what has been proposed in the new Qing history, the relation of core (i.e., Han in the Chinese context) with periphery is addressed in Chen's analysis; he suggests that the notion of reflective self-criticism is a solution as we "have our own inescapable identities to speak from within, so that the subject group we belong to will respond to the problems in question" (267). Yet, while the goal of the search for the "self" is to construct an imaginary anchoring point that helps reconstitute a critical subjectivity in the production of knowledge in non-Western contexts, we should accept that there are different understandings of the self. Therefore, the ultimate goal of self-analysis is to arrive at a process of constant inter-referencing (252–253).

A further investigation of the purpose of the anchoring effects of Asian perspectives in R&D is needed, as there is an increasing awareness of the global interconnectedness in today's academic field. In Chen's view (2010), Asian perspectives are important in terms of conceptually (re)positioning Asia in the process of globalization of knowledge production. Yet, we should not ignore the methodological relevance of Asian perspective to non-Asian academic communities, if we are aware of the interconnectedness of academic communities in the global era. Therefore, this chapter argues that the purpose of the anchoring effects of Asian perspectives is not to (re)establish subjectivity only but also to externalize the self in knowledge production. On this basis, it further notes that the following:

- The emphasis on local dimensions and indigenous perspectives is not protective in nature, and the main reason for reinventing Asian perspective is not to promote an academic protectionism. Instead, it serves the goal of promoting diversity in academic research through circulation and exchange of indigenous perspectives and culture.
- The application of local dimensions and indigenous perspectives is inclusive and transnational in terms of involvement. Local academic communities do not have exclusive access to indigenous perspective. Indeed, it is intriguing and important to note that the historical revision accentuated in the new Qing history is mainly proposed and promoted by researchers from the West (Waley-Cohen 2004). In this regard, local academic communities are even obligated to ensure high accessibility of indigenous perspectives to outsiders, when they consider inclusion of indigenous elements in academic research.
- The value of indigenous perspectives and elements in knowledge production is not to offer itself as a subject of study only. The critical role of indigenous elements in promoting innovation is to be used as a

Conclusion

In many systems, the global elements associated with managerial discourse have constituted an academic environment in which heavy emphases have been placed on performance measurement and quality indicators. The primary goal of this mixed process of internationalization and managerialization is to ensure that research productivity of universities would be increased and the HE sectors would remain competitive and connected with the international academic community in the era of globalization (Altbach and Balán 2007; Postiglione 2013). However, given the fact that the world of HE is not flat and academic resources are unevenly allocated across the globe, there is an unequal power relation in global HE (Altbach 1998; Lo 2011). Consequently, the global trends characterized by internationalization and managerialization in HE are seen as a form of neocolonialism that promotes a "new dependence culture" in academic field (Deem et al. 2008).

Following these thoughts, the ideas presented in this chapter aim to reemphasize the importance of local dimensions in HE development. Yet, we do not deny the essential role of global networks and international research collaboration in enhancing research capacity and visibility of Asian universities. Instead, while this chapter places an emphasis on local dimensions and indigenous perspectives, it clearly indicates the need for global-local dialectics in knowledge production. While we see the global flows of ideas and global knowledge networks as the superstructure of an open, cross-border intellectual system, we also need an understructure of local dimensions and indigenous elements that allows and facilitates a diversified context in which to advance R&D. Policy initiatives and institutional settings then play a role of network agents that pump both global and local elements around national systems in which knowledge is inherently holistic in perspective.

References

Altbach, P. G. 1998. *Comparative Higher Education: Knowledge, the University, and Development.* Hong Kong: Comparative Education Research Centre, University of Hong Kong.

Altbach, P. G., and J. Balán, eds. 2007. *World Class Worldwide: Transforming Research Universities in Asia and Latin America*. Baltimore, MD: Johns Hopkins University Press.

Baker, D. P. B., and G. Lenhardt. 2008. "The Institutional Crisis of the German Research University." *Higher Education Policy* 21 (1): 49–64.

Chen, K. H. 2010. *Asia as Method: Toward Deimperialization*. Durham, NC: Duke University Press.

Deem, R., S. Hillyard, and M. Reed. 2007. *Knowledge, Higher Education, and the New Managerialism: The Changing Management of UK Universities*. Oxford: Oxford University Press.

Deem, R., K. H. Mok, and L. Lucas. 2008. "Transforming Higher Education in Whose Image? Exploring the Concept of the 'World-Class' University in Europe and Asia." *Higher Education Policy* 21 (3): 83–97.

Dei, G. J. S. 2006. "Introduction: Mapping the Terrain—Towards a New Politics of Resistance." In *Anti-Colonialism and Education: The Politics of Resistance*, edited by G. J. S. Dei and A. Kempf, 1–23. Rotterdam: Sense Publishers.

Elliott, M. 2006. "Manchu Archives and the New Qing History." *National Palace Museum Quarterly* 24 (2): 1–18.

Ishikawa, M. 2009. "University Rankings, Global Models, and Emerging Hegemony: Critical Analysis from Japan." *Journal of Studies in International Education* 13 (2): 159–173.

Lo, W. Y. W. 2009. "Reflections on Internationalization of Higher Education in Taiwan: Perspectives and Prospects." *Higher Education* 58 (6): 733–745.

———. 2011. "Soft Power, University Rankings, and Knowledge Production: Distinctions between Hegemony and Self-Determination in Higher Education." *Comparative Education* 47 (2): 209–222.

Mohrman, K., W. Ma, and D. Baker. 2008. "The Research University in Transition: The Emerging Global Model." *Higher Education Policy* 21 (3): 5–27.

Postiglione, G. A. 2013. "Anchoring Globalization in Hong Kong's Research Universities: Network Agents, Institutional Arrangements, and Brain Circulation." *Studies in Higher Education* 38 (3): 345–366.

Waley-Cohen, J. 2004. "The New Qing History." *Radical History Review* 88 (Winter): 193–206.

Chapter 14

Research, Development, and Academic Culture in Chinese Universities
A Historical Reflection
Su-Yan Pan

Introduction

As drawn from the experience of European universities during the medieval period, a university can be mainly defined as a scholarly institution for independent thought, criticism, and creativity that is governed, in large measure, by its community members (Hetherington 1965; Jaspers 1959; Martin 1972). Research is seen as a scholarly activity that helps to define the principal functions—that is, creating new knowledge, pursuing truth, and transmitting culture—that are central to a university's identity (Newman 1959; Clark 1984). A university should maintain a certain distance and independence from the surrounding culture so that it may pursue truth without external interruptions from government, business, or religion (Moor 1993; Mori 1993).

In recent years, the relationship between university research and economic growth has become more closely connected and interrelated. Universities in industrialized countries have been under increasing pressure to produce an adequate supply of specialists and research outputs that are related to economic innovation (Chapman 1983). For example, Cantwell and Mathies (2012) noted that, in US universities, a growing emphasis has been placed on contributing to the innovation process, as a result of which academic research and development (R&D) expenditures have increased in recent years. In Australia, where some proponents have claimed that a market approach leads to greater efficiency and provides sharper incentives for managing research outputs, universities are challenged to use market instruments to steer and manage their academic research (Beerkens 2013), including external standards for and measures of research performance, output controls, competition for research grants, and discipline and parsimony in resource allocation (Salminen 2003). Likewise, the forces of globalization and neoliberal mentality have led to the use of market rules in education restructuring and university governance in the Asia Pacific region (Mok 1996; 2002; Mok and Welch 2003).

In addition, the last decade has witnessed growing government intervention and interest in higher education (HE), specifically as regards increased demands for accession and vocational training, the formation of alliances between business and universities, the use of social forces to ensure universities' quality and accountability, the need to supply highly qualified personnel to the labor market, the need for the regular updating and renewal of knowledge among existing workers, and the contribution of research to the economy (Maassen and van Vught 1994). As a result, there has been a change in university-state relations in industrialized countries (e.g., the United States and South Korea) from loose central control to increased state intervention in the expectation that the academic knowledge derived from university research will stimulate economic growth and national competitiveness in the globalized market economy (Kwon 2011). Consequently, the university has functioned as a productive element of the economy by training skilled personnel, developing new technology, and serving national interests (Husen 1994).

The alliance between the university, state, and market in research is often regarded as a threat to traditional academic values. Lobkowicz (1983) opined that external research forces limit universities' search for truth, which requires a tranquil detachment that must arise from within the university and cannot be enforced. Utilitarian considerations—valuing immediate utility and the direct impact of education on productivity—do not validate a university's mission. Bok (2003, 103) noted that market-driven research may generate outcomes that destroy academic excellence, including increased "secrecy [about] company-sponsored researches, biased or compromised research findings," and "commercial competition for profits" that do not always produce a beneficial outcome but "merely yield what the market wants." Schimank (2005) argued that the use of market mechanisms in HE has resulted in a growing sense of public unease about academic freedom, a loss of university autonomy, and an expanding opportunity structure that favors political intervention, all of which may threaten the most distinctive features of academic life.

Is it possible for a university to cooperate with the state and market and yet preserve the academic values of self-determination and privileged freedom in research? Answers from the existing literature tend toward pessimism. For example, according to Polin (1983) and Thorens (1993), scholars should guard their academic freedoms, including the right to decide what to teach and to research, the right to express what they see as scientifically valid, and the right to be free from political intervention or state ideological orientation. A university that cooperates with the state becomes an instrument of national purpose and is thus unable to critique that purpose, for an instrument is a means to, not an evaluator of, ends. Wolff (1992) even asserted that if the government wants a university to conduct war research or political stability studies or officer training, the professors and students of that university may decide that the government is *wrong* and that its desires should be resisted. Works by Tunnermann (1996) and Marginson (2008) suggested that research for purposes defined by the state and/or economic forces may result in a mission shift in academic values, whereby economic concerns and efficiency checking by state and market forces prevent university research from being a self-determined, truth-seeking process with privileged autonomy.

In summary, much has been discussed about the functions and nature of the university, as well as the purpose of research in relation to knowledge advancement, innovation, and economic development. Still, the topic remains under-researched in three aspects. First, while the extant studies provide an understanding of the possible tensions arising from the dynamic interactions among the state, market, and scholars, all of whom use competing approaches to shape the direction of research and academic culture, little is known about how these tensions are manifested and handled in specific institutional contexts. Second, the existing discourse on the relationship between research and academic culture mainly draws upon the experiences of universities in Western and developed countries and does not specifically explore or explain the issue in the context of China. Third, extant studies cannot explain a phenomenon observed at Tsinghua University (THU)—that by strategic negotiation and interplay with the state and market, it successfully attained a degree of academic freedom to decide the direction of its research and to improve its research capabilities. These research gaps are addressed in this chapter. With specific reference to THU and its efforts to excel in R&D, this chapter argues that linking the university with economic development is not necessarily the result of the university's passivity in the face of external societal pressures and that, by using the linkage proactively and skillfully, the university could gain resources, opportunities, and relative freedom to shape the direction of its research according to its scholars' vision, mission, and professional judgment.

To present the argument, the following sections first review how research culture was initially installed in modern Chinese universities, and then reshaped by the state, from the 1910s to the 2010s. This is followed by an illustration of the relationship between THU's and China's economic development, with specific focus on THU's research capacity and contribution to national development. Then, three examples are selected to show the tension between the state and scholars in designing its academic structure in different periods, how that tension was handled, and how the linkage between THU's and China's economic development has been an important factor in helping it strive for the freedom to decide the direction of its academic research. The chapter concludes by discussing the implications of its experience for our understanding of the impact of the dynamic engagement among the state, market, and scholars on shaping research, development, and academic culture.

Scholars, the State, and Market Forces: Shapers of R&D in China's HE System

The HE system in imperial China (prior to 1911) was weak in scientific research. Its core mission was to transmit basic knowledge, based on Confucianism, which scholars needed to pass imperial civil service examinations and to pursue bureaucratic careers (Borthwick 1983; Gao 1992). Between the 1910s and 2010s, a research culture was developed in Chinese HE system that reflected Chinese scholars' university ideals but was reshaped by state and market forces to serve the purposes of national defense, economic development, and competition for global capital.

Scholars' Ideas of the University and Liberal Approach to Research

Research culture was introduced into Chinese HE system in the early 1920s by Chinese scholars such as Cai Yuanpei, who had studied in Western universities before returning to China to serve the Chinese government. Similar to Western scholars such as Hetherington (1953) and Newman (1959), Cai (1993) regarded the university as an institution for pursuing knowledge and training personnel. In 1912, when Cai became the minister of education of the Republic of China (ROC, 1911–1948), he drew upon German and French experience to establish the 1912 Legislation for Higher Education, which emphasized that universities should be committed to research and to building up their capacity to advance knowledge (1991). Cai later became the president of Peking University and tried to broaden its curricular structure, install research into university programs, and separate the university from its role of preparing students for bureaucratic careers. He also introduced academic freedom into Peking University and hired scholars of different ideological stance including, for example, socialists, communists, and anarchists (1986).

Similar to Cai, Mei Yiqi and Zhang Bolin introduced research culture into their universities when they were presidents of THU and Nankai University, respectively. They saw a university as a scholarly institution where scholars meet to pursue advanced knowledge, generate new knowledge and culture, and pursue truth (Mei 1993; Sun and Li 1993, 157). They agreed that universities should be comprehensive enough to include multiple subjects and to integrate teaching and research as necessary for pursuing truth, while still maintaining autonomy and academic freedom (Gao 1992; Qu 1993).

Research institutes were established to develop research, mainly in the areas of Chinese studies, including Chinese history, literature, philosophy, and social issues (Wu 1925). Between 1912 and 1927, China did not have a strong, unified central government but was ruled piecemeal by various warlords' local and regional armies. Without the state's intervention (or attention), Chinese scholars initiated and determined the development of research in light of their understanding of the university's function of creating knowledge. During this period, China's scholars engaged in vigorous experimentation at all levels and established the "university" in terms of the defining values of autonomy and academic freedom to teach and research (Hayhoe 1996).

The State-Directed Research for National Development

Following the 1912 collapse of the Qing Dynasty, China languished without a unified or relatively strong central government until 1927, when the Kuomintang (KMT) under Chiang Kai-shek conquered the warlords in the southern and northern parts of the country; however, parts of eastern China, particularly the area surrounding Nanjing, fell under the control of the Communist Party of China (CPC) resulting in prolonged civil warfare. From 1927 on, the KMT reshaped research in universities to relate more directly to national economic tasks; the primary economic tasks for HE under the Nationalist government were to assist in national construction and defend the nation, first against CPC incursions and later against Japanese invasion. In May 1928, China's then leader, Chiang Kai-shek, declared at China's first national education conference, "Education in wartime has the responsibility of serving the nation at the turning point of survival or demise, prosperity or recession... Education should take up the task of turning the nation towards a bright future" (Shen 1994, 237).

In response, the Ministry of Education (MOE) prioritized the development of HE in applied sciences and technologies to provide the workers and technology that China needed to survive during wartime. In 1929, it confirmed that the integration of research and teaching was valuable to economic progress; subsequent legislation, passed in 1934, called on each college to have its own research institute and each graduate school to have three or more different subject areas (MOE 1974). In 1934, the MOE approved the establishment of research institutes for the development of applied knowledge at nine universities; the government sponsored twice as many research projects in applied sciences and technologies as it did in the humanities, law, and the arts (Yang 1971).

In the founding period of the People's Republic of China (PRC, 1949–), Mao Zedong (1965) expressed his *yi bian dao* (lean to one side) policy, which influenced Chinese HE to move away from Western experience and to instead to reorganize institutions of higher learning countrywide based on the Soviet model, which separated research from teaching in HE. Research activities were thus moved out of the universities to the Chinese Academy of Sciences (CAS) and other research institutes (Gao 1992).

This situation changed in the late 1970s, when Deng Xiaoping, Mao Zedong's successor, argued that science was a productive force for modernization and that key universities were to be centers of both teaching and research (1977); as a result, research activities were restored at universities. The state established research centers, grants, programs, and degrees and launched national schemes to help Chinese universities improve the quality of their research to meet international standards. These included the "863 Scheme," named after the March 1986 decision to improve research and foster economic modernization by introducing advanced foreign sciences and technology into China, and the 1994 "211 Scheme," which aimed to help approximately one hundred Chinese universities reach international standards in the twenty-first century. In 1995, the state council proclaimed its *ke jiao xing guo* (Reviving the Country by Science and Education) policy, as a part of the Ninth Five-Year Plan. The policy emphasized the importance of being "expert" in technological innovation to enhance national economic competitiveness in an era of economic globalization (State Education Committee 1996). Beginning in the late 1990s, universities and national research academies began to collaborate more closely. Academics from the Chinese Academy of Engineering and the Chinese Academy of Technology, for example, also worked at universities as academic leaders and more than 70 percent of the National Natural Science Fund was allocated to higher educational institutes (HEIs) (Zhou 2003).

Deng's successors continued to emphasize the significance of research and innovation as driving forces for economic development. Jiang Zemin's (2000) May 1998 call for universities to act as "incubator[s] of advanced technology" led to the "985" project, which provided generous financial support to help elite universities approach world-class university status (2001). In 2006, in his opening speech to the National Science and Technology Conference, then president Hu Jintao explicitly expressed the state's desire to turn China into a science powerhouse and his personal expectation that science and technology elites would lead the way (*People's Daily Online Reporter* 2007). In response to Hu, in 2007, six state council ministries and commissions[1] jointly promulgated the "Decisions on Further Strengthening the Work of Improving the Quality of Human Capital with Expertise Urgently Demanded by National Development," which urged HEIs nationwide to improve their quality of teaching and research and develop international cooperation in order to create qualified human capital in new energy technology, new industry, and cutting-edge research and innovation—areas considered key to China's goal of becoming an "innovation-oriented country" by 2020 (MOE 2007a).

Thus, despite changes in political regimes, the Chinese state has consistently played a role in shaping the direction and scope of research in Chinese universities, placing a strong emphasis on research in science and technology as a means of pursuing economic modernization. As in other developing states in East Asia, China has invested in domestic education to spur its economic growth (see details in Ashton et al. 1999), using universities as incubators for expertise and technologies to enhance its national strength and international competitiveness.

Market-Driven Research, Development, and Innovation (RDI)

The adoption of more open economic policies since the 1980s enhanced China's participation in the world economy, eventually leading to its joining the World Trade Organization (WTO) in 2001. Throughout this transition, the market economy emerged as a new factor shaping Chinese academic culture in relation to university research. This marketization of Chinese HE (Mok 2000; 2002) allowed universities to diversify their financial resources and to begin to run their organizations according to such economic rationales as "accountability," "effectiveness," "efficiency," and "competition." Universities began to vie for new competitive research grants, such as the National Natural Science Fund and the National Scheme of March 1986 funds, and generate income by collaborating with international enterprises and commercializing their R&D efforts. In the process, education became a commodity provided by competitive suppliers, research services were priced, and access to them began to depend on consumer calculations and ability to pay (Chinese Education Yearbook Editorial Board 1984).

To quicken the speed the commercialization of research outcomes, universities established enterprise parks that featured a complex blend of centers, institutions, companies, and production lines. The parks integrated research, development, and production, applied for patent rights for their research products, and even invested in the stock market (Zhou 2003). This enterprise culture was pioneered by universities with strong expertise in science and technology (e.g., Huazhong University of Sciences and Technology [HUST]) and was endorsed by the state after Zhou Ji became minister of education. A former president of HUST, Zhou (2006) stressed the importance of knowledge transfer and technological innovation in enhancing national economic competitiveness in a global age.

In addition, international trade allowed universities to profit from their high-tech products, in part due to the inflow of foreign-trained Chinese students. China has a long history of buying foreign HE by sending its students to study abroad, a brain gain strategy that has enabled it to access research universities in developed industrialized economies that are often sources of new knowledge, innovative technology, and well-educated human capital (Pan 2011). Between 1978 and late 2006, 1.067 million Chinese students and academics went abroad to study, the majority (approximately 792,000, or 74%) for postgraduate programs or as visiting scholars at Western universities, mostly to North America (32.1%) and Europe (28.9%) (MOE 2007b; *China Review Reporter* 2010). Recognizing that foreign-trained scholars could offer new knowledge skills to help China's high-tech sector grow, the state created "returning-student entrepreneurial parks"—exclusive high-tech development zones located near prestigious national universities strong in science and technology (such as Peking, Tsinghua, and Jiaotong universities) to facilitate cooperation between universities and entrepreneurs and hasten the transfer of new knowledge, technologies, and research outcomes. While these enterprises were recognized by the state as key engines for leading scientific innovation, upgrading industrial structures, and driving economic development in China (*Human Recourse Market News Reporter* 2010), the primary force driving their development was the profit motive. A survey by Zweig et al. (2004) showed that the opportunity to earn larger profits in China's domestic market is an important incentive for foreign-trained Chinese students to return home and run businesses. These students' primary income-generating strategy is to sell products and services based on technologies imported from developed countries, most of which, while new to China, are not new internationally. Internationally, registration in the NASDAQ stock market is an indication of the market value of, and influence wielded by, high-tech businesses; the majority of NASDAQ-registered Chinese companies were the product of entrepreneurial parks (*China Review Reporter* 2010). In this regard, R&D has mediated between China's high-tech industry and the global economic market.

Tensions Arising from Varying Interests of the State and Scholars regarding Research: THU as an Example

This section uses THU in Beijing as an example to illustrate the tensions generated from the engagement among the state and scholars. Pan has discussed the national significance of THU in testing the state's policies before they are implemented in the countrywide HE system (2006; 2007); as Altbach (2009) stated, "The saga of Tsinghua University is, in many ways, the story of Chinese higher education." This chapter focuses on the tensions arising from the various interests of the state and scholars regarding the function and position of research in Chinese HE, including tensions between universities' power of self-determination and state intervention, between the American and Soviet models of HE, and between China's global aspirations and its politico-ideological constraints in local context.

Tension between the University's Power of Self-Determination and State Intervention

During the 1920s and 1930s, THU was a largely self-governing academic community. It was founded jointly, in 1911, by the US and Chinese governments with funds from the Boxer Indemnity. It was the first school in China formally established to send its students and graduates abroad to complete or further their studies with the hope to bring back Western knowledge to hasten China's economic and social modernization. Beginning in 1922, the THU alumni began to return to teach after finishing their undergraduate and postgraduate studies in the United States, bringing with them not only Western learning but also the idea of university autonomy. The returnees objected to THU being ruled by a government-appointed president rather than by its professors (Su 1996) and agitated for the right to elect the university president; between 1920 and 1931, teachers and students expelled six presidents from the university (Compilation Group of Tsinghua History 1981).

During this period, THU did not rely on the Nationalist government for its funding but was financed by the United States from the remnants of the Boxer Indemnity, which was sufficient to cover all kinds of costs (Fang and Zhang 2001b, 652). Financial independence from the Chinese government was an important factor that enabled THU scholars to resist political intervention and pursue university autonomy (Pan 2009). To reduce conflict, the Nationalist government appointed Mei Yiqi as the president of THU; with teachers' and students' support, Mei served as president for 17 years (1931–1948) and built a culture in which the university was governed by its professors.

During Mei's presidency, following American practice, THU set up a Professors' Association, a Senate, and a University Council, which together served as its top internal decision-making bodies (Mei 1946). Academic decisions were made democratically (i.e., by majority rule), with both staff and students being involved in the decision-making processes. It established faculties of science, arts, and law according to its professors' wishes, based upon their educational experiences in American universities. As such, THU was governed much like a Western university and enjoyed a large degree of autonomy and academic freedom to decide what to teach and research (Compilation Group of Tsinghua History 1981).

This academic culture was challenged by the Nationalist government, which used unified national policy to reshape university curricular structure. The MOE, for example, required THU to set up a school of engineering to reflect the national policy of developing applied technology to foster national construction. In addition, Chiang Kai-shek personally asked Mei Yiqi to develop teaching programs for applied sciences and technologies, such as technical aeronautics and agriculture (Gu 1933; Lao 1934; Xin 1934).

Mei acted as a buffer between university scholars and the government. He explained to the THU faculty that while he felt embarrassed to be the government's messenger, he nonetheless believed that the university should not be isolated from society but should serve the nation, a view that was reflected in THU's motto, "self discipline and social commitment" (Mei 1993). He explained that, during wartime,[2] specialists in engineering were urgently needed and that THU should share the responsibility of providing expertise for national defense and salvation. However, he also critically judged Chiang's request believing that establishing teaching programs in agriculture and aeronautics was inappropriate because graduates from these programs would be jobless during wartime; instead, he suggested setting up research institutes to conduct investigations in domestic agriculture, industry, and population in order to develop the knowledge and expertise that would be needed to serve national reconstruction needs after the war (Mei 2013). Mei's explanations were acceptable to both the THU faculty and Chiang and as a result THU established its School of Engineering, which included teaching programs and research in civil engineering, engineering technology, electronic engineering, and military sciences. It also established research institutes in such areas as agriculture, radio communication, and metal materials. In return, THU received financial support from the Nationalist government to develop new disciplines and pursue new research avenues; for example, the State Committee on Aeronautics sponsored THU to establish the Institute of Technical Aeronautics. The function of these research institutes was to collaborate with the government and conduct research to resolve problems in national defense and construction projects, such as road construction, manufacturing military instruments, and transportation (Compilation Group of Tsinghua History 1981). Cooperation earned THU the government's trust and resulted in its having a large degree of autonomy and the freedom to maintain a governing culture dominated by professors during Mei's presidency. At the same time, THU was protected by the Nationalist government during the wars, which allowed it to build its capacity in applied sciences, engineering, and industrial and military technologies and to develop its reputation as "China's MIT" (Su 2000).

Tension between the American and Soviet Models of HE

Up until 1948, because of its academic affiliations with American HE, THU modeled American universities in its teaching and research arrangements. Its undergraduate education was a four-year program, faculties of arts, sciences, law, and engineering were established to provide students with a broad knowledge structure covering the social and natural sciences, and English was adopted as the medium of instruction. Teaching was integrated with research and research institutes were established to conduct research in Chinese studies, natural sciences, and applied sciences and technologies. The academic staffs were free to decide the course they would teach and the direction their research and publications would take. For example, staffs who had returned from the United States tended to use English literature as references for teaching and research and to publish papers in international journals (Compilation Group of Tsinghua History 1981).

This academic culture faced challenge in the early 1950s following the PRC government's adoption of the Soviet model of HE. Like other universities in China, THU was impacted by the nationwide reorganization of HEIs. By MOE fiat, THU's faculties of art, science, and law were merged with those of Peking University and its research institutes were moved to CAS; at the same time, it absorbed all of Peking University's and Yenching University's engineering departments and became a college of engineering (Fang and Zhang 2001b). When the MOE's decision was announced, THU's professors expressed their disapproval, questioning whether THU would still be a university if it did nothing but teach engineering. They argued that "Tsinghua is not only a center of teaching, but also a center of scientific thought" and that "scientific research is the principal foundation for raising the quality of teaching" (315). THU's president, Jiang Nan-xiang, who was also the vice minister and general secretary of the MOE and minister and general party secretary of the Ministry of Higher Education, communicated these concerns to the central government (Pan 2007); as a result, the MOE allowed the university to continue to conduct research in engineering.

THU's track record of contribution to national construction influenced the government's decision to involve the university in national research projects. Seizing upon this opportunity, it established research committees at the faculty and department levels, which in turn organized faculty to participate in research projects related to national and local economic construction. These included, for example, research projects connected with the Second Five-Year Plan of national construction, the application of the laser in technology, the establishment of experimental stations for nuclear energy, and the harnessing and control of the Yellow River. During the 1950s and 1960s, though there were no official relations between China and Western countries and though English was replaced by Russian as the primary foreign language to be taught in educational institutions nationwide, THU continued its academic exchanges with Western universities, including those in the United States. The exchanged materials included scientific and technological journals published by Western university presses, which gave it access to the cutting-edge international knowledge needed to advance research in China (Fang and Zhang 2001b).

China's need for advanced science and technology and THU's role in providing both knowledge and human resources to help the state allowed THU to develop and pursue research in these areas. In this period, it developed research in nuclear and space science and technology, which eventually helped China to make its first experimental shielding reactor, its first atomic and hydrogen bombs, and its first man-made satellite. By 1965, THU had established seven research institutes in the areas of nuclear technology, hydraulic engineering, civil engineering, architecture, radio electronics, and water conservancy (Fang and Zhang 2001a). Along with these successes, it became more advanced in science and technology and its scholars' expertise and participation in nation building helped it to gain relatively more freedom to develop the university further.

Tension between Global Aspirations and Politico-Ideological Constraints in Local Context

In the late 1990s, THU promoted the goal of moving from being a top-ranked national university in China to becoming an internationally recognized world-class university; more specifically, the original proposal, prepared by the strategic planning office of THU's CPC Committee, aimed at developing it into a "world-class socialist university" (Fang and Zhang 2001b). In 1997, when the proposal was first circulated within THU for consultation, its faculty suggested to remove the wording "socialist" from the mission statement, arguing that its aspirations should not be constrained by political or ideological boundaries. However, it had been common practice, even obligatory, since 1949 for Chinese universities to (at the very least) acknowledge their socialist nature in official documents; how, then, was the university to explain to the central government why THU was breaking that rule? According to the author's interview with the secretary for THU's CPC Committee in 2001, it avoided confrontation with the ruling party by asserting that "the wording of 'world-class socialist university' gives an impression that we just aim to become a world-class university among socialist countries; if so, we are already...one." In another interview, one vice president further explained that THU's aim was to become internationally recognized as a world-class university, which would "place the university on [the] international dimension, and...measure its educational quality by [criteria] widely accepted by the international academic community." THU's senior management staff realized that, to achieve a world-class status, THU had to play according to the rules of the game in the international academic community, which are defined and judged by international scholars rather than by any one political ideology. These explanations helped to justify THU's adoption of politically neutral language in its new vision statement.

THU's proposal and explanation was accepted and supported by Zhu Rongji, a THU graduate who later became premier of the state council (1998–2002). Zhu publicly encouraged THU to "bravely" build upon the experience of other excellent HEIs throughout the world to reach world-class standard (Pan 2009). Soon after Zhu became premier, in 1998, the PRC state launched the "985" project in its effort to build world-class universities in China.

Having received the state's endorsement, THU took action to integrate practices common in international HE, including the adoption of foreign experience for reference in policy making, an emphasis on learning English, promoting information and communication technologies in education, expanding international academic relations, and increasing tolerance of Western culture on campus (Pan 2009).

In particular, THU laid emphasis on innovative R&D and on becoming an internationally recognized research university. At a conference held at THU, in 2001, three thousand of its faculty members collectively decided that it should enhance research and innovation in order to produce new knowledge that China needed to improve its international economic competitiveness (THU 2001, 8, 29). To that end, it encouraged its academics to access external financial resources to improve research facilities cooperating with and seeking the financial support of international commercial enterprises and established joint research institutes with top international enterprises, including IBM, P&G, SMC, and Motorola (Hu 2000), to access opportunities to join in cutting-edge research. At times, this cooperation was also market driven, as some international firms attempted to reap the commercial benefits of commercializing THU's research outcomes in the Chinese market. THU recognized that cooperation with international firms was mainly based on the principle of mutual benefit: the firms benefited financially, while the university benefited by enhancing the quality of the hardware and software it used for innovative research (Fang and Zhang 2001b).

Discussion and Conclusion

Over the past century, R&D in Chinese universities has been shaped by the interplay of three actors—scholars, the state, and market forces—with varying degrees of interest in using research to pursue knowledge advancement, national development, and economic growth. With specific reference to THU in Beijing, this chapter has unfolded the tensions generated from the engagement between the state and scholars, and the parties' divergent interests in R&D. It has shown how THU skillfully handled the tensions between the university's desire for self-determination and state intervention, between the American and Soviet models of HE, and between global aspirations and local politico-ideological constraints. THU's experience offers an interpretive reflection on how the purposes of RDI have changed along with Chinese society and how, through this historical process, the nature of academic culture has been shaped in the context of China.

The case of THU helps to further the debate over whether it is possible for a university to cooperate with the state and market while preserving key academic values of self-determination and privileged freedom in research. Unlike the pessimistic views presented in the existing literature (as discussed earlier in this chapter), this chapter has demonstrated that linking the university to economic development is not necessarily a passive result of external societal pressures. Moreover, it has shown how, by using that linkage proactively and skillfully, the university gained resources, opportunities, and relative freedom to shape the direction of its research to accommodate its scholars' vision, mission, and professional judgment. First, the university was willing and able to increase its academic competence in the domestic HE community. Second, the university had the capacity to help national economic development in response to both domestic market demands and global imperatives. Third, its faculty members strived to voice their professional judgment regarding the function of, and approaches to RDI, and to affect the government's policy making.

The past two decades have seen increased interplay among universities, states, and market forces that has shaped the direction and scope of RDI. In this process, whether the university can retain its power of self-determination is an important concern, as is whether the university can make good use of research resources to innovatively pursue new knowledge that can improve both the quality of HE and the university's capacity to improve the society of which it is a part.

NOTES

1. Including the MOE, the State Development and Reform Commission, the Ministry of Finance, the Ministry of Personnel, the Ministry of Science and Technology, and State-owned Assets Supervision and Administration Commission.
2. In the early 1930s, Japan attacked North China, Manchuria, and finally launched a full-scale invasion of China in 1937.

References

Altbach, P. G. 2009. *Endorsements for University Autonomy, the State, and Social Change in China by Su-Yan Pan.* Hong Kong: Hong Kong University Press.
Ashton, D., F. Green, D. James, and J. Sung. 1999. *Education and Training for Development in East Asia: The Political Economy of Skill Formation in East Asian Newly Industrialised Economies.* London: Routledge.
Beerkens, M. 2013. "Competition and Concentration in the Academic Research Industry: An Empirical Analysis of the Sector Dynamics in Australia 1990–2008." *Science & Public Policy* 40 (2): 157–170.
Bok, D. 2003. *Universities in the Marketplace: The Commercialization of Higher Education.* Princeton, NJ: Princeton University Press.
Borthwick, S. 1983. *Education and Social Change in China: The Beginnings of the Modern Era.* Stanford, CA: Hoover Institution Press.
Cai, Y. 1986. *Cai Yuanpei Quanqi* [*Collections of Cai Yuanpei's Works*], Vol. 4. Beijing: Zhonghua Press.
———. 1991. "Tiyi Sheli Daxue Yuan An" ["Proposal for the Establishment of National Academic Council"]. In *Cai Yuanpei Jiaoyu Lunzhu Xuan* [*Selected Works of Cai Yuanpei*], edited by P. S. Gao. Beijing: People's Education Press.
———. 1993. *Cai Yuanpei Xuanji* [*Selected Works of Cai Yuanpei*]. Hangzhou: Zhejiang Educational Press.
Cantwell, B., and C. F. Mathies. 2012. "Expanding Research Capacity at United States Universities: A Study of Academic Research and Development Investment from 1990–2005." *Higher Education Quarterly* 66 (3): 308–330.
Chapman, J. W. 1983. "Introduction: The Western University on Trial." In *The Western University on Trial*, edited by J. W. Chapman, 1–25. Berkeley: University of California Press.
China Review Reporter. 2010. "Xinyidai Haigui Chengwei Zhongguo Canyu Quanqiuhua Zhongyao Cuihuaji" ["A New Generation of Returnees Help China Participate in Globalization"]. Available online at: http://chinareview-agency.net/doc/1012/8/4/7/101284732.html?coluid=49&kindid=972&docid=101284732&mdate=0409111952; accessed on May 18, 2013.
Chinese Education Yearbook Editorial Board. 1984. *Zhongguo Jiaoyu Nianjian 1949–1981* [*China Education Yearbook, 1949–1981*]. Beijing: China Encyclopedia Press.
Clark, B. R., ed. 1984. *Perspectives on Higher Education: Eight Disciplinary and Comparative Views.* Berkeley: University of California Press.
Compilation Group of Tsinghua History. 1981. *Qinghua Daxue Xiaoshi Gao* [*History of Tsinghua University*]. Beijing: Zhonghua Shuju.
Deng, X. (1977) 1983. "Some Comments on Work in Science and Education." In *Deng Xiaoping Wenxuan* [*Selected Works of Deng Xiaoping*], Vol. 2. Beijing: People's Education Press.
Fang, H. J., and S. J. Zhang, eds. 2001a. *Qinghua daxue zhi* [*Annals of Tsinghua University*], Vol. 2. Beijing: Tsinghua University Press.

———. 2001b. *Qinghua daxue zhi* [*Annals of Tsinghua University*], Vol. 1. Beijing: Tsinghua University Press.

Gao, Q. 1992. *Zhongguo Gaodeng Jiaoyu Sixiang Shi* [*Historical Review of Chinese Ideals of Higher Education*]. Beijing: People's Education Press.

Gu, Y. X. 1933. "Zhuanmen Rencai de Peiyang" [The Preparation of Personnel with Specialisms"]. In *Qinghua Daxue Shiliao Xuanbian* [*Selected Compilation of Historical Document of Tsinghua University*], Vol. 2, edited by Compilation Group of History of Tsinghua University. Beijing: Tsinghua University Press.

Hayhoe, R. 1996. *China's Universities, 1895–1995: A Century of Cultural Conflict*. New York: Garland Publishing.

Hetherington, H. 1953. *The Social Function of the University*. London: Lindsey Press.

———. 1965. "University Autonomy." In *University Autonomy: Its Meaning Today*, edited by International Association of Universities, 1–38. Paris: International Association of Universities.

Hu, D. C. 2000. "Yu Haiwai Qiye Hezuo, Cujing Yiliu Daxue Jianshe" ["Cooperating with Overseas Enterprises, the Construction of World-Class University"]. *Qinghua Daxue Jiaoyu Yanjiu* [*Tsinghua Journal of Educational Research*] 2:1–4.

Human Recourse Market News Reporter. 2010. "Liuxue Huiguo Renyuan Jian Haigui Chuangyeyuan Yu 150 Jia" ["Returnees Have Established More Than 150 Returning-Student Entrepreneurial Parks across China"]. Available online at: http://news.sohu.com/20100406/n271328712.shtml; accessed on May 16, 2013.

Husen, T. 1994. "The Idea of the University: Changing Roles, Current Crisis, and Future Challenges." In *The Role of the University: A Global Perspective*, edited by T. Husen, 7–31. Tokyo: United Nations University.

Jaspers, K. 1959. *The Idea of the University*. Boston: Beacon Press.

Kwon, K. 2011. "The Co-evolution of Universities' Academic Research and Knowledge-Transfer Activities: The Case of South Korea." *Science and Public Policy* 38 (6): 493–503.

Lao, G. (1934) 1991. "Shenlun Yinianji bu Fenxi" ["A Perspective on No Faculty and Department Difference in the First Year Undergraduate Education"]. In *Qinghua Daxue Shiliao Xuanbian* [*Selected Compilation of Historical Document of Tsinghua University*], Vol. 2, edited by Compilation Group on the History of Tsinghua University. Beijing: Tsinghua University Press.

Lobkowicz, N. 1983. "Man, Pursuit of Truth and the University." In *The Western University on Trial*, edited by J. W. Chapman, 27–39. Berkeley: University of California Press.

Maassen, P., and F. van Vaught. 1994. "Alternative Model of Governmental Steering in Higher Education." In *Comparative Policy Studies in Higher Education*, edited by L. Goedegebuure and F. van Vught, 35–63. Utrecht: Center for Higher Education Policy Studies.

Marginson, S. 2008. "Academic Creativity under New Public Management: Foundations for an Investigation." *Educational Theory* 58 (3): 269–287.

Martin, W. B. 1972. "Universities and Their Range of Concern." In *World Yearbook of Education 1972/3: University Facing the Future*, edited by W. R. Niblett and R. F. Butts. New York: Evans Brothers.

Mei, Y. 1993. *Mei Yiqi Jiaoyu Lunzhu Xuan* [*Collected Works of Mei Yiqi's Thought of Education*]. Beijing: People's Educational Press.

———. 2013. *China's Universities*. Beijing: Beijing Institute of Technology Press.

Mei, Z. 1946. "Huainian Xianfu Mei Yi-Qi Xiaozhang" ["To Remember My Father, President Mei Yiqi"]. In *Shiji Qinghua* [*Tsinghua University in a Century*], Vol. 2, edited by L. J. Zhuang. Beijing: Guangming Daily Press.

Ministry of Education (MOE). 1974. *Disici Zhonghua Minguo Jiaoyu Nianjian* [*Chinese Education Yearbook*], Vol. 4. Taipei: Zhengzhong Press.

———. 2007a. *Jiaoyubu Guanyu Jinyibu Jiaqiang Yingjin Haiwai Youxiu Liuxue Rencai Gongzuo de Ruogan Yijian* [*A Number of Decisions on Further Strengthening the Work of Attracting Back Outstanding Students from Overseas*]. Beijing: MOE. Available online at: http://www.chinabaike.com/law/zy/bw/gw/jtb/1341374.html.

———. 2007b. *Liuxue Gongzuo* [*Works on Education Abroad*]. Beijing: MOE. Available online at: http://www.moe.edu.cn/; accessed on May 17, 2007.

Mok, K. H. 1996. "Marketization and Decentralization: Development of Education and Paradigm Shift in Social Policy." *Hong Kong Public Administration* 5 (1): 35–56.

———. 2000. "Marketizing Higher Education in Post-Mao China." *International Journal of Educational Development* 20 (2): 109–126.

———. 2002. "Policy of Decentralization and Changing Governance of Higher Education in Post-Mao China." *Public Administration and Development* 22:261–273.

Mok, K. H., and A. Welch, eds. 2003. *Globalization and Education Re-structuring in the Asia Pacific Region*. London: Palgrave Macmillan.

Moor, R. A. 1993. "Academic Freedom and University Autonomy: Essentials and Limitations." In *Academic Freedom and University Autonomy*, edited by European Centre for Higher Education, 35–50. Bucharest: UNESCO.

Mori, W. 1993. "The Universities' Responsibilities to Society: International Perspectives." In *Academic Freedom and University Autonomy*, edited by European Centre for Higher Education. Bucharest: UNESCO, European Centre for Higher Education.

Newman, J. 1959. *The Idea of a University*. Garden City, NY: Doubleday.

Pan, S. Y. 2006. "Economic Globalization, Politico-cultural Identity, and University Autonomy: The Struggle of Tsinghua University in China." *Journal of Education Policy* 21 (3): 245–266.

———. 2007. "Intertwining of Academia and Officialdom and University Autonomy: Experience from Tsinghua University in China." *Higher Education Policy* 20 (2): 121–144.

———. 2009. *University Autonomy, the State, and Social Change in China*. Hong Kong: Hong Kong University Press.

———. 2011. "Education Abroad, Human Capital Development, and National Competitiveness: China's Brain Gain Strategies." *Frontiers of Education in China* 6 (1): 106–138.
People's Daily Online Reporter. 2007. "Innovation-Oriented Country." Available online at: http://english.peopledaily.com.cn/90002/92169/92211/6281108.html; accessed on May 19, 2010.
Polin, R. 1983. "Freedom of Mind and University Autonomy." In *The Western University on Trial*, edited by J. W. Chapman, 39–45. Berkeley: University of California Press.
Qu, S. P. 1993. *Zhongguo Daxue Jiaoyu Fazhan Shi* [*History of Development of Chinese Higher Education*]. Shan Xi: Shanxi Education Press.
Salminen, A. 2003. "New Public Management and Finnish Public Sector Organizations: The Case of Universities." In *The Higher Education Managerial Revolution?* edited by A. Amaral, V. L. Meek, and I. M. Larsen, 55–69. Dordrecht; Boston; London: Kluwer Academic Publishers.
Schimank, U. 2005. "'New Public Management' and the Academic Profession: Reflections on the German Situation." *Minerva: A Review of Science, Learning and Policy* 43 (4): 361–376.
Shen, X. Y. 1994. *Dongdang Zhuanxing zhong de Mingguo Jiaoyu* [*Education and Social Transformation in the Republic of China*]. Henan: Henan People's Press.
State Education Committee. 1996. *Maixiang 21 Shiji de Zhongguo Gaoxiao* [*The Development of China's Higher Education Institutions in the 21st Century*]. Beijing: Capital Normal University Press.
Su, Y. F. 1996. *Cong Qinghua Xuetang dao Qinghua Daxue: 1911–1929* [*From Tsinghua College to Tsinghua University: 1911–1929*]. Taipei: Institute of Modern History, Academia Sinica.
———. 2000. *Kangzhan Qian de Qinghua Daxue: 1928–1937* [*Tsinghua University before Wartime: 1928–1937*]. Taipei: Institute of Modern History, Academia Sinica.
Sun, P. Q., and G. J. Li. 1993. *Zhongguo Jiaoyu Sixiang Shi* [*History of Chinese Educational Thoughts*]. Shanghai: Eastern China Normal University Press.
Thorens, J. 1993. "Proposal for an International Declaration on Academic Freedom and University Autonomy." In *Academic Freedom and University Autonomy*, edited by European Centre for Higher Education. Bucharest: UNESCO, European Centre for Higher Education.
Tsinghua University (THU). 2001. *Wei 21 shi ji zhong guo xian dai hua jian she pei yang quan mian fa zhan de gao ceng ci ren cai de zhong he yan jiu yu shi yan yan jiu bao gao* [*A Research Report about the Experiment and Research about the Training of High-level All-round Developed Personnel for Modernization of China in the 21 Century*]. Beijing: Tsinghua University.
Tunnermann, C. 1996. "A New Vision of Higher Education." *Higher Education Policy* 9 (1): 11–27.
Wolff, R. P. 1992. *The Ideal of the University*. New Brunswick, NJ: Transaction Publishers.
Wu, M. 1925. "Qinghua Kaiban Yanjiuyuan zhi Zhiqu ji Jingguo" ["The Establishment of the Research Institution of Chinese Classics in Tsinghua

College"]. In *Qinghua Daxue Shiliao Xuanbian* [*Selected Compilation of Historical Document of Tsinghua University*], Vol. 1, edited by Compilation Group on the History of Tsinghua University. Beijing: Tsinghua University Press.

Xin, R. (1934) 1991. "Lun Diyinian Bufen Yuanxi" ["A Perspective on No Faculty and Department Difference in the First Year Undergraduate Education"]. In *Qinghua Daxue Shiliao Xuanbian* [*Selected Compilation of Historical Document of Tsinghua University*], Vol. 2, edited by Compilation Group of History of Tsinghua University. Beijing: Tsinghua University Press.

Yang, M. S. 1971. *Kanzhanqian Gaodeng Jiaoyu Shiliao* [*Historical Document of Higher Education before the China-Japan War*]. Taipei: Dang Shi Hui.

Zedong, M. 1965. *On the People's Democratic Dictatorship: Selected Works of Mao Tse-tung*, Vol. 4. Beijing: Foreign Language Press.

Zemin, J. 2000. *Lun Kexue Jishu* [*About Science and Technology*]. Beijing: Zhongyang Wenxian Press.

———. 2001. "Zai Qingzhu Qinghua Daxue Jianxiao Jiushi Zounian Dahuishang de Jianghua" ["Speech Given in the Ceremony of the 90th Anniversary of the Establishment of Tsinghua University"]. Available online at: http://www.tsinghua.edu.cn; accessed on June 3, 2002.

Zhou, J. 2003. "Lishixing de Kuayue, Xingzhengtu de Zhongren: Zhongguo Gaodeng Jiaoyu Gaige yu Fazhan de Huigu he Zhanwang" ["Progresses and Tasks of the New March: Development of Higher Education in China"]. *Mainland-Hong Kong Academic Exchange* 3 (57): 3–8.

———. 2006. *Higher Education in China* [*Foreign Language Teaching and Research Press, Trans.*]. Singapore: Thomson learning.

Zweig, D., C. Chen, and S. Rosen. 2004. "Globalization and Transnational Human Capital: Overseas and Returnee Scholars to China." *The China Quarterly* 179:735–757.

Chapter 15

Conclusion
Research Trends in Higher Education in Asia Pacific

John N. Hawkins and Ka Ho Mok

Over the past few decades, we have witnessed significant changes taking place in higher education (HE) policy and governance across different parts of the globe to address the changing economic and societal needs in the increasingly globalized economic context. Realizing the importance of enhancing the quality of HE would form a cornerstone in any strategy for national development. In response, universities have been under pressure to engage proactively in research and knowledge-transfer activities to enhance their global competitiveness (Psacharaopoulos and Patrinos 2002; Carnoy 2003; Hanushek and Woessmann 2007; Bajunid 2011; Gopinathan and Lee 2011; Hallinger 2011; Tjeldvoll 2011; Mok 2013). In particular, the rapid emergence of East Asian universities, both as domestic as well as regional centers of knowledge consolidation and production, has become a prominent trend in the last decade (Bajunid 2011; Gopinathan and Lee 2011; Mok and Cheung 2011). As a consequence, regional policy makers are focusing increasingly on HE strategies that will enhance higher levels of knowledge production and capacity development for sustaining future social and economic growth (Mok 2013).

Before the massification stage of HE emerged it was commonly thought that research in HE was reserved for only the elite level of the tertiary sector, the so-called research university, and that its goal was relatively straightforward. This sector shared some essential characteristics as follows (Bienenstock 2008):

- High-quality faculty committed to research
- Recruitment of high-quality graduate students
- A supportive intellectual climate
- High-quality facilities to support research
- Sufficient funding to remain competitive and up-to-date
- A supportive leadership with a vision

Trow (1974) noted long ago that as HE moved from elite to mass education, its social role changed as well, especially the role of research and expansion of knowledge. With more emphasis being placed on research and knowledge transfer, multidisciplinary and interdisciplinary research themes and projects have become increasingly popular. The classic model of the research university in the immediate post-WWII period, referred to in chapter 3, was that of a faculty that functioned in an environment of freedom to teach and conduct research on topics of their choice, weaving together teaching and research, and funded generously by both local sources (either state/provincial/public funds or endowments as well as governmental and private contract and grants). But, as we have seen in our study here, this rather linear and clear-cut view of the role of research and innovation in HE has become much more complex. Now we can see that several factors impinge on how research and innovation are viewed in the twenty-first-century HE systems in the Asia and Pacific region. Similar to the experiences of HE systems moving from elite to massification, and even to post-massification in some Western countries, the Asia Pacific region has witnessed unprecedented growth in HE over the past decades, particularly from the 1980s onward. For instance, South Korea has been witnessing an extremely rapid expansion of HE (see Table 15.1). The number of enrollments of HE in 2007 was more than quintuple of that of 1980. Similarly, Japan has seen a steady development in HE in terms of number of new entrants of higher education institutions (HEIs) in the first decade of the twenty-first century (see Table 15.2). In China, with its rapid expansion of HE launched in 1999, only 4 percent of the 18- to 22-year-old cohort or about 3 million (three- and four-year degree) students attended postsecondary institutions in 1996, but this rose to 24 percent of the same age cohort, or about 27 million students by 2009 (Carnoy et al. 2013, 48).

The rapid increase in student enrollments in HE has inevitably posed challenges to the purposes and roles of universities in teaching and learning, research and knowledge-transfer activities. Recognizing HE as a vital tool

Table 15.1 Number of student enrollments in HEIs in South Korea (1996–2010)

1980	1990	2000	2002	2004	2006	2007
647,505	1,691,681	3,363,549	3,577,447	3,555,115	3,545,774	3,558,711

Source: Data from *China Statistic Yearbook*, years as above. Tables created by authors.

Table 15.2 Number of new entrants in HEIs in Japan (1996–2010)

2000	2005	2006	2007	2008	2009
599,655	603,760	603,054	613,613	607,159	608,731

Source: Data from *China Statistic Yearbook*, years as above. Tables created by authors.

to stimulate economic growth, Gooch observed, "Efforts to raise standards and encourage collaboration are gaining pace. Raising standards at higher education institutions across ASEAN...is considered a key aspect of the effort to train the skilled workforce necessary for economic development. A recent World Bank report found that while higher education participation in less prosperous Southeast Asian countries has increased sharply in recent decades, the number of graduates is still too low for countries such as Cambodia and Vietnam...[which] are neither delivering graduates with the skills nor producing the research required to address labor market and innovation needs" (2011, 7).

It is against this particular dynamic context in Asia that HEIs are increasingly finding that they have multiple missions and it is becoming equally difficult to assign priorities to those missions—first and foremost being the future of research. Enhancing research capacity in HEIs that are undergoing transformation of mission, for example, from teachers' colleges (with emphasis on pedagogy and instruction) to regular HEIs, is just one example. These challenges have implications for faculty recruitment, retention, and retraining among other issues. The same would be true for mission creep in systems where the balance between teaching, research, and service exists and the reward structure favors research over the others.

There has been a dominant paradigm regarding the role of research in HE, largely established in Europe and the United States and now being imitated in other settings especially in the Asia and Pacific region. It raises a number of questions about the appropriateness of this model especially in the context of the added pressure of not only how to conduct research but to conduct "innovative" research that strives to reach world standards (Hawkins 2012). Rankings and the striving to achieve world-class university status help drive this movement. As the ecology of research in HE changes in the region, questions are raised about the idea that "one size fits all" is the best policy to follow in the transformation of HE in the complex setting of Asia. One outcome of this dominant paradigm is the "craze for publications" in Asian HEIs, which has had a profound influence on the various actors in HE (the university, the role of the state, the market under the increasingly neoliberal political economy, and so on). Caution is urged with respect to the untoward expansion of research and development (R&D), as quality assurance becomes an issue with respect to the number of journals, their quality, the appropriateness of the research that is conducted, and the role of each of the actors. Mok and Hallinger argued with strong evidence that a growing number of Asian universities have begun to deploy additional resources to promote research and knowledge-transfer activities in order to enhance their global ranking and address the internationalization agenda commonly perceived as a very important driving factor for enhancing quality in HE (2013). Such pressures for research and production of internationally refereed outputs have inevitably affected the way academics operate in the university sector. In order to perform well in competitive grant applications and production of international outputs, many academics have felt pressures and stresses especially when those contract renewals and promotions are increasingly determined by grants and outputs. Placing more weight on research would lead to less attention being given to teaching and learning, hence there is a tension between research and teaching commonly emerging across different Asian HE systems (Chou 2014; Mok 2014). The rise of a new "academic regime" is an area for future study and analysis.

There are special issues related to those settings where the political economy is making a transition from a commodity-based economy to that of knowledge production. All of this has implications for the culture of HEIs as they attempt to make this transition; there are forces both supportive and resistant to these changes; implications for R&D are significant.

The rise of academic capitalism and implications for how this movement contributes to what has become known as the "disrupting" movement affecting HE is at the cutting edge of the transformation of the role of research and innovation in HE. This is a complex phenomenon and in the book we have attempted to make sense of this with various levels of analysis including new typologies.

This is directly related to the linkage between entrepreneurship and the idea of the entrepreneurial university. Case studies of Hong Kong and Taiwan bring this phenomenon into sharp relief suggesting that there is an evolving linkage between university-industry-business relationships and the desire for both innovation and entrepreneurship. As indicated above, this has also contributed to blurring of the missions of HE in many settings in Asia. Ambiguity exists among scholars some of whom see promise in such relationships for the health and vitality, as well as practical value, of HE and those who see such pragmatic relations as threatening the very nature of what HE is all about.

This is also not just an issue for what are commonly known as research universities but is also reflected in the short cycle area of community colleges as well as their increasing response to the needs of their local communities to contribute the kind of innovative teaching and curriculum as well as community projects that make for higher levels of community engagement and problem solving.

The three-way linkage between HE (at all levels), the state, and the private sector has come to dominate the current model of HE transformation and the role of research, development, and innovation. The reformulation of research toward the triple linkage model is occurring in tandem and possibly supported by the worldwide focus on rankings or league tables. It is not easy to achieve the triple linkage model of research for many universities and this is especially true in light of current economic tensions in the region. The complexity of these linkages and the cost involved in putting them together are considerable and there are documented cases where it has been tried and failed (*University World News* 2009). Yet, the Organization for Economic Co-operation and Development (OECD), among others, views this model of research and the economic tensions as an important opportunity that may result in the birth of new industries aided and launched by HEIs that are successful in pulling together the three critical elements. What Osborne refers to as "creative destruction" may come to characterize a whole new set of industries that emerged out of the previous period of crisis (Microsoft, Nokia, etc.) (2009).

One major critique of this reformulation is that it is somewhat exclusive and likely to be achieved primarily by the institutions in the more developed nations that are located near government funding sources and corporate entities. Will the triple linkage model exacerbate the research divide between rich and poor nations, states, communities, and universities? Not necessarily, says at least one scholar who offers a new vision of how high-level triple linkage research can be shared and participated in globally (Vest 2007). Heavily influenced by his experience as the CEO of Massachusetts Institute of Technology (MIT), he calls this the "global meta university" and suggests that new media and technology can make possible widespread dissemination and participation in research without each institution having to achieve a high level of the triple linkage.

Vest suggests that the innovative use of technology can help to democratize research for HEIs of different sizes and locations. Antecedents for this kind of meta approach to research were such developments as JSTOR (i.e., Journal Storage), funded by Mellon in 1990 to build an online trusted archive of over a thousand academic journals, thus allowing smaller HEIs to collaborate and mount research projects that their own meager library resources would not allow. Then, of course, came the MIT open courseware, funded by Hewlett and Mellon, and "pledged to make available on the web, free of charge to teachers and learners everywhere, all of the approximately 2,000 subjects we have on our campus" (Vest 2007, 96). Included in this effort were all syllabuses, course calendars, well formatted and detailed lecture notes, examinations, problem sets and solutions, and lab and project plans as well as video lectures. The China Open Resources for Education (CORE) program as well as other such projects in Singapore, Taiwan, and Korea attempt something similar. One point that needs to be raised here is that when reflecting on the three-way linkage of university-state-market relationship, we should really go beyond this conventional theoretical model by exploring how the civil society and community at large would contribute to the development of knowledge and practice through the "catchment" of the wider society and the engagement of the civil society. Chan and Mok's chapter in this volume has pointed to the missing link by ignoring the contributions that the civil society and community at large could contribute to university development. Such a reflection draws us to the following question: Does this suggest that research with a big "R" and innovation may be made more available to HEIs previously left out of such efforts, thus expanding the notion of the knowledge society on a global scale? This is clearly a key HE research agenda item for the future.

References

Bajunid, I. A. 2011. "Leadership in the Reform of Malaysian Universities: Analyzing the Strategic Role of the Malaysian Qualifications Agency." *Journal of Higher Education Policy and Management* 33 (3): 253–265.

Bienenstock, A. 2008. "Essential Characteristics of Research Universities." In *Universities as Centers of Research and Knowledge Creation: An Endangered Species?*, edited by H. Vessuri and U. Teichler, 33–40. Rotterdam: Sense Publishers.

Carnoy, M. 2003. "Globalization and Education Reform." In *Globalization and Education: Integration and Contestation across Cultures*, edited by N. Stromquist and K. Monkman, 43–61. Oxford, UK: Rowman and Littlefield.

Carnoy, M., P. Loyalka, M. Dobryakova, R. Dossani, I. Froumin, K. Kuhns, J. Tilak, and R. Wang. 2013. *University Expansion in a Changing Global Economy: Triumph of the BRICs?* Stanford, CA: Stanford University Press.

China Statistic Yearbook. Beijing: China Statistics Press.

Chou, C. P., ed. 2014. *The SSCI Syndrome in Higher Education: A Local or Global Phenomenon*. Rotterdam: Sense Publishers.

Gooch, L. 2011. "ASEAN Nations Put Education Front and Center." *The New York Times*, October 30.

Gopinathan, S., and M. H. Lee. 2011. "Challenging and Co-opting Globalization: Singapore's Strategies in Higher Education." *Journal of Higher Education Policy and Management* 33 (3): 287–299.

Hallinger, P. 2011. "Riding the Tiger of Higher Education Reform in Asia Pacific: Where Are We Heading?" Keynote presentation at the Annual Regional Higher Education Leadership Summit, Singapore, October 18–21.

Hanushek, E., and L. Woessmann. 2007. *The Role of Education Quality for Economic Growth*. Policy Research Working Paper No. 4122. World Bank. Available online at: http://ssrn.com/abstract=960379.

Hawkins, J. N. 2012. "The Transformation of Research in the Knowledge Society." In *The Emergent Knowledge Society and the Future of Higher Education*. London; New York: Routledge.

Mok, K. H. 2013. *The Quest for Entrepreneurial Universities in East Asia*. New York: Palgrave Macmillan.

———. 2014. "Promoting the Global University in Taiwan: University Governance Reforms and Academic Reflections." In *The SSCI Syndrome in Higher Education: A Local or Global Phenomenon*, edited by C. P. Chou, 24–47. Rotterdam: Sense Publishers.

Mok, K. H., and A. Cheung. 2011. "Global Aspirations and Strategizing for World-Class Status: New Forms of Politics in Higher Education Governance in Hong Kong." *Journal of Higher Education Policy and Management* 33 (3): 231–251.

Mok, K. H., and P. Hallinger. 2013. "The Quest for World Class Status and University Responses in Asian's World Cities." *Journal of Higher Education Policy and Management* 35 (3): 230–237.

Osborne, A. 2009. "GLOBAL: Invest in R&D to Profit from Crisis." *University World News*, June 21. Available online at: http://www.universityworldnews.com/article.php?story=20090618194546998&query=Global%3A+invest+in+R%26D+to+profit+from+crisis.

Psacharaopoulos, G., and H. Patrinos. 2002. *Returns to Investment in Education: A Further Update*. Policy Research Working Paper No. 2881. World Bank. Available online at: http://ssrn.com/abstract=367780.

Tjeldvoll, A. 2011. "Change Leadership in Universities: The Confucian Dimension." *Journal of Higher Education Policy and Management* 33 (3): 219–230.

Trow, M. 1974. "Problems in the Transition from Elite to Mass Higher Education." In *OECD Policies for Higher Education*. Paris: OECD.

University World News. 2009. "New Zealand: Uni-research Institute Merger Abandoned." *University World News*, June 21. Available online at: http://www.universityworldnews.com/article.php?story=20090618194833585&query=New+Zealand%3A+Uni-research+Institute+merger+abandoned.

Vest, C. M. 2007. *The American Research University from World War II to World Wide Web*. Berkeley: University of California Press.

Contributors Biographies

Prompilai Buasuwan is an associate professor in the Program of Educational Administration, Faculty of Education at Kasetsart University and is an assistant to vice president for international affairs of Kasetsart University. Her main research interests are quality of education, partnership in education, internationalization of education, and educational policy analysis and evaluation. She has done various projects with international organizations, research funding agencies, universities' networks, and consortiums. She is a coordinator of "Kasetsart Initiative" international network for partnership and collaboration with participating members from over 20 countries and also a core member of Thailand Evaluation Network, Comparative and International Education Society of Thailand.

Sheng-Ju Chan is a professor in the Graduate Institute of Education and chief executive officer of the International Master Program in Educational Leadership and Management Development at the National Chung Cheng University, Taiwan. His areas of special interest are higher education policy, comparative education, and higher education management. He is the author of over a dozen publications in Chinese and English and a policy advisor to the Ministry of Education in Taiwan for higher education. His recent articles focus on cross-border education, internationalization, and student mobility in Asia, which were published in well-known journals such as *Asia Pacific Journal of Education*, *Higher Education Policy*, and *Journal of Higher Education Policy and Management*, and so on. Specializing in education in East Asia, Dr. Chan is the associate editor of international journal of *Asian Education and Development Studies* published by Emerald. He is also the coeditor of a book series, Higher Education in Asia, supported by Springer.

Dr. Robert Franco, an ecological anthropologist, has published scholarly and policy research on the changing meaning of work, service, schooling, housing, and leadership for Samoans at home and abroad; health disparities confronting Samoan, Hawaiian, and Pacific Islander populations in the United States; the meaning and management of water in ancient Hawai'i; and sociocultural factors affecting fisheries in Samoa and the Northern Marianas. In 2009, he was lead editor in the publication of American Samoa's first written history. At Kapi'olani Community College, University of Hawai'i, he serves as director of institutional effectiveness and shapes an innovative ecology of learning. With institutional commitment and support from federal and foundation sources, the college has emerged as a leader in service-learning for improved student engagement, learning, and achievement. Nationally, he is a senior consultant and trainer for Campus Compact and has assisted in the development of the Carnegie Community Engagement Classification. He is a Faculty Leadership Fellow for National Science Foundation's (NSF) Science Education for New Civic Engagements and Responsibilities initiative and leads the Community College Affiliate Program of the National Council for Science and the Environment. He also leads the national Teagle Foundation project on stimulating civic and moral responsibility for diverse, equitable, healthy, and sustainable communities.

Annette Gough is a research professor in the School of Education at Royal Melbourne Institute of Technology (RMIT) University and was previously head of the school. Prior to her appointment at RMIT she was in the faculty of education at Deakin University for 15 years. She has also been an adjunct or visiting professor at universities in Canada, South Africa, and the Hong Kong Institute of Education (HKIEd). She has been chief investigator on three Australian Research Council linkage projects and numerous other research projects for the Victorian Department of Education and other government and nongovernment bodies. She has also worked with UNESCO, UNEP, and UNESCO-UNEVOC on several research and development projects. Her research interests span environmental, sustainability and science education, research methodologies, posthuman, and gender studies. She has over 120 publications (books, chapters, and articles as well as curriculum materials) and is frequently invited as a keynote speaker at international conferences related to environmental/sustainability education.

John N. Hawkins is professor emeritus at the Graduate School of Education and Information Studies at the University of California, Los Angeles (UCLA), and codirector of the Asian Pacific Higher Education Research Partnership (APHERP) located at the East-West Center, Honolulu, Hawaii. He served as chair of the Graduate School of Education and head of the Division of Social Sciences and Comparative Education at UCLA. He served as dean of international studies at UCLA for 13 years and has served as a director of the UCLA Foundation Board, director of the East-West Center Foundation Board, and director of the J. F. Oberlin

Foundation Board, Japan. He was on the faculty of Vanderbilt University and Sciences Po in Paris. He is coeditor of the new Comparative and Development Education Series of Palgrave MacMillan. He has served as president of the Comparative and International Education Society, and editor of the *Comparative Education Review* published by the University of Chicago Press. He was educated at the University of Hawaii, University of British Columbia, and Vanderbilt University (PhD, 1973). He is a specialist on higher education reforms in the United States and Asia and the author of several books and research articles on education and development in Asia. He has conducted research throughout Asia since 1966 when he first visited the People's Republic of China and Japan.

Dr. Molly N. N. Lee is an education consultant from Malaysia. She is the former program specialist in higher education at UNESCO Asia and the Pacific Regional Bureau for Education in Bangkok. Prior to joining UNESCO Bangkok, she had been a professor of education in Universiti Sains Malaysia, Penang. Her professional expertise is in higher education, teacher education, information and communication technology (ICT) in education, and education for sustainable development. Her recent academic publications include: "Management of Research and Innovation in Malaysia," "Globalizing Practices in Asian Universities," "Centralized Decentralization in Malaysian Education," "Teacher Education in Malaysia: Current Issues and Future Prospects," "The Impact of Globalization on Education in Malaysia," "Case Studies of National and Regional Implementation Schemes Related to the Use of ICT in Education: The Case of Malaysia," and others.

Mario F. Letelier is a mechanical engineer from Universidad Técnica del Estado, Chile, and has MASc and PhD degrees from the University of Toronto. Over the years, he has pursued interests in the fields of non-Newtonian fluid mechanics, engineering education, and quality assurance in higher education. He is presently the director for the Center for Research in Creativity and Higher Education at the University of Santiago, Chile. Among his past activities are membership of the National Commission for Accreditation's board in Chile, presidency of the Chilean Society for Engineering Education, and participation in many boards and commissions associated to policy design and implementation. At present his main areas of teaching and research are heat transfer in viscoelastic flows in noncircular tubes, and professional learning processes with special focus on interdisciplinary studies aiming at making science and engineering science learning more effective in relation to Chile's needs for faster economical growth.

William Yat Wai Lo is assistant professor in the Department of International Education and Lifelong Learning, HKIEd. He writes on higher education policy with a focus on the effects of globalization and internationalization on East Asia. His recent sole-authored publication is *University Rankings: Implications for Higher Education in Taiwan* (Springer 2014).

Professor Joshua Ka Ho Mok is chair professor of comparative policy and concurrently vice president of research and development of the HKIEd. Before joining the HKIEd, he was associate dean and professor of social policy and faculty of social sciences at the University of Hong Kong (HKU). Being appointed as founding chair professor in East Asian Studies, Professor Mok established the Centre for East Asian Studies at the University of Bristol, UK, before taking the position at HKU. Professor Mok is no narrow disciplinary specialist but has worked creatively across the academic worlds of sociology, political science, and public and social policy while building his wide knowledge of China and the region. Professor Mok has published extensively in the fields of comparative education policy, comparative development and policy studies, and social development in contemporary China and East Asia. In particular, he has contributed to the field of social change and education in a variety of additional ways not the least of which has been his leadership and entrepreneurial approach to the organization of the field. His membership on numerous editorial boards and commissions in key scholarly societies contribute to the recognition that he is among the best in his field. He is a founding editor of *Journal of Asian Public Policy* and Comparative Development and Policy in Asia Book Series (published by London: Routledge, Taylor & Francis Group). In the last few years, Professor Mok has also worked closely with the World Bank and UNICEF as international consultant for comparative development and policy studies projects. He is also a former part-time member of the Central Policy Unit, HKSAR government.

Deane Neubauer is professor emeritus of political science at the University of Hawai'i, Manoa (UHM), senior research scholar at the Globalization Research Center, UHM, and codirector of the APHERP. He holds a BA from the University of California, Riverside, and an MA and PhD from Yale University. He has long been interested in the conduct of policy within and between democratic national states, an interest that has over time focused on comparative democratic institutions, policy processes, health care, food security, education, and more recently the development and conduct of globalization. He was the charter dean of social sciences at UHM and, in 1999, the founder of the Globalization Research Center and the Globalization Research Network, a collaboration of four US universities. He has also served as chancellor of UHM and as the vice president for academic affairs for the ten-campus University of Hawaii system. His current work examines the varieties of national policy expressions in health care, food security, and higher education within the contemporary dynamics of globalization with particular attention to nations in the Asia/Pacific region.

Su-Yan Pan is an associate professor in the faculty of liberal arts and social sciences at the HKIEd. Her research interests include interdisciplinary areas of higher education, citizenship education, international academic mobility, and educational policy making. Her research and publications in these fields place great emphasis on the cross-fertilization of Western and Chinese perspectives in understanding and explaining issues such as higher education and social change, university autonomy, human capital formation, the university-citizenship relations, and China's global power strategy.

Bordin Rassameethes received his PhD in management of technology from Vanderbilt University in the United States. He holds a MS degree in management from North Carolina State University, US, and BS in computer science from University of Miami, US. He has been working in the field of technology management, which includes electronic commerce, information technology, rural informatics, and supply chain management. He is currently a vice president of Kasetsart University (Sri racha Campus) and has served as project manager for numerous research and consulting projects. He has published more than 30 articles in refereed journals, 5 books, and over 100 articles in magazines. He also serves as a columnist in Thailand *Bloomberg Businessweek* and is advisor editor of three international journals.

María José Sandoval graduated as an industrial engineer from the University of Santiago, Chile, and is masters in science in innovation management and entrepreneurship from University of Manchester, UK. She worked at the Center for Research in Creativity and Higher Education of the University of Santiago, Chile, from 2007 to 2014, participating in the formulation and implementation of several innovation projects in higher education and institutional development. In addition, she has authored or coauthored many publications in conference proceedings and books related to the educational area. Her main areas of work have been related to institutional accreditation, curricula development, institutional improvement, and faculty training. Her main interests lie in the areas of innovation and entrepreneurship and in the relation between university and industry.

Stu Sutin is clinical professor of administrative and policy studies at the University of Pittsburgh, where he also serves as associate director, Institute for International Studies of Education. He is former president of the Community College of Allegheny County, president of Bank of Boston International, and senior vice president and international department head of Mellon Bank. He is senior editor and coauthor of *Increasing Effectiveness of the Community College Financial Model* (Palgrave Macmillan 2011) and coauthor of *Value-Based Education: A Vision for a Higher Education Business Model* (American Enterprise Institute 2012; White Paper).

Po-fen Tai is a professor in the Department of Sociology at Fu Jen Catholic University, New Taipei City, Taiwan. Professor Tai graduated in 2000 from the Graduate Institute of Building and Planning at National Taiwan University. She has published several studies dealing with Asian cities, international migration, and poverty. From 2012 to 2014, she was the chairperson for the Taiwan Higher Education Union. Recently, she has written about problems related to Taiwan's higher education system.

Chang Da Wan (C. D. Wan) is a research fellow at the National Higher Education Research Institute (IPPTN) and a doctoral candidate at the Department of Education, University of Oxford. He is bachelor of economics from the University of Malaya and master of social science from the National University of Singapore. His main interests include higher education and economics and recent research projects focus on doctoral education, research management, academic profession, private higher education, transition into higher education, and internationalization of higher education. He was a team member of the Review of the Malaysian National Higher Education Strategic Plan.

Index

academic capitalism, 79, 140, 151, 248
academic freedom, 46, 54, 128, 179, 226–9, 234–5, 237, 239
academic regime, 61–79, 248
    ideal types, 67–71
accountability, 12, 51, 143–4, 149, 178, 186, 226, 232
accreditation, 3, 13, 16, 84, 88, 101, 110
Arizona, 57, 170
ASEAN, 200, 247
Asian financial crisis, 65, 115
associate degree, 53
Australia, 11–26, 63, 226
    Australian Children's Education and Care Quality Authority, 13, 16
    Australian Institute for Teaching and School Leadership, 13, 15–16
    Australian Laureate Fellowship, 18
    Australian Parliament Senate Committee, 12
    Australian Universities Quality Agency, 15
    Better Schools Plan, 11–12
    Charles Sturt University, 24
    Deakin University, 22
    Discovery Early Career Researcher Awards, 18–19, 23
    Early Years Quality Fund, 12
    Excellence in Research for Australia, 13
        Field of Research codes, 18–23, 27
    Future Fellowship, 18, 23
    Higher Education Research Data Collection, 13, 20, 24–5
    Linkage Projects, 18–19, 21–3
    Monash University, 22–3
    National Competitive Grants Program, 18
    National Health and Medical Research Council, 18, 23
    National Plan for School Improvement, 12
    National Research Priority areas, 16–17, 20
    Office of Learning and Teaching, 18–19, 23
    Office of the Chief Scientist, 12, 17
    Queensland University of Technology, 21, 23–4
    Royal Melbourne Institute of Technology, 20–5
    A Smarter Australia report, 13–14
    Tertiary Education Quality and Standards Agency, 12, 15–16
    University of Melbourne, 15, 21, 23
    University of Queensland, 22–4
    University of Sydney, 21, 23–4
    University of Tasmania, 22
    University of Western Australia, 15
    Victoria University, 24

big data, 104–6
    AbouttheData.com, 105
big science, 34, 105

bioenvironmental model, 63
blue-sky research, 65
Bologna Process, 3
Boyer, Ernest, 43, 155, 159–60. *See also* Carnegie Foundation
categories of scholarship, 160
brain drain, 70–1
brain gain, 232
brain train, 3

California, 43, 54, 57, 111, 170
  Cal Tech, 41
  California Master Plan, 1, 5, 43–5
  California State University (CSU), 2, 43
  San Jose State University, 111
  three-tier system, 43
  University of California, 2, 39, 43, 46, 54, 111, 156
  University of California at Los Angeles, 39, 46
Cambodia, 247
Canada, 17, 117
  University of Ontario Institute of Technology, 118
chaos theory, 98
Chief Innovation Officers, 4
Chile, 81–91
  Center for Research in Creativity and Higher Education, 85
  Corporation for Development, 83
  National Commission for Scientific and Technological Research, 82–3, 89
  National Council for Innovation and Competitiveness, 83
  National System of Higher Education Quality Assurance, 88
China, 2–3, 36–7, 39, 41, 44, 61–3, 65, 67–9, 71–8, 82, 115–17, 119, 124–7, 130, 219–20, 227–39, 246–7, 250
  211 project, 36–7, 45, 230

863 Scheme, 230
985 project, 36–7, 45, 231, 238
1912 Legislation for Higher Education, 229
Beijing, 233, 239
Boxer Indemnity, 233–4
China Open Resources for Education, 250
Chinese Academy of Sciences, 36, 126, 230, 236
Chinese republican nationalists, 219
Communist Party of China, 229–30, 237
Confucianism, 228
Five-Year Plan, 125–6, 230, 236
Han Chinese, 219–21
Hong Kong University of Science and Technology joint projects, 126
Huazhong University of Sciences and Technology, 232
imperialism, 219–20, 228
innovation-oriented country, 231
Jiaotong University, 232
joint research institutes, 238
Kai-shek, Chiang, 229–30, 234
Kuomintang, 229–30
Manchuria, 219–20, 239
Ministry of Education, 230, 234, 236, 239
Ministry of Science and Technology, 126
Nankai University, 229
Nansha Information Technology Park, 126
National Natural Science Fund, 231–2
National Scheme of March 1986, 230, 232
Nationalist government, 230, 234–5
New Qing history, 215–22
Peking University, 229, 232, 236

People's Republic of China, 230, 236, 238
Qing dynasty, 219, 229
Shanghai, 115
Shenzhen, 115, 125–6
Tsinghua University, 227–30, 233–9
Yenching University, 236
Yuanpei, Cai, 228–9
Zedong, Mao, 230
city-state, 63, 115–16, 120, 124, 129, 131
civic engagement, 100, 109, 155–6, 158–9, 161–8, 170, 172–3
commercialization, 5, 65–6, 78, 116, 120–1, 123–4, 131, 183, 185, 192, 209–10, 232
community college, 2, 43, 52–3, 55–6, 155–72, 205. *See also* technical college
community engagement, 44, 155–73, 249–50
Community Engagement Classification, 44, 160, 163
complexity theory, 98
creative society, 199–212

disrupting movement, 95, 102, 104, 248
disruptive innovation, 95–7. *See also* sustaining innovation
Do It Yourself (DIY) model of education, 101, 105, 110

elite model, 15, 33, 67–8, 72, 76–8, 246
emerging global model, 41
English, 70, 72, 87, 168, 235–6, 238
Europe, 3–4, 17, 36, 41, 63, 82, 117, 125, 156–7, 225, 232, 247
European Union, 82
expatriate, 70, 78

Florida, 53, 57
Four Tigers, 44, 137
France, 62, 229

Germany, 62, 156, 229
global financial crisis, 26, 116
globalization, 4, 6, 53, 97–8, 104, 106, 141, 203, 216, 218, 221–2, 226, 231
gross domestic product, 65, 69, 72, 82–3, 130, 137, 177

Hawaii, 57, 165–8, 171
  Hawaii-Pacific Islands Campus Compact, 158, 165
  Kapi'olani Community College, 155–6, 160, 165–8, 170–2
  KELA model, 168–70
  Office for Institutional Effectiveness, 168
  University of Hawaii, 2, 158, 168
health care, 57, 105, 122
Hong Kong, 2, 5, 40, 115–33, 137–8, 149, 248
  Center for Innovation and Technology, 122
  Chinese University of Hong Kong, 117–18, 122, 126–7, 132
  City University of Hong Kong, 120–1, 127
  colonial period, 116
  Earmarked Research Grants, 130
  Enterprise Support Scheme, 124
  four traditional economic pillars, 115
  Hong Kong Applied Science and Technology Research Institute, 118–20, 126, 132
  Hong Kong Business Angel Network, 118
  Hong Kong Jockey Club Institute of Chinese Medicine, 119
  Hong Kong Polytechnic University, 118

Hong Kong—*Continued*
   Hong Kong R&D Centers
      Program, 119
   Hong Kong Science Park, 117–19,
      124–6
   Hong Kong University of Science
      and Technology, 40, 118,
      121–3, 126–7
   Hong Kong Venture Capital and
      Private Equity Association, 118
   Innovation and Technology
      Commission, 118–19
   Innovation and Technology Fund,
      118–20, 123, 132
   joint HEIs, 125
   New Technology Training Scheme,
      119
   Open Innovation Network, 122
   Pearl River Delta, 120, 125–6
   R&D centers, 120
   Research and Development Cash
      Rebate Scheme, 119
   Research Grant Council, 127, 130
   Small Entrepreneur Research
      Assistance Program, 118, 124
   Technology Transfer Office,
      121–2
   University Grants Committee,
      120–2, 129–30
   University of Hong Kong, 40,
      117–18, 121–2, 126–7
   Vocational Training Council, 119

immigration, 68, 70–1
income, 13, 17–20, 23–5, 39, 46, 57, 65–6, 81–2, 86–7, 118, 122, 130, 137, 140, 151, 177, 211, 232–3
incubation programs, 117, 147–8
India, 3, 40–1, 62, 69, 72, 75
information and communication technology, 120, 137, 184, 211
institutional autonomy, 3, 46, 54, 77, 149, 152, 195
internationalization, 3, 4, 149, 186, 218, 222, 248
Internet, 98, 100, 109
internships, 100, 109, 119, 128, 139, 141–2, 172, 208
ivory tower, 202, 204

Japan, 2, 34, 37–9, 41, 61–3, 65, 67–78, 82, 137–8, 167, 208, 219, 230, 246–7
   Global Centers of Excellence, 37–8
   Japanese model, 63
   Ministry of Education, Culture, Sports, Science, and Technology, 38
   Top 30 Program, 33, 37
   Toyoma Plan, 37, 45
   University of Tokyo, 39
   World Premier International Research Center Initiative, 38

knowledge economy, 34, 64, 71, 106, 115–16, 120, 136–7, 142–4, 146, 150, 199, 205, 209, 248
knowledge society, 1, 34, 98, 104, 152, 162, 199, 204–5, 212, 239
Korea, 2, 5, 39–41, 61–3, 65–8, 70–8, 117, 121, 127, 137–8, 226, 246–7, 250
   Brain Korea, 21, 39–40, 45
   Seoul National University, 39

laissez-faire, 34, 85–6, 89, 91, 190
language, 70–2, 77, 106, 171, 189, 219–20, 236
liberal arts colleges, 32, 55, 100, 109, 183–4
Louisiana, 57, 170

Malaysia, 177–97
   Academic Staff Training Scheme, 178, 188
   Accelerated Program for Education Excellence, 178–9

INDEX

Advisory Committee on World
 Class Programs, 182–3, 187
Center of Drug Research, 187–90
Centers for Research Initiatives,
 183–4, 186, 194
deputy vice chancellor of research
 and innovation, 183–6
Engineering Campus, 180, 184
Health Campus, 180, 184, 187
Higher Institution Centers of
 Excellence, 187
Innovation and Commercialization
 Office, 183, 185
Institute for Research in Molecular
 Medicine, 187–90
Institute of Postgraduate Studies,
 190–2
Kelantan, 180
Key Performance Indicators, 188,
 190, 192, 195–6
Ministry of Science, Technology,
 and Innovation, 189–90
MyBrain15, 178
National Higher Education
 Research Institute, 187–9, 193
National Higher Education
 Strategic Plan, 178
Nibong Tebal, 180
Penang, 180
Personal and Professional
 Development, 191
Postgraduate Academic Support
 Services, 191–2
Research, Creativity, and
 Management Office, 183–4
Universiti Sains Malaysia, 177–97
Universiti Sains Malaysia research
 institutes, 187
University Management
 Committee, 186
University Research Committee,
 183
University Research Council, 183
USAINS, 183, 185

marketization, 5, 34, 232
Massachusetts, 54, 249
 Framingham State University, 54
 Harvard, 39, 41, 45–6, 54
 Massachusetts Institute of
  Technology (MIT), 41, 102,
  249–50
massification, 1, 3, 5, 44–7, 52, 54–6,
 58, 210, 245–6
massive open online course (MOOC),
 96, 101–4, 107, 110–11
 examples of, 96, 102
 iTunes U, 102, 106
 Udacity, 96, 111
military, 84, 157, 235
mission creep, 1, 5, 43–5, 247

NASDAQ stock market, 233
neoliberalism, 34, 36, 140, 226, 248
New York, 53, 159, 171
 Teagle Foundation, 170
Newman, John Henry, 31
nongovernmental organizations, 35,
 207–8, 212, 217
North America, 3, 63, 95, 232

Organization for Economic
 Co-operation and
 Development (OECD), 1, 66,
 83, 189, 199, 249

peer review, 21, 43, 130
Pennsylvania, 53, 56, 159
 Community College of Allegheny
  County, 56
 University of Pennsylvania, 159
PhD degree, 23, 44, 178, 186, 188
privatization, 5, 66, 70, 78, 140
publications, 13, 20, 37, 42, 61–2, 66,
 68, 71–2, 74–8, 88, 90, 165,
 190, 192, 236, 248
 citation impact, 61–2
 impact factor, 86, 88, 191
 publish or perish, 39, 45, 76

Quacquarelli Symonds ranking, 40

rankings, 4, 31–2, 40–1, 70, 87, 128, 137–8, 248–9
Russian language, 236

salary, 66, 68
scholarships, 68, 83, 158
Science, Technology, Engineering, and Mathematics (STEM), 4, 12, 17, 167
Science Citation Index, 39, 46
science parks, 117–19, 124–6, 139, 141, 146–7, 232
Singapore, 5, 40, 61–3, 67–75, 77–8, 115, 127, 137–8, 149, 250
    National University of Singapore, 40
small- and medium-sized enterprises, 118, 139, 210
Social Science Citation Index, 39, 46
socialism, 63, 71, 73, 76, 229, 237
socialist model, 63, 76
South Africa, 63
student debt, 52, 57–8, 111
sustaining innovation, 96. *See also* disrupting innovation

Taiwan, 2, 5, 61–3, 65–78, 117, 121, 127, 135–52, 248, 250
    Accountability Assessment, 143–4
    Department of Technological and Vocational Education, 139, 142
    Division and Center of Technology Promotion, 148
    Dynamics of industry-academy cooperation, 149–50
    entrepreneurship education programs, 148
    hard science, 136, 151–2
    Hsinchu Science Park, 139, 146–7
    incubation centers, 145–9
    Major League IAC, 146–7
    Ministry of Economic Affairs, 141, 145–8
    Ministry of Education, 139, 141–8
    Model University of Technology Program, 142
    National Chiao Tung University, 139
    National Chung Cheng University, 147–8
    National Kaohsiung First University of Science and Technology, 142
    National Science Council, 141, 146–7
    National Tsing Hua University, 139, 147, 237, 232–3, 236
    Silicon Valley of the East, 137
    Unemployment, 148
technical college, 52, 55, 142–3. *See also* community college
tenure, 39, 42–6, 52, 67–8, 76, 78, 185
Thailand, 199–212
    Bangkok, 200
    Bangkok University, 206, 209
    creative economy institutions, 206
    Design Thailand 2019, 200
    Foresight National Research Council of Thailand, 209
    Kasetsart University, 206–11
    Knowledge Network Institute of Thailand, 200
    National Economic and Social Development Plan, 200
    Office of Higher Education Commission, 205, 208
    Panyapiwat Institute of Management, 209
    public-private partnership, 200–1, 204, 206–8, 210, 212
    Research and Innovation for Technology Transfer to the Rural Communities Project, 205
    Stock Exchange of Thailand, 208, 210

Index

Thailand Consortium of Business Schools, 209
think tank, 100, 109, 183, 187
Thomson Reuters, 61
triple helix, 2, 35, 64, 131, 149, 151
triple linkage model, 35, 249–50
tuition, 51–2, 54, 57–8, 157, 210

UNESCO, 135, 189
United Kingdom
    Institute for Public Policy Research, 13, 62, 140, 188
    Oxford University, 121
    University of Leeds, 121
    Warwick University, 140
United States, 1, 4, 17, 32–6, 39, 41–3, 45, 51–61, 82, 84, 98, 102, 117, 138, 156, 173, 219, 226, 234, 236, 247. *See also under individual states*
    Accreditation Board for Engineering and Technology, 84
    American Association for Higher Education, 159
    American Association of Community Colleges, 55, 155, 157–8, 160, 164–6
    American Association of Junior Colleges, 157
    American College Testing (ACT), 55
    American Council on Education, 159
    Association of American Colleges and Universities, 155, 159, 164–6
    Association of American Universities, 54, 155, 159–60
    Bayh-Dole Act of 1980, 34
    Brown University, 158
    Campus Compact, 155, 158–60, 163–5
    Carnegie Foundation, 44, 155, 159–64
    Center on Budget and Policy Priorities, 57
    Chicago school of economics, 34
    Community College Survey of Student Engagement, 164, 168, 170
    Cornell University, 55
    Department of Education, 52
    Education Commission of the States, 158
    Georgetown University, 158
    GI Bill, 55, 157
    Horizons Project, 164, 166
    Johnson Foundation, 159
    Medicaid, 57
    middle college, 56
    Morrill Act, 156
    National Science Foundation, 33, 84, 155, 165–6
    National Survey of Student Engagement, 165
    National Task Force on Civic Learning and Democratic Engagement, 164–5
    New England Resource Center for Higher Education, 159
    Office of Scientific Research and Development, 33
    President Lincoln, 156
    President Roosevelt, 33
    Science Education for New Civic Engagements and Responsibilities, 155, 165–6
    Stanford University, 96, 102, 121, 158
    town versus gown issues, 155
    Truman Commission, 55, 157
    University of Michigan, 159
    University of Minnesota, 159
    University of Texas, 53–4
    University of Virginia, 53
    Vannevar Bush model, 33, 35–6
    W. K. Kellogg Foundation, 159–60
    Western Association of Schools and Colleges, 99, 167
    Wingspread Conference, 159, 161, 164

Vietnam, 247

Western model, 63
World Bank, 44, 76, 247
World Trade Organization, 231

world-class universities, 14, 31, 36–41, 43–4, 46, 64, 76, 144, 150, 204, 210, 218, 231, 237–8, 248
WWII, 33, 35, 41, 246

GPSR Compliance

The European Union's (EU) General Product Safety Regulation (GPSR) is a set of rules that requires consumer products to be safe and our obligations to ensure this.

If you have any concerns about our products, you can contact us on

ProductSafety@springernature.com

In case Publisher is established outside the EU, the EU authorized representative is:

Springer Nature Customer Service Center GmbH
Europaplatz 3
69115 Heidelberg, Germany

www.ingramcontent.com/pod-product-compliance
Lightning Source LLC
LaVergne TN
LVHW051914060526
838200LV00004B/143